THE DEADLY CONNECTION

THE DEADLY CONNECTION

Nuclear War & U.S. Intervention

New England Regional Office
of the
American Friends Service Committee
Edited by Joseph Gerson

**Foreword by
Bishop Thomas J. Gumbleton**

new society publishers

Philadelphia, Pennsylvania

New Society Publishers
4722 Baltimore Avenue
Philadelphia, PA 19143

ISBN: 0-86571-067-8 Paperback
0-86571-068-6 Hardcover

Cover Design by Brian Prendergast

Printed in the United States

New Society Publishers is a project of the New Society
Educational Foundation and a collective of Movement for a New
Society. New Society Educational Foundation is a non-profit, tax-
exempt public foundation. Movement for a New Society is a
network of small groups and individuals working for fundamental
social change through nonviolent action. To learn more about
MNS, write: Movement for a New Society, 4722 Baltimore
Avenue, Philadelphia, PA 19143. Opinions expressed in this book
do not necessarily represent positions of either the New Society
Educational Foundation or Movement for a New Society.

The Deadly Connection: Nuclear War and U.S. Intervention is published by the New England Regional Office of the American Friends Service Committee as a contribution to much needed public discussion of U.S. military and foreign policies. These policies contain the potential for wholesale slaughter of millions of people and the devastation of our nurturing planet, not to mention a blasphemous threat to all that we hold sacred about human life, values and ideals.

Articles and speeches by 23 authors are included in this book. A number of chapters were first prepared as talks given at the conference on "The Deadly Connection" held in Cambridge on December 4 and 5, 1982 under the auspices of the New England regional office of the American Friends Service Committee and other organizations. There are therefore some references in this book which have been overtaken by later events. To a degree they are a historical record, as well as a reflection of the 1982 conference. Several other chapters are reprinted from other publications, and others were especially written for this book.

The views of the various authors are their own, and they are presented here as challenging perspectives on a common peril. The AFSC commends them to readers, not necessarily as statements which the AFSC endorses, but as stimulating thoughts and analyses of concerned and informed scholars and activists who seek a better world. We hope that their views will generate wider public discussion and that they will lead to constructive ideas and actions for peace and justice.

Publisher's Note

The Deadly Connection explores in depth the relationship between U.S. nuclear policy and past, present, and future U.S. military intervention around the globe. In doing so, it provides food for thought about the future of U.S. policy and how we might be able to change it. If that were all it provided, *The Deadly Connection* would be a worthy contribution to crucially important public policy debates.

But hidden behind the "deadly connection" is yet another web of connections and relationships which bear further reflection. What are the connections between our own lifestyles in the United States and the earth's diminishing resource base? How does our standard of living relate to the exploitation of people in the Third World? What is the connection between our chosen economic systems and the need for the protection of available markets for goods and services abroad? Is it possible to talk about the long-term possibilities for peace without asking how our habits and ways of thinking contribute to the maintenance of a war system which makes that peace even more difficult to attain? Is there any connection between long-term U.S. foreign and military policy and the relative silence of the American people in the face of an intensifying worldwide cycle of poverty, alienation, violence, and human degradation?

If we agree that such connections exist, it becomes clear that breaking them will require a choice: one rooted in the certain knowledge that not choosing, or choosing half measures, will likely result in the same apocalyptic results as embracing the "deadly connection" in its entirety, as our national leaders from both political parties have done for two generations. It is in the hope that you our readers will understand the historic choices before you that New Society Publishers is proud to publish *The Deadly Connection: Nuclear War & U.S. Intervention*.

David H. Albert
for New Society Publishers

Bishop Thomas J. Gumbleton

Foreword

In 1976, the Vatican submitted a statement to the Secretary General of the United Nations as its contribution to the special session of the U.N. on Disarmament scheduled for 1978. This was one of the clearest and strongest condemnations of the nuclear arms race ever made by any individual or collective body of the Roman Catholic Church.

> The arms race: it is to be condemned unreservedly.....it is an injustice....It is an act of aggression which amounts to a crime, for even when armaments are not used, by their cost alone, they kill the poor by causing them to starve.

It is no exaggeration to call this a "deadly connection." And thank God more and more people are responding to it out of a deep compassion for the poor.

But another "deadly connection" has not been made so clear and has not been as forcefully condemned. The collection of articles in this book will help all of us explore the possible links between the nuclear arms build-up and U.S. intervention strategies in industrialized and Third World nations. As the case is set forth for this "deadly connection," many of us might well be shocked and dismayed. But ought we not expect to find such a connection? In his talk in Edmonton, Alberta in the fall of 1984, John Paul II described how the nations of the "North" amass to themselves "the imperialistic monopoly of economic and political supremacy" at the expense of others. As one of those nations it seems highly likely that we would use whatever strategy seems necessary to maintain that monopoly.

One of the stated purposes of this book is to bring the whole peace movement together. Because of a failure to identify the "deadly connection," too often the movement is fragmented. Clearly there is a need to develop coordinated strategies of opposition to unwarranted and unjustified intervention on the part of the United States together with opposition to the nuclear arms build-up. There must be an overall strategy of peace to counteract the overall strategy of war.

The "deadly connection" further reinforces what the Catholic bishops' pastoral letter on peace cited as the "initial insight" of the very first communities of the disciples of Jesus, namely, that it is an illusion to think any use of violence or lethal force can be selective and restrictive. Once any nation claims to be bringing peace through violence or force, we can be sure that there will be no real peace, nor will there be justice upon which genuine peace must be built. Instead, in a world with nations heavily armed with nuclear weapons, there will only be continuing turmoil and ultimately the war through which the "deadly connection" will bring about the end of the world as we know it.

All of us must oppose all violent strategies for the direct and indirect use of nuclear weapons and the military interventions that seek to maintain the "imperialism of the North." Instead, we must seek to find every way to promote peace through genuine efforts for nonviolent revolution. This alone will bring justice among the nations, and finally some hope of peace in the world.

20 May 1985

Editor's Acknowledgements

This book is the result of the encouragement, support and work of many people, more than can be listed here. Lani Gerson, Leon Gerson and Hannah Gerson were each supportive and helpful in their own ways. Mark Reader and Tony Polumba each made invaluable contributions to the concept and development of "Deadly Connection" work. I will always remain indebted to friends and longtime colleagues from Arizona and to Paul Cravedi and Wilfred Desan.

The New England Regional Office of the American Friends Committee, its staff and committee members, have encouraged work on the Deadly Connection since its inception in 1982. Special appreciation must be noted for Doug Hostetter's thoughtful support, Jenny Rankin's work on the conference and its transcripts, and Phyllis Cohen's labor at the word processor under the capricious pressure of deadlines. Andrea Ayvazian and Courtney Cazden read this volume, made innumerable recommendations for its improvement on behalf of the New England Office of the AFSC, and were supportive in difficult moments. Bruce Birchard, Chris Wing, Roberta Levenbach, Corinne Johnson, Joe Elder and John Sullivan made many helpful suggestions.

I am obviously indebted to the many authors of the articles in this volume. Carol Greenwald, Margaret Lazarus, Renner Wunderluch, members of the Deadly Connection film collective, will recognize some of the language and the theses of the book. *MERIP Reports* is also due a special thanks for allowing the reprinting of Chistopher Paine's article "On the Beach". David Albert of New Society Publishers is due his share of credit for seeing the value of this book and bringing it from potential to product.

Contents

THE DEADLY CONNECTION

Part I
the Meaning of the Deadly Connection

Introduction

Speak truth to power.

From a charge to
eighteenth century Friends

We must follow with firmness in the footsteps of the heart,
Always joined in the struggle, facing hope.

Roque Dalton

In recent years the term "deadly connection" has become something of a slogan or cliché for the peace movement, meaning many things for many people. As described at some length in this volume, our conception of the "deadly connection" is the extraordinarily close relationship between U.S. nuclear war policy and U.S. foreign intervention. Its four principal components are the historical use of nuclear blackmail, a first strike nuclear war policy which serves as a shield to protect U.S. intervention in the Third World, the erosion of the "firebreak" between nuclear and conventional war, and intervention in industrialized and Third World nations to build and to maintain U.S. bases and installations necessary for fighting nuclear war. Like all other aspects of militarism and the arms race, the deadly connection has demanded a heavy price from our civil society and from our economy.

"The Deadly Connection: Nuclear War and U.S. Intervention" was the title of a conference held in Cambridge, Massachusetts in December 1982 which has inspired more than thirty similar conferences and a "new wave" within the U.S. peace movement. It has been the subject of numerous magazine articles and a frame of reference for several audio-video productions, was voted a priority for educational work by the national freeze movement and the Mobilization for Survival. It has helped to unify and give greater depth to the American peace movement. Yet it remains too little understood.

There are many ways to trace the origins of the idea of the deadly connection. Its roots can be found in the lessons learned about the United States during the Vietnam War, in the struggles of the peace movement during the 1950s and early 1960s against the then emerging nuclear arms race, and in the basic human need to understand how and why things work. Its more immediate origins lie in the Middle East and in some of the fault lines of the United States' peace movement.

As a Jew and as a person deeply concerned about war and peace, life and death, I was driven to learn about the sources of conflict and the possibilities for peace in the Middle East. Between the volatility of the Israeli-Palestinian-Arab conflict and the centrality of oil in the modern world, it seemed that many of the most crucial questions of war and peace—of human survival—lay in the Middle East. I first travelled to the Middle East in 1965, a time when there was new hope for the possibility of Israeli-Palestinian-Arab reconciliation, and later had the good fortune to join the staff of the American Friends Service Committee, one of the few organizations active in the United States which had both long experience in the Middle East and a commitment to work for Middle East peace in the United States.

In the late 1970s and early 1980s I worked closely with friends and colleagues in the AFSC in helping to build New England's disarmament and Freeze movements. But there were frustrations that many of us grounded in the Middle East felt. Disarmament and freeze activists gave scant attention to the peoples of the Middle East, or to the danger that the Middle East was a likely trigger for nuclear war. There had been nuclear alerts during Middle East wars in 1956, 1970, and 1973. While nuclear war could begin by accident, it would more likely develop out of a confrontation between the United States and Soviet Union over what they perceived to be their "vital interests." And the Middle East, in the words of the noted scholar Eqbal Ahmad, is "the center of the geopolitical struggle for world power."

The concept of the deadly connection grew directly from the U.S.-approved Israeli invasion of Lebanon in June 1982 and from the massive "March for Disarmament and Human Needs" held in New York City that same month. I had again travelled to Israel and Lebanon for the American Friends Service Committee in

December 1981 and heard from many there that the war was coming. On June 6, following the attempted assassination of the Israeli ambassador to London, apparently by Iraqi agents, the Israeli army and air force invaded Lebanon. By June 12 thousands of Lebanese and Palestinian civilians had been killed and wounded, many with planes, bombs, and anti-personnel weapons built in the United States. In addition to fighting Palestinians and Lebanese, the Israeli military also found itself engaged with the Syrians who had occupied Lebanon in 1976, ostensibly to protect the Christian population of the strife-torn nation.

On June 12, when we marched through New York's concrete canyons into Central Park, it was not yet clear that the Syrians and Soviets would stand aside as the Israelis drove on and into Beirut. We faced the possibility that the superpowers would find themselves forced to support their Middle East clients, just as they had done during the 1973 Middle East War. In the final days of that war, President Nixon placed U.S. forces on a DEFCON 3 alert to prevent the Soviets from coming to the aid of the defeated, encircled, and starving Egyptian Army, which was trapped in the Sinai Desert.

On June 12 in Central Park only one woman had the insight and courage to say anything from the podium about the war then raging in Lebanon. No one was moved to say that the Israeli-Syrian confrontation could trigger the nuclear holocaust we had come to prevent. While people left encouraged by our numbers and thrilled by the demonstration, some of us were not as excited. We knew people on all sides of the war in Lebanon, and we could not ignore the war's human and possibly nuclear dimensions. The June 12 march, which was one of the American peace movement's greatest achievements, also revealed serious shortcomings. Our silence spoke all too loudly.

I spent much of the summer following the June 12 march trying to understand what had and had not happened in New York and learning about the relationship between nuclear war and foreign intervention. The information was sparse. The best resource then available, Daniel Ellsberg's "Call to Mutiny", is included in this book. In conversations with friends and colleagues, I explored whether the AFSC should initiate a conference for people in the peace movement to explore the relationship between U.S. nuclear war policy and U.S. foreign intervention. If we had not been fully true to the moment in New York, it was more a result of our ignorance than our malice.

In September 1982 representatives from a number of Boston-based organizations responded enthusiastically to an AFSC invitation to consider and plan what became the first "deadly connection" conference. These organizations included the Massachusetts Council for a Nuclear Weapons Freeze, the Central America Solidarity Association, Catholic Connection, Mobilization for Survival, and Oxfam. With their help we secured commitments from an impressive array of speakers and assembled three hundred representatives from more than one hundred local, regional, and national peace organizations. People left the conference with a new understanding of the relationship between nuclear weapons and U.S. foreign policy.

Five of the basic lessons we have learned in "deadly connection" work are reflected in this volume. To begin with, Nagasaki was not the last time the United States "used" its nuclear arsenal. President Nixon's nuclear alert of 1973 and President Eisenhower's discreet threats to use nuclear weapons during the Korean war were not unique exceptions to U.S. post-war policy. Our commanders in chief have repeatedly threatened to use nuclear weapons against the Soviet Union and Third World nations to retain U.S. control over "The Grand Area", the sphere of influence won as a result of World War II which extends from our shores to the borders of the Soviet Union and China.

Second, we have learned that although the nuclear arms race is suicidal, it has not been as unthinking as many of us first believed. It has been fueled by the United States's effort to obtain a first strike capability, the ability to destroy, or threaten to destroy, the Soviet Union without fear of retaliation. In Randall Forsberg's words: "The arms race has nothing to do with defense, little to do with deterrence, and everything to do with a monopoly of U.S. intervention in other countries." Euromissiles, MX, and other first strike weapons have been deployed to create a shield allowing the United States to intervene in Third World nations with reduced fear of Soviet retaliation. The Soviet Union, with its inferior but all too powerful nuclear arsenal, has done its best to raise a nuclear umbrella, based apparently more on deterrence rather than a first strike capability, over Eastern Europe as well as the Soviet Union itself.

Thirdly, the "firebreak" between conventional and nuclear war is rapidly disappearing. Some tactical nuclear weapons, like conventional weapons of earlier eras, can destroy relatively confined areas. They can be used as anti-tank, anti-ship, and anti-aircraft weapons. On the other hand, new "conventional" weapons, like concussion bombs and vacuum bombs, are beginning to approach nuclear weapons in their destructive capacity. The incentive and ability to keep a conflict "conventional" is thus being reduced. The problem of keeping wars "conventional" is further complicated by the introduction of "dual capable" weapons which can fire both nuclear and conventional munitions.

Fourth, we have also learned that the protests in Japan against the deployment of Tomahawk cruise missiles, New Zealand's ban on visits by nuclear-powered or nuclear-armed vessels, and European resistance to the deployment of Pershing II and cruise missiles are struggles for national sovereignty *and* survival. They result from U.S. intervention in industrialized and Third World nations to build and to maintain the technological infrastructure for fighting nuclear, as well as conventional, wars. The nuclear arms race itself has thus become another driving force for intervention.

Finally, we have recognized that in the post-Vietnam War era the U.S. peace movement allowed itself to become divided into two wings, one focusing on disarmament and the other on intervention in the Third World. They rarely communicated, cooperated, or learned from one another. The lesson is being learned that focussing individual or organizational efforts on only the nuclear arms race, or on only one manifestation of intervention, often fragments and weakens the struggle for peace, justice, and survival. In Pam Solo's words, "it takes two wings to fly," but the wings need to be well coordinated.

The essays contained in this book clearly indicate that every U.S. and Soviet intervention carries with it the potential of theater or strategic nuclear war. As Carol Bragg's essay, "Central America and the Deadly Connection" explains, the United States not only attempted to intimidate the people of Central America with nuclear weapons in the past, but does so today. Daniel Ellsberg reminds us that "the whole panoply of new arms and deployments, the usable neutron warhead and the Rapid Deployment Force to the Pershings and the MX serve to implement presidential claims to have wired the Middle East to a Doomsday Machine."

The articles contained in this book explain these dimensions of the "deadly connection" in U.S. policy in considerable detail. Some refer to, but do not explore in depth, Soviet use of nuclear blackmail to retain its "sphere of influence." Information about the Soviet use of nuclear blackmail is extremely limited. Those who can document and add to what is included in this volume would be making a valuable contribution to the struggle for survival.

The authors of the articles contained in this book are not without their disagreements and varying emphases. Daniel Ellsberg asserts that nuclear blackmail has worked thus far for U.S. policy makers, while Ngo Vinh Long asserts that it failed in Vietnam. Unlike other authors in this volume, Stuart Schaar and Kassahun Checole draw the reader's attention to a new and potentially dangerous dynamic: the rise of "second tier" powers which will soon be able to threaten nuclear wars.

It should also be noted that some of the articles included here were first prepared as talks for the December 1982 Deadly Connection conference. Others were written specifically for this volume, and several are being reprinted here because of their singular importance. Their style is therefore uneven, and there is some overlap in the content of the articles. Many readers will, therefore, find the book most useful as an anthology of related and critically important articles and will choose to focus on particular articles rather than read the book from cover to cover. For an explanation of the roots and the long history of U.S. intervention, readers might want to look at books by William Appleman Williams, Howard Zinn, Richard Barnett and John M. Swomley, Jr., among others.

What will it take to survive? The essays in the final section of this book, as well as the proposals in earlier sections of the book, provide clues, not answers. The peace movement has a lot of thinking and strategizing still to do. Part of the answer to what must be done lies in the need to reconsider the value of life, what it means to live, and what energies we are willing to commit to save our lives, our children's lives, and the lives of people we have met or will never meet.

Yet the need for clear strategies remains. Jack O'Dell's speech describes the necessity for the disarmament and anti-intervention movements to find ways to cooperate and to "embrace the human needs dimension of the struggle for peace." The working paper prepared by Melinda Fine, Everett Mendelsohn, Jennifer Leaning and Pam Solo offers a reconceptualization of the meaning of security. In the era of the national security state, it is essential that the peace movement launch efforts to redefine the parameters of the public debate and to redefine the national consensus. Until the people of the United States, who have suffered no foreign invasion since the War of 1812, have a clearer understanding of what our security really requires, we are unlikely to pose a fundamental challenge to the Military-Industrial-Complexes which dominate and threaten life. The essay on the defeat of Navy plans to base a battleship task force and nuclear weapons in Boston Harbor illustrates both the "deadly connection" dimension of new offensive weapons systems and how ordinary people can prevail if they have vision and commitment. What can we do? We can begin to learn about and to understand better the threats to our, and to others', survival. We can teach, organize, write to and meet with our Congressional representatives, declare nuclear free zones, go to jail, demand an end to the war in Central America, assist people in need of sanctuary, and learn and speak about the Middle East. What will it take to survive? Being stubborn enough to pursue the meaning of things, being brave enough to speak to our neighbors and friends, being patient enough to walk in endless marches, being bold enough to think and act as if our lives and those of our children were more important than reasons of state or corporate dividends.

Joseph Gerson
Cambridge, Mass.
30 March 1985

Joseph Gerson

What is the Deadly Connection?

In recent years efforts to halt and reverse the nuclear arms race
have won vast popular support and have forced the Reagan
administration to the arms control negotiating table in Geneva.
They have, however, been weakened by the fact that few
disarmament and arms-control activists or leaders have
understood the relationship between the nuclear arms race and
the global ambitions of the United States. Similarly, efforts to
halt and to restrain U.S. intervention in the Third World have
too often proceeded in ignorance of the nuclear ramifications of
"conventional" conflicts in Asia, the Middle East, Latin America,
or Africa.

The resources of the peace movement are powerful but few.
Compared to the government, the corporations, the universities
and the think tanks which comprise the military-industrial
complex, we are a poor and largely part-time force within society.
Our strength derives from our understanding of what is at stake
in the nuclear arms race and wars of intervention, and from our
commitment to life. If we are to respond authentically to the
threats which face us and the human family as a whole, it is
essential that we better understand the forces that threaten
survival.

In the last decade the peace movement has moved its attention
from one issue to another, too rarely understanding the underlying
relationships among our many concerns. After the Indochina War
too few people were able to remember the lesson that "Vietnam
was not an aberration." Many forgot what we had learned about
the nature of power in the United States. Work for a nuclear
weapons freeze, against U.S. intervention in Central America, and
for the resolution of conflicts in the Middle East proceeded with

little cooperation and with little interest about how the arms race and wars of intervention might be connected.

Wars in the Third World and the escalating nuclear arms race are directly related. There are often secret nuclear dimensions to U.S. intervention. President Eisenhower, for example, dispatched Strategic Air Command bombers armed with nuclear warheads to Nicaragua in 1954 to reinforce the CIA coup in neighboring Guatemala.[1] Explicit threats of nuclear attacks played a significant role in U.S. strategy during the Korean and Indochina wars. Three of the four explicit threats of nuclear war directed at the Soviet Union cited in the Brookings Institution's study *Force Without War* were related to conflicts in the Middle East.[2] Nuclear weapons have thus been used on many occasions since the bombings of Hiroshima and Nagasaki. There is, unhappily, a hidden "logic" to the apparently senseless and suicidal nuclear arms race. It is this "logic"—the uses of nuclear weapons to build and retain a global "sphere of influence"—which must be understood and repudiated.

The Reagan administration is leading a campaign begun in the mid-1970s to reconstruct a first-strike nuclear weapons shield. It is motivated by the desire to regain freedom of action to intervene anywhere in the Third World which our government exercised during the period immediately following World War II. The power to threaten annihilation that comes with such a shield, it is believed, would prevent the Soviet Union from directly challenging U.S. intervention in any region thought to be vital to our national interests. Our government is also producing and deploying weapons which have all but eroded the "firebreak," the distinction between nuclear and conventional war. And, as the United States seeks to destabilize the democratic government of David Lange in New Zealand and to stabilize the Marcos dictatorship in the Philippines, it becomes clear that the United States government chronically intervenes in industrialized Western nations and the Third World to build and to maintain the technological infrastructure needed to fight nuclear war. A theoretical "first-strike" nuclear weapons capability, the loss of the firebreak, and intervention to secure and maintain bases and installations are the central elements of the "deadly connection", the direct relationship between nuclear war and U.S. foreign intervention.

A Hidden History

In the closing days of the 1973 "October" Middle East War, President Nixon publicly ordered U.S. military forces to a

"DEFCON 3" nuclear alert. In doing so, he threatened the world with nuclear holocaust and at the same time illuminated a pattern of U.S. policy in the atomic era: the exercise of nuclear blackmail. As when Nixon informed the nation that he had ordered the 1973 nuclear alert, the threatened use of nuclear weapons against the Soviet Union and essentially defenseless Third World nations has at other times been public knowledge. More often, these threats have been made, implicitly or explicitly, to our "enemies" and hidden from the American people.

The public record[3] now reveals more than twenty occasions when U.S. presidents threatened to resort to nuclear war during crises. The pattern began in March 1946 when, according to President Truman, he threatened to drop the "superbomb" on the Soviet Union if it did not evacuate Kurdistan and Azerbaijan within forty-eight hours.[4] The Soviets had occupied these provinces of Northern Iran during World War II with U.S. and British approval, but they were slow to depart at the war's end. According to President Truman their withdrawal began within twenty-four hours of his threat. While there were no witnesses present at the meeting in which Truman claims to have delivered the threat to then ambassador Gromyko, thus opening its veracity to question, it set the pattern for future administrations. According to Daniel Ellsberg, a principal architect of U.S. nuclear war policy in the Kennedy administration, the Truman threat was accepted as fact by succeeding presidents and became a model for their foreign and military policies.

Truman's successor, Dwight Eisenhower, continued the pattern of nuclear blackmail, sometimes in the light of the media, and sometimes covertly through diplomatic channels. Shortly after his 1952 election, President Eisenhower secretly threatened China with a nuclear attack unless it agreed to a settlement of the Korean War on terms favorable to the United States. Writing in his memoirs, Eisenhower recalled that "...to keep the attack from becoming overly costly, it was clear we would have to use atomic weapons... one possibility was to let the Communist authorities understand that in the absence of satisfactory progress we intended to move decisively without inhibition in our use of weapons.... We would not be limited by any worldwide gentleman's agreement.... At truce negotiations at Panmujom, we dropped the word, discreetly of our intention." Eisenhower was similarly discreet in 1954 when he sent Strategic Air Command bombers to Nicaragua to back up the CIA-sponsored coup in neighboring Guatemala, and later in 1958 when he instructed the

Joint Chiefs of Staff to resort to nuclear war, if necessary, to contain the antimonarchist revolution in Iraq.[5]

Eisenhower was rather more public in 1954 when he had his secretary of state and vice president publicly offer the French tactical nuclear weapons to break the siege of their forces at Dienbienphu in Vietnam. Fortunately, the French had the good sense to decline the offer.

"The Cuban Missile Crisis" of 1962 was the most visible and terrifying exercise of nuclear diplomacy. During the crisis, President Kennedy brought the world to the brink of destruction when he refused a Soviet offer to withdraw the intermediate range missiles they were installing in Cuba in exchange for a commitment from the United States to withdraw similar U.S. missiles from Turkey. Unknown to the Russians, the U.S. missiles in Turkey were obsolete and already slated for retirement. According to Kennedy aides, the odds that the U.S. would launch a nuclear attack during the crisis were between one third and one half.[6]

The record of the Nixon administration is replete with public and secret threats of nuclear war. Four years before the 1973 Middle East War, the president and Secretary of State Kissinger planned to threaten North Vietnam with nuclear weapons in order to force a settlement of the war. In his memoirs H.R. Haldeman, Nixon's chief of staff, recalled a conversation with the president: "He said, 'I call it the madman theory Bob. I want the North Vietnamese to believe I've reached the point where I might do anything to stop the war. We'll just slip the word to them. . . . We can't restrain him when he is angry—and he has his hand on the nuclear button—and Ho Chi Minh himself will be in Paris in two days begging for peace.' "[7] Daniel Ellsberg, then a consultant to the Pentagon, has since argued that the November 1969 Mobilization demonstration, which brought five hundred thousand protesters to Washington, D.C., convinced Nixon that the American public would not support such an attack on the Vietnamese. Thus his threat was neutralized.

A year later President Nixon announced at a press conference that he had threatened the Soviets with nuclear retaliation should Syria intervene in the September 1970 Jordanian-PLO civil war. The fear in Washington was that Syrian forces would cross the Jordanian border to support the PLO. Three years later, as referred to above, Nixon placed U.S. forces on a DEFCON 3 alert following the ceasefire ending the October War. This was in the last days of the Watergate Crisis. This threat was designed to prevent the Soviet Union from intervening to break the Israeli siege of the Egyptian Third Army. The Egyptian forces had already been defeated and were being denied food and water in the Sinai Desert.

In recent years the Carter Doctrine proclaimed that the United States would use "any means necessary"[8] to retain its primacy in the oil-rich Persian Gulf. This commitment has been reiterated by the Reagan administration. It is reinforced by the costly drive to obtain a first-strike capability against the Soviet Union and by the deployment in Comiso, Italy of cruise missiles targetted against the Middle East and North Africa.[9]

It should be noted that the United States is not the only country to have used nuclear blackmail. Press reports indicate that Britain threatened Argentina with nuclear weapons during the 1982 Falklands War.[10] While information about the Soviet Union's use of nuclear threats in connection with foreign intervention is difficult to obtain, the record is clear that during the Suez crisis in 1956 the Soviets threatened Britain and France with nuclear weapons to induce them to withdraw their forces from Egypt. (This threat was followed by a U.S. nuclear threat against the Soviet Union.) The Soviets also threatened China with nuclear attack on a number of occasions.[11] As "second tier" nations such as Israel, Pakistan, and South Africa obtain and develop nuclear weapons and delivery systems, the use of nuclear blackmail will spread with potentially disastrous consequences for us all.

First Strike: Shield for Intervention

Speaking at the first deadly connection conference, held in Cambridge, Massachusetts in 1982, Randall Forsberg, the author of the proposal for a bilateral U.S.-Soviet nuclear weapons freeze, surprised her audience by asserting that "the nuclear arms race has nothing to do with defense, it has little to do with deterrence, except in the sense of deterring the Soviet Union's intervention while permitting our own."

The public debate in the United States on issues relating to nuclear war policy has, for the most part, proceeded in the belief that deterrence is the goal of the U.S. government. Deterrence means that the United States and the Soviet Union both believe that should one nation unleash its nuclear arsenal it would certainly be destroyed in a retaliatory attack. Another name for this policy is "mutual assured destruction" or MAD. Most of the public debate in the United States is grounded in the belief that our government builds nuclear weapons only to deter a Soviet attack or a Soviet invasion of Europe.

In fact, the United States' nuclear arsenal is seen by our national security managers as a "seamless web," a highly integrated apparatus with offensive as well as defensive capabilities. The acquisition of new and more powerful nuclear weapons systems in recent years has been explained to the American people as essential for defense, deterrence, or uses as a "bargaining chip" for negotiations. While some of these weapons systems do have defensive capabilities, the principal reason they are being deployed is for their role in supporting the U.S. commitment to develop and to maintain a "first-strike" capability against the Soviet Union.

A first-strike policy is one that is designed to deliver a *totally disarming blow*, one which eliminates the possibility of enemy retaliation. A first-strike capability requires that the United States be able to destroy *all* of the Soviet Union's land based missiles, bombers, command, control, and communications centers, and submarines armed with nuclear weapons, before any of them can retaliate.

The *threat* of a devastating and totally disarming first strike against the Soviet Union allows the U.S. to use its nuclear weapons as a shield to allow it to intervene in Third World nations with little or no fear of the Kremlin countering its moves. Even if it is doubtful that the United States would be capable of *totally* disarming the Soviet Union, if the Soviets believed that our leaders thought they could launch a first-strike blow—Nixon's "madman" theory—they would use extreme caution in countering U.S. moves. Their behavior would have to be extremely guarded even when their most vital national interests were at stake. It is interesting to note that U.S. nuclear blackmail appears to have been far more successful when used against the Soviet Union than against popularly based struggles for "national liberation," as in Vietnam.

Until the late 1960s, the Soviets' nuclear arsenal was neither large enough, nor reliable enough, to challenge U.S. nuclear superiority.[12] As in the early years of the nuclear era and again at the time of the 1973 Middle East War, Soviet leaders apparently felt that they had to accept the will of the U.S. government or face total annihilation. The United States maintained superiority into the 1970s, but by the end of the decade, with the Soviet nuclear arsenal capable of launching a devastating retaliatory blow, the United States' ability to intimidate Soviet leaders in times of crisis was considerably diminished.

The year 1979 marked a turning point in U.S. nuclear war policy. The fall of the Shah of Iran created panic and turmoil among U.S. national security managers. They conjured up images of Soviet forces pouring into what was described as a "power vacuum" across the Soviet border. The Carter administration was incapable of dispatching enough troops half way around the world quickly enough to block such an invasion. In a period of rough nuclear parity, U.S. threats of resorting to nuclear war could be matched by threats of Soviet retaliation. On paper, and in theory, there were no assurances that the United States could emerge the victor from a nuclear confrontation.

This crisis in 1979 added momentum to a serious effort to revise U.S. military policy. Not only did President Carter move to create the dual-capable Rapid Deployment Force to enable the U.S. to fight conventional or nuclear wars in the Middle East, but he signed Presidential Directive No. 59. This document committed the United States to a first-strike nuclear war policy. Efforts to build and to deploy a first-strike nuclear arsenal, including MX, Trident II, Pershing II, and complementary cruise missiles, were accelerated.

In the field of first-strike weapons, the Reagan administration has moved from design to deployment. Missiles with pinpoint accuracy and the ability to destroy hardened missile silos are now deployed around the world, on the ground, in the air, and beneath the sea.

With his call for "Star Wars," President Reagan has launched an initiative which could further enhance the ability of U.S. forces to launch a first strike against Soviet missiles. Few experts believe that a perfect defense capable of protecting the civilian population of the United States could possibly be developed within the next twenty or thirty years. However, a partially effective anti-ballistic missile system, whether space- or earth-based, would have a better chance of destroying a smaller number of incoming missiles which managed to survive a U.S. first strike attack than it would in assuring the destruction of missiles launched in a massive Soviet first strike.[13] Star Wars would thus be a key component of a first-strike strategy, although its backers seldom mention this fact. In the classical pattern, a weapons system with an offensive role is being promoted on the basis of its theoretical defensive capabilities, while its usefulness in an offensive first-strike strategy is publicly ignored.

As was the case in the first three decades following the bombing of Hiroshima and Nagasaki, diplomacy based on a first-strike policy is less dependent on first-strike weapons working than on Soviet and other governments' fear that our leaders *believe* they would work, and that they are desperate enough to use them. The

public commitment to a first-strike policy thus serves as a shield
to intimidate the Soviet Union and to ensure the United States
freedom to intervene anywhere in the Third World. This is a policy based on bluff. The bluff can be called a limited
number of times, possibly only once. While such a policy may
work to the temporary advantage of the U.S. government, any
strategy that places a proud and powerful superpower like the
Soviet Union in a permanent condition of military inferiority and
humiliation is, of necessity, fundamentally destabilizing. At the
very least, this dangerous offensive policy fuels a perilous
escalation of the nuclear arms race.

Erosion of the Firebreak

If the interventionary forces rely on a nuclear shield, they can
also serve as the tripwire for its use. Changes in technology are
eroding the firebreak between conventional and nuclear war,
increasing the likelihood of a conventional battle escalating into
a nuclear war.

We have been led to believe that our political and military
leaders have established a "firebreak," an impenetrable barrier
between conventional and nuclear war. Nuclear weapons, we are
told, exist only to prevent our enemies from attacking us or our
allies. We have been assured that, because of the destructive
capabilities of nuclear weapons, our leaders will do everything
they can to prevent conventional war from escalating into nuclear
war. Unfortunately, radically new battlefield weapons have been
developed which all but destroy the firebreak. With the exception
of Michael Klare's prolific writing on this subject, the erosion of
the firebreak has been largely unnoticed.[14]

As Michael Klare explains, U.S. forces are being equipped with
a new generation of what he describes as "near-nuclear"
conventional weapons.[15] Cluster bombs, vacuum bombs, and
concussion bombs combine anti-personnel weaponry with
advanced guidance systems, thus providing near total accuracy
and remarkable devastation. Many of these weapons have the
destructive capability of the smallest U.S. nuclear weapons.

At the same time, some nuclear weapons are becoming more
like conventional weapons in their ability to destroy small and
contained targets. More than ten thousand tactical nuclear
warheads and hundreds of dual-capable sea-launched cruise
missiles are deployed around the world. These include neutron
bombs, which produce relatively contained blast effects but high
radiation levels and can kill massive numbers of people while

leaving cities and oil fields intact. The Rapid Deployment Forces are regularly trained in fighting tactical nuclear war.

To make the situation more perilous, many weapons systems are dual-capable, able to fire both conventional and nuclear warheads. Military commanders now refer to the "integrated battlefield," a place where soldiers and sailors have the ability and the temptation to transform conventional battlefields into nuclear conflagrations at a moment's notice. In some battlefield conditions, commanding officers may opt to use "small" nuclear weapons rather than "large" conventional weapons, believing it the more compassionate choice. In other situations, field commanders may make desperate decisions to go nuclear rather than face the loss of their troops. Regardless of where on the planet the firebreak is broken, there cannot be any assurance that once the firebreak has been breached the escalation can be contained.

Infrastructure and Intervention

Linked with the first-strike nuclear shield and the erosion of the firebreak, there is a third clear connection between U.S. nuclear war policy and U.S. foreign intervention. This is the pattern of intervention in industrialized and Third World nations to build and to maintain the technological infrastructure needed to fight nuclear, as well as conventional, war. Such intervention is not unique to the nuclear age. Hawaii and the Philippines were seized in the nineteenth century because their ports were seen as essential for the United States to project its power across the Pacific to Asia. Nonetheless, as people in Pacific, North Atlantic, and West European host nations seek to secede from the American nuclear war machine, they have frequently found their democratic rights and even their sovereignty sacrificed in the name of "security." Prime Minister Lange of New Zealand put it bluntly: "To force an ally to take nuclear weapons when it doesn't want them is exactly the sort of totalitarianism we're supposed to be arming against."¹⁶

The United States has more than one thousand foreign military bases and installations strategically located around the world. By comparison, the Soviet Union has less than one hundred.¹⁷ U.S. facilities include command, control, and communication stations, homeports and support bases for naval power projection, air force bases, and launching pads for intermediate range missiles. Each base or installation is designed to play a role in reinforcing U.S. intervention by conventional or nuclear forces. In some cases, the role is public knowledge. In other cases, such as the revelations that the U.S. was preparing to introduce nuclear weapons into Canada, Iceland, Spain, and other countries in times of crisis, U.S. plans to use bases to support nuclear warfighting have been hidden even from some of its closest allies.[18]

The Philippines, poised at the strategic crossroads between the Pacific and Indian Oceans, is the most obvious and well-known example of U.S. intervention to obtain and maintain strategic "assets." Seized from Spain in 1898 to support merchant ships and gunboats en route to Asia, this former U.S. colony received its independence from the United States only after it modified its constitution to allow for the presence of U.S. bases. Four decades later the Philippines hosts twenty-three U.S. bases including Subic Bay, the largest naval depot in the world, which play a critical role in supporting the power projection of the nuclear navy into Asia and the Middle East. Clark Air Force Base, the largest in East Asia, has served as a storage facility for U.S. nuclear weapons. To assure continued U.S. access to these bases, the CIA intervened in the 1950s to assure the election of President Magasaysay.[19] Since then the U.S. government has extended extraordinary support and financial backing to the Marcos dictatorship, even after it suspended the constitution and imposed martial law in 1972.

Closer to the Asian mainland, Japan, in the words of Prime Minister Nakasone, serves as "an unsinkable aircraft carrier" for the United States. The United States has 119 bases on this small island nation. These bases, plus a new constitution which renounces recourse to war, were the price exacted from Japan as a condition for ending the post-war occupation.

Yokosuka Harbor, twenty miles from downtown Tokyo, is the command, control, and communications center for the U.S. navy and its nuclear arsenal in the northwest Pacific. Sasebo, another Japanese port, opens to the East China Sea. It is a major base for U.S. warships, including aircraft carriers and submarines bearing Tomahawk cruise missiles. Despite massive protests and widespread support for a nuclear free Japan, successive Japanese administrations have avoided their constitutional responsibilities by refusing to inquire of the United States whether naval vessels and aircraft carry nuclear weapons when they come to Japan. Former U.S. ambassador to Japan, Edwin Reischauer, Admiral Gene LaRocque, and others with firsthand experience have testified that the United States regularly brings nuclear weapons into Japan. There is also evidence of major U.S. nuclear weapons accidents having occurred in Japan.[20]

The situation is much the same in Europe, the Middle East, the Caribbean, and Central America. U.S. support for the Colonels' Junta in Greece, beginning in 1967, and for brutal military regimes in Turkey, have underlined to Europeans the lengths to which the United States will go to maintain its bases on the southern front of NATO and the approach to the Middle East. People in Comiso fear that the deployment of cruise missiles in Sicily makes them a target for a preemptive Soviet strike or an attack by Libyan or terrorist bands anxious to strike U.S. nuclear forces in the Mediterranean.[21]

In 1984 the European Nuclear Disarmament Movement published a report detailing the militarization of the North Atlantic. Despite a Danish-United States agreement that U.S. bases in Greenland would be closed at the end of World War II, the U.S. air force retained its presence there through back door diplomacy and then the 1949 creation of NATO. In the early 1950s, three major U.S. bases were built on the pretext of shuttling troops to and from the war in Korea. Greenland is now a major link in the U.S. command, control, and communications strategy for nuclear war, despite the opposition of many Danes and their subjects in Greenland.

A similar scenario was followed in Iceland. Popular opposition to Iceland's entry into NATO forced its government to set conditions for its membership. Primary among these conditions was that there would be no foreign troops in Iceland during peacetime. Peacetime in Iceland ended with the Korean war. In the words of Vigfus Gierdel, a leading Icelandic peace activist, Iceland is "essentially an occupied country," serving as a major base for the U.S. nuclear navy, the air force, and military telecommunications.

The 1979 plan to deploy 572 Pershing II and cruise missiles in Britain and Western Europe, as part of the U.S. effort to regain leadership of NATO and to enhance U.S. first-strike capabilities, ignited the creation of the largest peace movement in European history. Despite the opposition of the majority of people in Britain, Germany, Italy, Holland, and Belgium, many of these missiles have been deployed. In Western Europe, as in the Pacific, the imposition of U.S. first-strike weapons and preparations to fight theater nuclear wars are making the people of host nations first-line nuclear targets. Additionally, in the words of Ulrich Sonn of the German Fellowship of Reconciliation, these missile deployments "seriously threaten our political sovereignty."

In Conclusion

The deadly connection lies at the heart of the nuclear arms race and U.S. military intervention around the world. There are no simple solutions for untangling it or for defusing the nuclear triggers placed around the world. There are, however, lessons that can be taken from the analysis of the deadly connection. Organizers at the local and national levels have begun to use the deadly connection as a tool in their work for peace and survival.

The first and most obvious lesson is that the either/or equation of disarmament and anti-intervention work is inappropriate and counter-productive. On June 12, 1982, this dichotomy led the organizers of our nation's largest peace demonstration to remain silent as thousands were killed during the U.S.-approved Israeli invasion of Lebanon. They were silent as the superpowers drifted toward confrontation in the early days of that war, with the U.S. backing Israel and the Soviets backing Syria. Three years later this either/or distinction has led to the weakening of the disarmament movement as many committed activists abandon the bilateral nuclear weapons freeze campaign to work against U.S. intervention in Central America. If we are to build the alliances and coalitions necessary to seriously challenge the war system of our society, we need to do our homework and to undertake basic education—if not basic training.

The concept of the deadly connection has informed several organizing efforts. In New England, New York, and Gulf and West Coast ports, it has helped local organizers understand the multiple missions of the Reagan administration's battleship task forces. Strategy built on an understanding of the strategic, interventionary, and economic implications of "homeporting" has led to the creation of coalitions embracing the nuclear weapons freeze and other disarmament organizations, groups working in solidarity with Central America, and community institutions and activists committed to economic development that benefits *all* the citizens of a community. In another area, long neglected by the peace movement, people are beginning to learn about the importance of addressing developments in the Middle East. They are learning that we may all pay the ultimate price if we ignore the region's conflicts and the interventionary role of our government there.

Observation and history teach us that all empires, all "grand areas," and all "spheres of influence" are but passing moments in the human experience. Yet they are realities that too often determine how people live, and how they die. When we consider the growth, evolution, and fall of the Greek, Roman, Dutch, Spanish, French, and British empires, we are reminded that as they declined they caused immense human pain and suffering. In each of these empires the seeds for future societies were sown as the old structures declined. With "the American century" drawing to a close, those of us living in the United States have a particular responsibility. It is we who will determine, in many ways, whether our leaders will be able to lash about with weapons of mass destruction, be they "conventional" or nuclear, taking much of the world with them in a desperate effort to retain their princely powers.

Notes

1. Barry M. Blechman and Stephen S. Kaplan, *Force Without War: U.S. Armed Forces as a Political Instrument*, (Washington, D.C.: The Brookings Institution, 1978), 48.
2. Ibid., 47.
3. Ibid., memoirs of past presidents and their cabinet officials, *Time* magazine, and the daily press.
4. Daniel Ellsberg, "Call to Mutiny," first published in *Protest and Survive*, ed., E.P. Thompson and Dan Smith, (New York: Monthly Review Press, 1981).
5. Blechman and Kaplan, *Force Without War*, 238, 256.
6. Theodore Sorenson, *Kennedy*, (New York: Harper and Row, 1965), 705.
7. H.R. Haldeman, *The Ends of Power*, (New York: Times Books, 1978), 81-85.
8. President Carter's "State of the Union Speech,"January 23, 1980.
9. "Cruise: Why the Arabs Should Worry," *The Middle East Magazine*, London, January, 1984, 16.
10. "The Belgrano Cover-Up," *New Statesman*, London, 31 August 1984.
11. Todd Gitlin, "Time to Look Beyond Deterrence," *The Nation*, 22 December 1984.
12. There is now a plethora of books and articles recounting the history of the nuclear arms race and the U.S. lead throughout. Among the more interesting are *The Price of Defense* by the Boston Study Group, (New York: Times Books, 1979); "The Freeze and Beyond: Confining the Military to Defense as a Route to Disarmament" by Randall Forsberg, *World Policy Journal*, Winter, 1984; and "Nuclear Samizdat" by Roy and Zorhes Medvedev, *The Nation*, 16 January 1982.
13. E.P. Thompson, "The Real Meaning of Star Wars," *The Nation*, 9 March 1985.
14. Michael T. Klare, "Securing the Firebreak," *World Policy Journal*, Spring, 1985; "Leaping the Firebreak," *The Progressive*, September, 1983; "The Inescapable Links: Interventionism and Nuclear War,"

CALC Report, November, 1983; "The Global Reach of the Superpowers," *South*, August, 1983.

15. Michael T. Klare, "Intervention and the Nuclear Firebreak in the Middle East," *MERIP Reports*, No. 128, Vol. 14, No. 9, November-December, 1984.

16. *Boston Globe*, 2 March 1985.

17. William M. Arkin and Richard W. Fieldhouse, *Nuclear Battlefields: Global Links in the Arms Race,* (Cambridge, MA: Ballinger Publishing Co., 1985), 264-267.

18. *New York Times*, 13 February 1985 and 14 February 1985.

19. Stephen Rosskamm Shalom, *The United States in the Philippines*, (Philadelphia: ISHI Press, 1981), 91-93.

20. See publications by the Japanese Council against Atomic and Hydrogen bombs. The Author also has a photograph used in a slide program prepared by the U.S. Air Force's 313th Air Division indicating missile accidents at the Kadena and Naha bases in 1969 and 1970.

21. Ben Thompson, "COMISO," an END Special Report, London, 1982.

THE

Part II

First Strike Policy & U.S. Intervention

DEADLY

CONNECTION

Randall Forsberg

Behind the Facade:
Nuclear War and
Third World Intervention

My personal goal is to see war ended completely, throughout the world, to see complete disarmament. Nothing left but perhaps police forces. This has been my goal since I first became involved in working for peace in early 1968, when I moved to Sweden, and happened into a job at the newly formed Stockholm Peace Research Institute. Watching television reports from Vietnam, I was not only sad but angry, which is an important distinction. I not only felt that war is awful, but that it was being perpetrated deliberately, voluntarily, by free choice, by some policymakers in this country, and that if it could be created by some individuals, it could be ended by individuals.

I am going to examine the connection between nuclear weapons and intervention and what we can do about both, by means of giving a biography of my own growing understanding of the connection between these areas and about what can be done about them.

As I worked at the Stockholm Peace Research Institute, learning about armaments and warfare, it wasn't at all clear exactly how individuals could do something about this. In Stockholm, I worked with statistics of military spending and military forces. I did detailed studies of the military production complex, what weapons had been developed and produced by the United States and the Soviet Union in the 20th century. What are the size of their industries? How rapidly do they produce new weapons? What types of new weapons do they produce? Where are they?

As I learned all of this statistical information, it wasn't clear to me what people could do politically. What was even less clear was how the continuation of this system could be rationalized by the people on top. Over a period of six years, I grew to understand in great detail the enormous amount of resources that were being poured into the arms race, how they were competing in other areas, and how they were roughly comparable—if you took the United States and Western Europe on the one hand, and the Soviet Union and Eastern Europe on the other hand. Here were these two enormous military blocks, spending vast amounts of money, producing more tanks, more aircraft, more ships, more nuclear weapons, keeping roughly in balance with one another, all to no end. And I thought, why do they do this? Why don't they just both cut by 50%? Why don't negotiations result in a 25% cut on each side? We keep the same balance, but we will save some money that we need for other things. Or a 50% cut on the two sides—that would be even better, or 75%. Still keeping in balance, not letting war break out, not making the same mistakes we made in World War II, not being naive, not being pacifists, just being rational. That was the state of mind in which I came to MIT in 1974 to do graduate work in political science, specializing in what was called "defense policy"—what I called "military policy and arms control".

It took me a year to find the answer to the question, "why?" I learned it one day toward the end of the first year. I spent a full semester in a course on nuclear strategy, which taught me that we had many more nuclear weapons than were needed for deterrence of an out-of-the-blue nuclear attack. But the course didn't really illuminate for me *why* we had many more nuclear weapons than were needed for that purpose. During the spring semester I took a different sort of course, in conventional military forces, non-nuclear forces, the Army, the Navy, the Air Force, which absorb, together with overhead, about 80% of our military budget and a comparable portion on the Soviet side. A much larger share than the nuclear arms race. Now, this course on conventional military forces was taught by the man who for 20 years wrote the Annual Report of the Secretary of Defense, working Monday through Wednesday in Washington and teaching at MIT on Thursday and Friday.

The spring course spent a lot of time talking about ground forces in Europe. We started out with an overview of the budgets. We then focussed on the Army. We looked at divisions; we looked at battalions; we looked at tanks and firepower and forward lines of battle and logistics and so on. There was an intensive look at who was going to win the next World War II in Europe. That went on for about 7 or 8 weeks. Then we spent about 3 weeks on the Air Force. We did the same thing with fighter aircraft knocking each other off, and attack aircraft bombarding the

troops of the other side—looking at the standoff in that area. I
had learned, more or less, what I expected to learn from my studies
in Sweden: that the purpose of these two enormous forces on the
two sides was to prepare to again fight a World War II in order
to deter World War III from happening. It still seemed as illogical
to me as ever.

Then, on the last day of the course, we looked at the Navy.
Maybe we had two sessions on the Navy—one session on the part
of the Navy that was going to help fight this war in Europe by
resupplying the convoys over the North Atlantic and destroying
Soviet submarines that would come out into the North Atlantic
in order to sink the convoys. We tied this chess game in the North
Atlantic to the one in Europe.

Then at the very end, in the last hour of this course, we started
talking about aircraft carriers and amphibious assault ships which
are large, floating military bases. Aircraft carriers carry lots of
fighter and attack aircraft and can float around the world, and
they stand off shore and bomb the ground or fend off fighter
aircraft. The aircraft carriers can fight an air war in any part of
the world. Amphibious assault ships are large landing docks for
ground troops, for Army troops and their tanks and artillery and
helicopters. They, too, can float anywhere around the world, so
you don't need a base on the ground. These things are very large.
They are very expensive. We are the only country in the world
that has them, and we don't have too many—13 aircraft carriers,
5 of the very largest amphibious assault ships, and about 20 or
23 of the next larger size. Neither has any counterpart in any other
country. They are very vulnerable because they are large, and they
are slow. They are also very vulnerable because the Soviet Union
soon after World War II saw the potential offensive power of
these floating military bases and developed, not just tens or scores,
but hundreds of anti-ship cruise missiles. These are the older type
of cruise missiles, essentially an unmanned airplane, radio-guided,
flying in the air, with nuclear warheads, hundreds of them aimed
at these 13 aircraft carriers and 25 amphibious assault ships. This
was made plain in the course, and it was observed that we probably
would not want to use these floating bases in a war with the Soviet
Union.

They could be used, however. They are stationed in the North
Atlantic and in the Mediterranean. The aircraft carriers carry not
only conventional bombs, they also carry a large arsenal of nuclear
bombs, usually about 2 per plane, or about 200 weapons per
aircraft carrier. This means that they are the single most potent
nuclear weapons system in the world. One aircraft carrier has 200

warheads. Those warheads can be loaded into the carrier's attack planes which could fly into the Soviet Union and attack Soviet cities. This is why the Soviet Union has its maritime patrol aircraft (bomber aircraft designed essentially to fly over the ocean), and its surface ships, and its submarines—all armed with nuclear, anti-ship cruise missiles designed to attack those aircraft carriers before their attack aircraft take off and fly towards the Soviet Union. The floating military bases could be used. The carrier admirals argued that they would be used against the Soviet Union, but other people, even the military, don't think so.

Where have they been used? In Vietnam, in Korea. Where could they be used without the threat of a nuclear attack which would eliminate them very quickly? Not against the Soviet Union, but against Third World countries. Against developing countries that don't have nuclear weapons, that have small military forces. An aircraft carrier has only 80 aircraft on it: the Soviet Union has several thousand combat aircraft. A developing country might have 20, or 40, or 10, or zero modern supersonic combat aircraft. If two aircraft carriers, like those sitting in the Persian Gulf right now, are dispatched against one of the smaller, developing countries in the Middle East, these two carriers would wipe out their air force in no time and would be free to bomb them. The same thing is true with the amphibious assault ships. They are very vulnerable and really can't be used against strong opposing military forces. But if they were sent against an nth-ranked developing country, they could be used with impunity.

I listened in this class, and I said to the teacher, "These are not for use against the Soviet Union." And he said, "Yes, next question." And I said, "But, I thought our military policy was to defend, if not ourselves, at least Europe, or somebody, against the Soviet Union. These weapons are only for us to use against, not a comparable military power—the only comparable military power is the Soviet Union—not even the next rank of military powers, European countries, Japan, or perhaps China, but against very weak, little, puny developing countries. We are maintaining very large military forces to intervene unilaterally and impose our will on these weak little countries."

He didn't like that. He again tried to go on to the next question. About ten minutes later I raised my hand again, and I said, "How come no one ever explains this? How come when we have policy discussions of military forces and military strategy in the newspaper, on television, in Washington, or wherever, it is never made clear which of our forces are for defense and which of our forces are for intervention? It's all just thrown together in a soup.

It's all dealt with as though it were one, coherent, single-purpose whole—our defense—which is how it's rationalized to the American people. Why isn't it explained more clearly?" He deliberately misunderstood my question, and he said, "If you think I don't do a good job teaching this course, I'm sorry. Next question." I thought he had done a very good job—I understood it perfectly well.

It took me several years to really understand what was going on in the nuclear arms race. I went back and looked again at the conventional military forces. I saw it is not just the aircraft carriers, not just the amphibious assault ships of the Marines, it is the Marines themselves. And the lighter parts of the Army are today being trained to operate in desert environments. They are not being trained to operate in Europe. There are no desert environments in Europe. A large part of our conventional military forces, perhaps 50%, is not even ostensibly intended for our defense.

If you ask any knowledgeable military officer (some aren't knowledgeable), if you get high enough up, and they've studied military strategy and know what they're doing, most of these officers would agree that about half of our conventional military forces are not oriented to defending ourselves. Defense isn't even in question. It doesn't arise.

The Soviet Union has no capacity to get to this country with conventional military force. So, no part of American military forces has anything to do with the defense of this country. The conventional forces are all for use overseas. The nuclear forces are for revenge. Nuclear weapons can't defend us if the Soviet Union launches an attack: we have no defense against a nuclear attack. We have no conventional attack to fear. So there is no attack against which we can defend. The only attack that might affect us is one against which we have no defense.

But conventional forces, to the extent that they are for defense of Europe in the first instance, are only about half of our conventional budget. This means a very large part of our military spending is going to non-defensive use of our military force. Then I came back to the nuclear forces again. I had known since 1972, when the SALT I Treaty was ratified, that ballistic missile defense was banned, allowing the two countries to be clearly, explicitly and openly hostage to a nuclear attack by the other with no possibility of defense. When that treaty was ratified I thought, we've reached a fork in the road. Everyone can see that if all nuclear weapons are to deter a Soviet nuclear attack on our cities by threatening a retaliatory attack on their cities, we have 500

or 1,000 times more nuclear weapons than we need to obliterate
the major cities in the Soviet Union. If that's all our nuclear policy
is about, which was implicit in the SALT I Treaty, then they won't
have any rationale for building any more nuclear weapons, and
the nuclear arms race, at least, will stop. It didn't stop.
But they did come up against a logical wall for the first time
in the postwar period. They could not rationalize any new weapons
beyond what we already had without explaining that the reason
we needed some new weapons was to attack, not cities, but
military targets. We had more than enough weapons to obliterate
all the cities in the Soviet Union. If we needed still more nuclear
weapons, it was because the cities are not really the targets. It
is the military forces that are the targets, as they have always been
in warfare.

If you were a general looking at nuclear forces on the other
side that could wipe out your cities, would you be interested in
wiping out the cities on the other side? As a military planner?
Of course not. As a general, what you want to do is wipe out
the nuclear forces on the other side so that your own cities are
safe, and the other side is disarmed. If you were a general, your
priorities would be: get nuclear weapons to obliterate the inter-
continental nuclear forces on the other side so that the U.S. is
safe. Once that is assured, get more nuclear weapons to obliterate
the intermediate range nuclear weapons on the other side. Then
Europe is safe. When you have that many nuclear weapons, you
should get some more nuclear weapons so that you can obliterate
all of the airfields in the Soviet Union, just in case they might
take some extra stocks of nuclear bombs, put them on shorter
range tactical airplanes (of which they have many thousands) and
still get them over here by hook or by crook. They could certainly
get to Europe. So obliterate those airfields. There are about 5,000
airfields in the Soviet Union, scattered across the country, so that
is a big demand. Of course, you also have to attack the stockpiles
of nuclear weapons, the plutonium production plants and the
facilities where nuclear weapons are made. You wouldn't want
to leave out the conventional military forces. You could disarm
them with nuclear weapons, but they could still come rolling over
Europe with all their tanks. So, now you start on the Army bases,
and you get all the Navy ports, and the rest of the tactical air
support, and while you're at it, you might as well get the command
and control, the communications, the bridges.

The list is infinite. I have been told that the potential list
available to the Single Integrated Operational Plan of targets in
the Soviet Union contains upwards of 100,000 potential targets.

So, from the point of view of ending the nuclear arms race, we have decades worth of options. And, once all the potentially interesting targets are covered, it can be done in many different ways—in case they develop some of those means, or they're not handy or convenient, or you lose touch with them. So, with attacking military targets, you have a recipe for a permanent arms race. And James Schlesinger announced in the Annual Reports for fiscal year 1975, in the spring of 1974, that we need some options.

We have always had options. We have always been acquiring more weapons for options, but we have also had this kind of schizophrenia in Washington and in the arms control community. It is as if the right and left parts of the brain, or the country, have not been talking to each other. We have nuclear deterrents: we only strike second, only for retaliation. We would never want to use nuclear weapons. That's what our strategic forces are all about: second-strike deterrence. That's all. Tactical nuclear weapons? Overseas? On howitzers, on aircraft carriers? Antisubmarine torpedoes with nuclear warheads, anti-aircraft missiles? Oh, of course we have a first use policy for tactical nuclear weapons. That's not our territory, that's not our lives, that's not our part of the military establishment—that's all other stuff that goes on overseas.

That was the schizophrenia that prevailed for the period from 1960 to 1974. During that period, the official line in the military under McNamara and in the arms control community, was that our strategic nuclear forces are second-strike forces. All we wanted to do was deter an attack on our cities by threatening to retaliate in kind. Our nuclear forces had no other purpose, and under that rationale, they couldn't make any more nuclear weapons. So, James Schlesinger said in 1974, we don't actually only want to be able to attack Soviet cities. We would like an option to go after some Soviet missiles. He started a debate that is still going on today and which has escalated since 1974. The debate was not introduced by Reagan, but it has become more and more clear, pointed, terrible and dangerous. The debate continues to grow increasingly dangerous as new developments become more clear. Inter-continental nuclear forces are aimed at pre-emptive, widespread, first-strikes against the nuclear forces of inter-continental range and against the command and control systems of the Soviet Union.

Around 1977 or 1978, I began to bring these two things together. It had taken me 6 years to understand that the purpose of our conventional force was not only, perhaps not primarily, defense of ourselves or Europe against the Soviet Union. Defense is a purpose. But defense and deterrence of war were not the only purpose, and they were not the active purpose. The probability of war in Europe is very, very low. Not zero. No one expects war. Roosevelt, Stalin, Churchill and Truman at the end of World War II carved up Europe into spheres of influence which are extremely stable. "You stay out of my internal meddling and I'll stay out of your internal meddling." The Soviet Union can send troops into Czechoslovakia and Hungary, and if they could get away with it, Poland. They will not be challenged by NATO. That is their sphere of influence; it is established. It is clear, it is finite. There is the same thing on the Western side, which we haven't seen with that degree of blatancy, but which could happen. Henry Kissinger recommended that if the Socialists and Communists together were to come to power in Italy, we should be prepared to use NATO forces to get them out. If they were freely elected, we should force a *revolution of the government*—which is the mirror of what the Soviet Union has done in Eastern Europe.

I saw that this non-defensive use of conventional military force was, in fact, related to the use of nuclear weapons against targets other than cities. I saw that connection in the following way. What is the reason for using nuclear forces against military targets, if the function of nuclear forces is to prevent an attack on cities? How does our attacking military targets prevent a Soviet attack on American cities? That doesn't make sense. We don't need nuclear forces aimed at military targets in the Soviet Union, to do so increases the likelihood of a Soviet attack on American cities. The chances are it would escalate out of control and we'd all be blown up.

What then was the purpose of our having nuclear forces designed to attack military targets? On the battlefield, in the air, at sea, at intermediate range, at inter-continental range? What was the purpose behind the national policy of having these forces? As I learned more about conventional and nuclear war, I came upon the area of tactical nuclear warfare and first-use policy. I realized the purpose of having nuclear forces to attack military targets is to threaten escalation. We are going to escalate. If we have this war in Europe, it is going to be an extremely bloody war which nobody can win. It will be devastating. This is just a conventional war. But if we suddenly escalate to a pre-emptive nuclear strike against their forces, maybe we can obliterate them. That is the fuzzy theory behind the first use of nuclear weapons in Europe. If it gets out of control, we can escalate to the next level. Or, if you are a smart general, you might not want to wait until it gets out of control. You might think through, as you do in a bridge game or chess game, the possibilities of things getting out of control and decide to begin, not with an attack on tanks over the next hill, but with an attack on those inter-continental forces that threaten our cities. And, while you're at it, at the same time, you might as well attack the forces that could threaten European cities and, indeed, attack as much as you possibly could. Because you might not have another chance. Because you couldn't tell where the weapons on the other side would be aimed if you didn't destroy them first.

I saw that escalation has nothing to do with deterring a nuclear attack on cities, *it is the opposite*. Escalation has to do with conventional warfare, with relating nuclear warfare and conventional warfare. Now I come to the final piece of this story.

If there is not going to be another war in Europe, if it is very stable, and if it is very clear that the spheres of influence are divided up and are not going to lead to war, why did they keep improving nuclear capability for escalation, for a counterforce attack? Where is the area in which this escalatory capability— the ability to escalate to nuclear war from conventional war— will actually come into play? I looked back. I read again, for the twentieth or thirtieth time, the Annual Report of the Secretary of Defense, where they explain why they need nuclear capability. What would we lose, what would we risk, if we did not have nuclear capabilities for attacking military targets on the other side? What would be at risk in the world? Surely, with the arsenals that we have now, with 25,000 nuclear weapons, there is more than enough horror to insure that another World War II in Europe (extremely unlikely in any case) will not break out. We don't need to get more or better nuclear weapons in order to deter another World War II in Europe with the threat of nuclear escalation. The weapons we have are fine for that purpose. What is it that we could do better if we obtain weapons that are even better for escalation?

I came to the conclusion that the only place the new generation of nuclear weapons actually plays a role, an active role in international politics, is in backing up intervention on our part and deterring intervention on the part of the Soviet Union. The only area where we can actually imagine conventional forces being used, by either country, is in unilateral intervention. By the Soviet Union in Eastern Europe or the Third World; by the United States, primarily in the Third World.

Suppose there were no nuclear forces, and there were a civil war in Iran, and the United States sent in troops to ensure that the socialist side did not win. What would prevent the Soviet Union from sending its troops over the border and getting into a direct war with the United States? Nothing would prevent them: they would do that. No doubt they would continue the history of nation-state behavior along those lines. Why shouldn't the United States send troops over to Afghanistan and kick the Soviet Union out? Suppose that we only had a few nuclear weapons, 200 missiles on submarines that couldn't be touched by the other side, so there's no point in going after them first because you couldn't find them anyway.

Suppose those were the only nuclear weapons in the world: 200 U.S. nuclear weapons on submarines aimed at Soviet cities and 200 nuclear weapons on Soviet submarines aimed at U.S. cities, and there were no other nuclear weapons. Would the Soviet Union be able to go into Iran and challenge a U.S. intervention there? Would they be afraid that a direct war between the United States and the Soviet Union, a direct conventional war, might lead to a nuclear holocaust in which all our cities would be obliterated? There would be some fear of that.

The Soviet Union might think, ah, they won't risk it. We'll have a limited war, geographically limited and limited in means. That is what 20th century wars are like. We have limited means and limited goals. There have been no all out wars since World War II. There have been no all out wars since nuclear weapons were invented. We cannot have all out wars any longer. But we can continue to play power politics games with limited war, as long as we keep it appropriately limited.

Why don't we increase our nuclear weapons then? And just keep adding more until you reach the point where it is clear, it is perfectly clear and indisputable, that it is too dangerous for one superpower to challenge the intervention of the other. When territory is claimed by the one that intervenes first, or the one that's been there traditionally, or the one that *does* care, the claimant can take the land. In Afghanistan it is not worth it for us to challenge the Soviet Union. It has no value, no geographic value, no resources, no wealth, no military value, nothing. But even in places where it is worth it, like Iran, when one of the superpowers gets in first, the other one cannot fight. Or even worse, suppose there is not a balance. There is instead superiority, real nuclear superiority. This is the goal.

Does the concept of fighting and winning a nuclear war make sense anymore? It never did, but it was more plausible in the 1940s and early 1950s, when nuclear weapons were not on a five-minute alert, when they couldn't be launched on a few minutes' notice, when there were not upwards of 10,000 intermediate range and inter-continental range weapons aimed at all of the major targets in the northern hemisphere. It was more thinkable then. Today, it doesn't make sense to talk about efforts for nuclear superiority, for fighting and winning nuclear wars. As soon as anything like that starts, the weapons on the other side, rather than being pre-emptively destroyed, can be launched on warning of attack. What general, not even in his right mind, but with some shred of rationality left, would dare launch a pre-emptive strike on the other side's nuclear forces, knowing that unless they decide to sit on their hands, the other side is going to launch their weapons before they're hit? No general.

If there were a general who would do that, he would be insane. Insane people are not deterred by revenge or logic or rationality. There is no rationale any longer for developing nuclear weapons designed for a pre-emptive, disarming, first strike against the other side. Nevertheless, that is exactly what U.S. policy is. We are developing the MX and Trident II in order to obliterate Soviet inter-continental forces. Our new weapons in Europe and our weapons on submarines will help obliterate Soviet intermediate-range forces. We are developing a new generation of tactical nuclear weapons which are aimed at the tactical weapons and conventional forces on the other side.

What is the theory behind this? Suppose that at every level of nuclear warfare, at every amount of weapons or at every geographic range, the United States has the capability to obliterate Soviet nuclear capability, but that the Soviet Union, at best could only destroy part of our capability. Then we might not merely have a standoff in intervention—where the side that gets in first or the side with the sphere of influence can intervene and it won't be challenged by the other side. We might have a monopoly on intervention. The United States could intervene wherever it wanted to, but the Soviet Union would be deterred from intervening, because of the risk that we would dare to challenge Soviet intervention. The Soviet Union would know that at every level of escalation of war, we had a significant and obvious advantage. This is the golden era of superiority that the Reagan Administration longs for, one which can never be recaptured. This is what is driving the nuclear arms race. It has nothing to do with defense, it has little to do with deterrence, except in the sense of deterring their interventions while permitting our own. This is not manufactured, it is not an extreme interpretation. Knowing a little bit about weapons and strategy, you can read this yourself if you read the Annual Report of the Secretary of Defense and you look at the goals of our new nuclear weapons.

Talk given at the Deadly Connection conference, 4 December 1982.

Daniel Ellsberg

Call to Mutiny

The notion common to nearly all Americans that "no nuclear weapons have been used since Nagasaki" is mistaken. It is not the case that U.S. nuclear weapons have simply piled up over the years —we have over 30,000 of them now, after dismantling many thousands of obsolete ones—unused and unusable, save for the single function of deterring their use against us by the Soviets. Again and again, generally in secret from the American public, U.S. nuclear weapons *have* been used, for quite different purposes: in the precise way that a gun is used when you point it at someone's head in a direct confrontation, whether or not the trigger is pulled.

By Harry Truman's own telling, it was just seven months after Nagasaki that he so used the Bomb in the "postwar" world. As he recalled, the effect was immediately as successful as on the first occasion, with no need this time to pull the trigger.

The issue was, as it happens, Russian influence in northern Iran, where the Soviets were prolonging their wartime occupation and supporting separatist regimes in Azerbaijan and Kurdistan, in pursuit of Russian oil leases in that area comparable to those of the British in the south. One version of Truman's account was revealed to *Time* by Senator Henry Jackson in January 1980, the week, by no coincidence, that the Carter Doctrine was announced. *Time* gave the story the heading, "Good Old Days for the Middle East":

> In a little-known episode of nuclear diplomacy that Jackson said he had heard from Harry Truman, the President summoned Soviet Ambassador Andrei Gromyko to the White House. Truman told Gromyko that Soviet troops

should evacuate Iran within 48 hours—or the U.S. would use the new superbomb that it alone possessed. "We're going to drop it on you," Jackson quoted Truman as saying. They moved in 24 hours.

Truman's memory may be faulty in this recounting: Barry Blechman, who believes it was, reports at least seven public or private occasions when Truman discussed what he called his "ultimatum" over Iran, the earliest of these in 1950, but there are inconsistencies and a lack of any supporting evidence. This is not the case with any other of the episodes to be discussed below, for which this anecdote is, in the form Truman presented it, nevertheless archetypal.

The most recent of these, thirty-five years later, brings us back to the very same region and adversary. When outgoing Secretary of Defense Harold Brown told interviewers in January 1981, and President Ronald Reagan reiterated in February—using the same words—that what will keep Russia out of northern Iran and other parts of the Middle East in the 1980s is "the risk of World War III", the threat-strategy each was at the same time describing and implementing was somewhat more complex than that which Truman recollected, but not by much.

And there is no lack, this time, of corroborating elucidations of the nuclear component to the policy. A year earlier, in the weeks before and after Carter's State of the Union message announcing his "doctrine" for the Middle East, the White House almost jammed Washington talk shows and major front pages with authorized leaks, backgrounders, and official spokesmen all carrying the message that the president's commitment to use "any means necessary, including military force" against a further Soviet move into the Persian Gulf region was, at its heart, a threat of possible initiating of tactical nuclear warfare by the United States.

Just after the president's speech, Richard Burt of the *New York Times* (now a high Reagan official), was shown a secret Pentagon study, the most extensive military study of the region ever done by the government, which lay behind the president's warning. It concluded, as he summarized it, "that the American forces could not stop a Soviet thrust into northern Iran and that the United States should therefore consider using 'tactical' nuclear weapons in any conflict there." (*New York Times*, February 2, 1980).

Even before the president spoke, this same conclusion was reflected in White House backgrounders given to *Los Angeles Times* reporters Jack Nelson and Robert Toth. Heralding the president's message, "White House and other senior officials dealing with national security," told them that "if the Soviet Union carried its expansionism into Iran or Pakistan, the United States would have little choice but to oppose it militarily." These officials went on to say what the president, speaking to the public a few days later, did not put into words: such a war with the Soviet Union "would almost certainly become a nuclear war" (*Los Angeles Times*, January 18, 1980). This information was the lead front-page story, under the headline "Russia vs. Iran: U.S. Ponders Unthinkable". The same story reprinted next day in the *San Francisco Chronicle* bore the headline, "Doomsday Talk in Washington."

The revelation in *Time* of Senator Jackson's old conversation with Truman, appearing on newsstands the day before the president's speech, was part of this same chorus. It was particularly well suited to administration purposes—evident in the unusual publicity given to threats usually kept highly secret —of legitimizing and gaining public acceptance for the president's own policy. The Truman anecdote displayed a precedent of nuclear threats against the Russians, involving Iran (or really, in both cases, the transcendent issue of Middle East oil), invoking just the image of feisty, now-popular Harry Truman (re-elected against all odds, now enshrined in history after the lowest ratings in popular support until Jimmy Carter) that the president sought to associate with his own shift to a new Cold War: above all, a precedent of success.

But there was still another reason to evoke the memory of Harry Truman in this context. For all the talk and posturing, for all the military analyses, plans, and recommendations, even the deployments, the question remained: Could the Russians, could anyone, come to believe that the president of the United States, if challenged, might really *carry out* such threats, accepting the prospect *at best*—if the war, improbably, stayed regionally limited—of annihilating the local population along with troops? Indeed, was he not bound to the contrary—as most Americans still imagine, quite falsely—by an explicit or at least tacit "no first use" commitment, never to be the first to use nuclear weapons in a crisis or non-nuclear conflict?

It was the official function of William Dyess, Assistant Secretary of State for Public Information, to interpret the president's meaning to the public in the week following the speech, and to address in particular just these questions. In an arresting exchange on television (*Newsmakers*, NBC Television, February 3, 1980) one day after Burt's leak of the Pentagon study, Dyess answered the second question crisply and correctly, and the first as well:

> Q: In nuclear war are we committed not to make the first strike?
> Dyess: No sir.
> Q: We could conceivably make an offensive. . .
> Dyess: We make no comment on that whatsoever, but the Soviets know that this terrible weapon has been dropped on human beings twice in history and it was an American president who dropped it both times. Therefore, they have to take this into consideration in their calculus.

But the Soviets, better than most, know a good deal more than this about past uses and near-uses of U.S. nuclear weapons. What Dyess might have mentioned (but almost surely does not know) is that in the thirty-six years since Hiroshima, every president from Truman to Reagan, with the possible exception of Ford, felt compelled to consider or direct serious preparations for possible imminent U.S. initiation of tactical or strategic nuclear warfare, in the midst of an ongoing, intense, non-nuclear conflict or crisis.

The Soviets know this because they were *made* to know it—often by explicit threats from the Oval Office, even when White House considerations of use of nuclear weapons was secret from other audiences—since they or their allies or client states were the intended targets of these preparations and warnings. Moreover, the Soviets will recall that the U.S. Strategic Air Command was established in early 1946 with the function of delivering nuclear attacks upon Russia when so directed, a time when it was publicly proclaimed by the president and high military that the Soviet Union was not expected to possess operational nuclear weapons systems for a decade or longer. SAC's *only* mission in that initial period—which included the formation of NATO—was to threaten or carry out a U.S. first strike: *not at all* to deter or retaliate for a nuclear attack on the United States or anywhere else.

It is not the Russians but the rest of us who need to learn these hidden realities of the nuclear dimension to U.S. foreign policy. Here, briefly listed, are most of the actual nuclear crises that can now be documented from memoirs or other public sources (in most cases after long periods of secrecy; footnotes indicate the most accessible references):

> Truman's deployment of B-29s, officially described as "atomic-capable", to bases in Britain and Germany at the outset of the Berlin Blockade, June 1948.[1]

Truman's press conference warning that nuclear weapons were under consideration, the day after marines were surrounded by Chinese Communist troops at the Chosin Reservoir, Korea, November 30, 1950.[2]

Eisenhower's secret nuclear threats against China, to force and maintain a settlement in Korea, 1953.[3]

Secretary of State Dulles's secret offer to Prime Minister Bidault of three tactical nuclear weapons in 1954 to relieve the French troops besieged by the Indochinese at Dienbienphu.[4]

Eisenhower's secret directive to the Joint Chiefs during the "Lebanon Crisis" in 1958 to prepare to use nuclear weapons, if necessary, to prevent an Iraqi move into the oilfields of Kuwait.[5]

Eisenhower's secret directive to the Joint Chiefs in 1958 to plan to use nuclear weapons, imminently, against China if the Chinese Communists should attempt to invade the island of Quemoy, occupied by Chiang's troops, a few miles offshore mainland China.[6]

The Berlin Crisis, 1961.[7]

The Cuban Missile Crisis, 1962.[8]

Numerous "shows of nuclear force" involving demonstrative deployments or alerts—deliberately visible to adversaries and intended as a "nuclear signal"—of forces with a designated role in U.S. plans for strategic nuclear war.[9]

Much public discussion, in newspapers and in the Senate, of (true) reports that the White House had been advised of the possible necessity of nuclear weapons to defend marines surrounded at Khe Sanh, Vietnam, 1968.[10]

Nixon's secret threats of massive escalation, including possible use of nuclear weapons, conveyed to the North Vietnamese by Henry Kissinger, 1969-72.[11]

The Carter Doctrine on the Middle East (January 1980) as explained by Defense Secretary Harold Brown, Assistant Secretary of State William Dyess, and other spokesmen,[12] reaffirmed, in essence, by President Reagan in 1981.[13]

Although the current warnings and preparations for nuclear war in the Middle East are the most *public* threats since the crises over Berlin and Cuba a generation ago, it follows from this listing that there has been no thirty-six-year moratorium upon the active consideration and use of nuclear weapons to support "nuclear diplomacy". Indeed, many of the recurrent circumstances were remarkably similar to the first use at Hiroshima.

In none of these cases, any more than in 1945, was there apprehension among U.S. officials that nuclear war might be initiated by an adversary or needed urgent deterring. In most of them, just as against Japan, the aim was to coerce in urgent circumstances a much weaker opponent that possessed no nuclear weapons at all. In the remaining cases the object—already important in August 1945—was to intimidate the Soviet Union in an otherwise non-nuclear conflict.

And even against the Soviets most of these threats were seen as effective, just as the first two bombs were. U.S. marines, who had fought their way out of Chinese encirclement at the Chosin Reservoir without carrying out Truman's 1950 warning, were never finally assaulted at Khe Sanh, in 1968. The Chinese accepted and kept our 1953 armistice terms in Korea; in 1958, they ceased abruptly their daily shelling of Quemoy. The Russians backed down over Berlin in 1961 and again, spectacularly, in Cuba the next year.

Whether the nuclear component of U.S. threats to escalate the level of hostilities was actually critical to the behavior of opponents is not the issue here. (That question is still hotly controversial for the 1945 case itself.) What matters, if we are to understand this record, is that presidents *believed* that past and current threats had succeeded: this was why, as they understood it, they or their predecessors had not been forced to carry them out, why they and their successors kept making such threats, and buying more and more first-use and first-strike nuclear weapons systems to maintain and increase the credibility and effectiveness of threats they expected to make in the future. It is why, after all, each president has refused to make a "no first-use" commitment, when the Soviet Union has proposed such a commitment bilaterally.

The objection to these tactics is not that such threats cannot possibly "work". However, it is important to observe that most of these known incidents—*and all of the apparently successful ones* (except Khe Sanh)—occurred under earlier conditions of American strategic nuclear superiority so overwhelming as to amount to monopoly.

Thus, in mid-1961, the year of the projected "missile gap" favoring the Russians, the United States had within range of Russia about 1000 tactical bombers and 2000 intercontinental bombers, ICBMs, Polaris missiles, and another 100 intermediate range missiles based in Europe. The Soviets had at that time some

190 intercontinental bombers and exactly *four* ICBMs: four "soft", nonalert, liquid-fueled ICBMs at one site at Plesetsk that was vulnerable to a small attack with conventional weapons. When Kennedy urged the American people to prepare fall-out shelters during the Berlin Crisis that year, it was not for a nuclear war that would be started by the Soviets. Nor was it to avert Soviet superiority or to deter a Soviet nuclear first strike, that Kennedy fixed on the figure of 1000 missiles as the projected size of the Minuteman force in November of that year, well *after* the intelligence community had concurred on the conclusive estimate that the Soviets possessed less than ten ICBMs.

Officially, the precise figure cited above for Soviet ICBMs in the period from early 1960 to early 1962—four—is guarded as a classified secret today just as it was twenty years ago; the number presented in nearly all public sources—"about fifty"—is wrong by an order of magnitude. The true figure remains secret for the same reason as before: because public knowledge of the *scale* of the "missile gap" hoax would undercut the recurrently-necessary tactic of whipping up public fears of imminent U.S. "inferiority" to mobilize support for vastly expensive arms spending intended, in fact, to assure continued and increased—or in the present instance, regained—U.S. superiority.

The Soviets did acquire a large and growing ability to devastate Western Europe from the mid-fifties on (with short- and medium-range bombers and rockets). But (a) the ability to disarm the opposing superpower of its strategic forces in a first strike, and (b) the ability to retaliate against the homeland of the opposing superpower in a second strike, were both capabilities strictly monopolized by the United States until the late sixties. Not until 1967 did the Russians begin to put their ICBMs into "hardened" concrete silos and deploy advanced missile submarines, thereby acquiring the second capability and depriving the U.S. of the first.

For most of two decades, it is now clear, the Soviets chose not to seriously challenge what amounted to U.S. strategic monopoly. But the cost to U.S. security interests of using that monopoly repeatedly, dramatically over Quemoy, Berlin, and Cuba—while increasing spending sharply to maintain it and refusing to put a ceiling on U.S. technological superiority by a comprehensive, bilateral test ban on warheads or missiles—was to discredit Krushchev's reliance on cheap bluffs and to help him lose his job. Brezhnev, displacing Krushchev in 1964, seems to have promised the Soviet military to spend whatever it would take to eliminate inferiority. The Soviets proceeded to outspend the U.S. in the seventies, as they finally duplicated the huge investments in strategic capabilities that the U.S. had made in the fifties and sixties. In the course of the decade, they succeeded in buying "rough equivalence" or parity, thus drastically eroding the credibility of the U.S. first-strike threat, and along with it, the credibility of threats to escalate lesser levels of conflict if necessary to avoid tactical defeat or stalemate.

Americans are now being mobilized for a massive attempt to buy back these two lost pillars of U.S. foreign policy. The damaged credibility is to be partially restored by adding to our sizeable (and unique) antisubmarine capability the highly precise counterforce capabilities for a disarming first strike against landbased forces represented by the MX, Trident II, Pershing, and cruise missiles (with antiballistic missile systems and civil defense as logical and likely complements, when the public is ready). So far (July 1981) Congress is not balking at a projected price tag of several hundred billion dollars, even though the significant superiority sought (under the consciously deceptive policy slogan of "avoiding inferiority") seems most unlikely to be achieved, in face of the evident Soviet determination to deny it.

Meanwhile, as the Nixon, Carter, and Reagan examples demonstrate, presidents continue to issue threats of U.S. nuclear initiatives, even in the era of superpower parity that has lasted now about a dozen years. The White House backgrounders cited earlier explain why, for the case of the Carter Doctrine. Thus the secret Pentagon study of U.S. capabilities in the Middle East is quoted by the *New York Times* as concluding: "To prevail in an Iranian scenario, we might have to threaten or make use of tactical nuclear weapons." The reason given is that the Soviets could move twenty-three divisions with 200,000 troops into their neighboring country within thirty days, confronting the 20,000 Americans and equipment that could be brought in by then with "more than a five-to-one advantage in forces." In the *Los Angeles Times* backgrounder, White House officials explained that even a local conflict with Soviet troops "would almost certainly become a nuclear war, because the United States has concentrated on its nuclear weapons rather than on matching the Soviet Union's massive strength in conventional warfare" (January 18, 1980).

Of course, as the leaked Pentagon study makes clear, even if the U.S. did match Soviet conventional strength in overall global terms, it could hardly aspire to do so in a region bordering Russia, any more than the Soviet Union, for all its vast army and growing navy, could ever hope to outweigh U.S. conventional strength on our own borders, in order, say, to block U.S. access to the oil in Mexico or Canada (or, for that matter, to protect states in the

Caribbean or Central America from determined U.S. intervention). This regional disadvantage for the exercise of unilateral U.S. military power in at least the northern part of the Persian Gulf region would not be reduced at all by instituting the draft, by enlarging a Rapid Deployment Force, or, indeed, by combat employment (as distinct from threat) of tactical nuclear weapons, with which the Soviet forces are well equipped.

It is in these unchanging circumstances that the deterrent tactic has recommended itself to a succession of U.S. administrations of *threatening* and preparing to initiate tactical nuclear warfare in the region, to escalate if necessary, risking Soviet preemption or counter-escalation. In plainer language, the tactic is to threaten regional annihilation, with a link to global holocaust. Within their persistent frame of reference, these policy-makers see simply no alternative.

Nor is this true only of the Middle East. Look again at the list of nuclear crises. In fact nearly *all* of them, except for Cuba, focus on countries bordering the Soviet Union or China (with Berlin actually within the Soviet zone of occupation). The current "dilemma" in the Middle East merely highlights the historical legacy of an earlier generation in which strategic nuclear monopoly permitted and encouraged the United States to claim rights to intervention in what amounted to a "sphere of predominant influence" that ran right up to the borders of Soviet or Chinese occupation *everywhere in the world*, including (from early 1946) northern Iran. Now, a decade after that monopoly has vanished, U.S. commanders-in-chief still feel compelled to defend and assure U.S. influence within that same immense, global sphere. They believe, and they are right to believe, they cannot do so everywhere without being ready to ignite thermonuclear war whenever "necessary".

Within that sphere of influence, the incentive to threaten or launch nuclear weapons to protect U.S. interventionary troops is not limited, either, to prospective confrontation with Russian forces. Again, the list of incidents above reveals a clear pattern. In *every* one of the half-dozen cases when U.S. or allied tactical units were surrounded or cut off and in danger of defeat—at the Chosin Reservoir, Dienbienphu, Berlin, Quemoy, Khe Sanh— the administration secretly gave consideration, far more seriously than was ever admitted to the public, to the use of tactical nuclear weapons to defend them. In the light of this secret history, it is worth reflecting on the potential nature of the Rapid Deployment Force, limited in size and equipment and intended for distant intervention, as a portable Dienbienphu. Perhaps its major function would be as an instrument of real and visible commitment to the possible first-use of nuclear weapons by the United States. Indeed, that is pretty much how its purpose is described to a careful reader of official statements. Analogy is often explicit to the nuclear "tripwire" function of U.S. forces stationed in Western Europe.

In an interview in his first weeks in office (*New York Times*, February 3, 1981), President Reagan was asked if the U.S. was "capable, now, militarily of backing-up" his threat to "use arms to prevent any Soviet move in the Persian Gulf to cut off oil to the United States."

Reagan replied that what he called for:

...is a presence in the Middle East...Not the stationing of enough American troops that you say we could stop the Soviet Union if they set out to advance logistically; we know that we couldn't do that.

What is meant by a presence is that we're there enough to know and for the Soviets to know that if they made a reckless move, they would be risking a confrontation with the United States.

Why wouldn't that be, he was then asked "an empty threat that the Soviets could see through?"

Reagan's reply:

Well, it's not—you don't just plant a flag in the ground and walk away and leave it. There would be Americans there. But I think there should be some kind of American presence Well, we're doing it right now with the Navy in the Indian Ocean. But I think we need a ground presence also.

But it's based on the assumption—and I think a correct assumption—the Soviet Union is not ready yet to take on that confrontation which could become World War III.

There are, currently, a few weak links in that threatened sequence, but measures to strengthen them are all included in the current defense budget. Production of "neutron" warheads is one: with their relatively precise killing zone, they are "optimal" for close-in nuclear defense of protected troops (not only against tanks, not only in Europe). Precisely accurate delivery vehicles for such low-yield warheads as air- or sea-launched cruise missiles are another.

But how might the Soviets be deterred from retaliating in kind, at least, to such short-range attacks on their forces (or on their allies)? Or, if some retaliation was unavoidable, how might it be kept to an "acceptable" level, the prospect of which would not deter the U.S.from the initial attacks? The Pentagon's answer is to be able to pose a threat of further escalation that is more credible than the Soviets can make.

This is where the Pershing and cruise missiles to be stationed in Europe come in, and precisely with reference to the Middle East. With their extreme accuracy, unmatched by anything the Soviets possess (an order of magnitude better than the Russian SS-20), these promise great effectiveness against military targets even with relatively small-yield warheads, which need not destroy nearby population centers. Thus, the theory goes, the Russians might be deterred from retaliating against a U.S. carrier that had just destroyed their forward units in Iran, by fear that the U.S. would then use the unique capabilities of its Pershings to eliminate "surgically" all the bases, depots, command posts, and reserves in Eastern Europe and western Russia that support Soviet Middle Eastern theater operations. The Pershings could (on paper) do this while leaving most Russian cities (and ICBMs) intact, thus daring the Soviets to *start* an all-out city-busting exchange by replying with their large-yield, "indiscriminate" warheads (all they have, supposedly). This they might not do, even in a retaliation limited regionally to Europe, for fear the U.S. might then take out their ICBMs and a good deal more, with the MX, Trident II, and air-launched cruise missiles newly bought for this purpose.

In the words of E.P. Thompson: "If all this sounds crazy, then I can only agree that crazy is exactly what it is." Yet there is a short-run, narrow-focus rationality, certain coherent, if reckless, logic to the traps the Pentagon planners are so carefully setting for themselves, and all of us on earth. If they did not develop and deploy these new first-strike weapons, they could no longer even pretend that threats to initiate, or escalate nuclear war *against Soviet forces* were anything but hollow. But if they do invest several hundred billion dollars to achieve a first-strike capability, the Soviets could not be sure they had not convinced themselves they had succeeded.

If all these threats really were hollow, and if presidents were content to let this be perceived, the strategy would not be so dangerous; but then, it could not possibly succeed. Because they do rely on such means to protect what they see as vital interests, and because they do face up, in a sense realistically, to the credibility problem posed by the real craziness of the threats, decision-makers take positive measures to enhance that credibility. And these measures tend to be committing, that is, actually do increase the likelihood that the threats will be carried out if they should happen to be defied.

Thus, the Carter Doctrine itself, the president's public pledge of effective action ("any means necessary") has this effect. More concretely, nuclear-armed carriers are deployed to the area where their vulnerability as tempting and urgent targets for retaliatory or preemptive attack by the Soviets (or others) commits the U.S. to the possibility of nuclear escalation just as much as does their own capability to launch nuclear strikes. Exactly the same is true for the presence in Europe of the far-from-invulnerable Pershing and cruise missiles (or, on the Soviet side, SS-20s), which makes quite realistically credible the prospect of escalation *by one side or the other* from a Middle East conflict to the heart of Europe.

And it is not only from the Middle East that a regional nuclear conflict can "spill over" into Europe; *all* the non-Soviet targets of U.S. nuclear warnings in the list above were allies or clients of the Soviet Union, and the possibility of such spill-over (e.g., by Soviet retaliation against Berlin or U.S. missiles in Turkey, or against Japan) was vividly present in the minds of U.S. planners, even in the bygone era of U.S. superiority.[14]

Carter and Reagan are right; their policy cannot safely be regarded by the Russians, or anyone else, as mainly bluff. To make first-use warnings in a world so loaded with nuclear weapons that both threaten and invite preemption is *really* to play Russian roulette, with a gun pointed at the heads of all our children. It was thirty years ago that their White House predecessors pioneered an essentially terrorist strategy based on threats of regional genocide: the indiscriminate, massive slaughter of innocents foreseeable even in the most "limited" one-sided nuclear war. Their own current pursuit of superiority—in the face of present parity and of Soviet efforts to maintain it—is intended to prolong that strategy into an era when such threats are vastly more dangerous than before: likely now to be suicidal as well as genocidal, yet more likely to be challenged, and then, to be carried out. For their deliberate arms policies *are* effectively committing, making it likely that sooner or later—unless U.S. threats always work perfectly, which they will not—a U.S. president will turn a non-nuclear conflict into a nuclear one, or a local nuclear exchange into a global one.

The whole panoply of new arms and deployments, the "usable" neutron warhead and the Rapid Deployment Force to the Pershings and the MX, serve to implement presidential claims to have wired up the Middle East to a Doomsday Machine, the same way Iranian captors of American hostages in Teheran claimed to have wired the U.S. Embassy for total demolition in the event of attack.

It is not reassuring to recall that the latter warning did not, in fact, deter President Carter from launching a "rescue" raid, despite official estimates that it would cost the lives of some and perhaps most of the hostages. (They all lived to come home, after all, only by an "act of Allah" in the form of a sandstorm, which did not, however, spare the lives of all the raiders.)

Nevertheless, such threats can work, in the larger case as well. The Russians may not tread, in some future year of crisis, on the nuclear tripwires that have been laid around their present zone of occupation, protecting "our" oil in the Middle East. But the scale of risk is different. By the Carter/Reagan policy, human life in the Middle East and every city in the northern hemisphere is held hostage.

Even when such a policy is challenged, the demolitions *may* not be triggered. But the historical political conditions for that deserve to be studied. The one clear example among past nuclear crises is the failure of Nixon's direct, secret threats to the Hanoi regime in 1969. As H.R. Haldeman has revealed (see note 11), Henry Kissinger conveyed the warning to the Vietnamese that Nixon would escalate the war massively, including the possible use of nuclear weapons, if they did not accept his terms, which Nixon describes in his memoirs as his "November ultimatum". Roger Morris, who worked on these escalation plans under Kissinger, reports seeing the actual mission folders, including photographs, for the nuclear targets recommended to the president; one of them was a railhead in North Vietnam a mile and a half from the Chinese border. Hanoi never did accept the terms of Nixon's ultimatum, and Nixon's discussion and his later actions indicate strongly that it was not a bluff. Why then was the escalation not carried out?

Nixon himself gives the reason, one only, in his memoirs. There were too many Americans on the streets, demonstrating nonviolently against the war, on October 15, and again on November 15, 1969, the days of the Vietnam Moratorium actions and the Washington March Against Death, which happened to straddle his secret November 1 ultimatum. Nixon realized by October 16, he reports, that the protest movement had so "polarized" public opinion that he would not have sufficient support for his planned escalation. As he saw it, the antiwar movement had kept him from ending the war—his way—his first year in office. From another point of view, the protest actions—

whose actual power and effect Nixon kept at the time as secret from the public as his ultimatum—had prolonged the moratorium on the combat use of nuclear weapons by a dozen years so far. But presidents learn, too, from such setbacks. In the era of parity (which had arrived a few years before Nixon took office) public support of nuclear threats is both harder to come by and more necessary—if the threat is to work—than in the golden age of U.S. near-monopoly. A demonstration, in advance, of public support of the threat policy seems now almost essential to its prospects of success (as well as to containing the political risks if it should fail). Following the onset of the emotional hostage crisis, the Russian invasion of Afghanistan provided a near-perfect occasion for Carter to bid for this public support, which had become urgent, in White House eyes, almost a year earlier with the fall of the Shah as protector of U.S. interests in the Gulf. (Almost equally ominous for the prospects of client dictators of the U.S. was the triumph of liberation forces over Somoza a few months later, July 19, 1979, in Nicaragua.)

By deliberately making *public* what the Soviets had undoubtedly always regarded as sufficiently obvious implicit threats of nuclear initiatives to preserve U.S. influence in the Gulf oil regions, Carter was also acting to legitimize such threats in future cases where the public was less likely to perceive either an urgent threat from a rival superpower or a "vital national interest". Such threats would be used primarily, as in the past, against adversaries who did not yet have any nuclear weapons with which to retaliate: in particular, to U.S. troops who were defending other Shahs and Somozas from their own people.

Before long some such threat would be called and carried out. Even if such a war, outside NATO or the Middle East, should be limited in area and intensity, it would be a precedent for other nuclear wars that eventually would escape any such limits. And the next such outbreak would not again wait thirty-six years; more likely it would not take thirty-six weeks for the earliest example of nuclear first-use to be repeated, by the U.S. or others.

The onset of this fatal epoch of limited—and then less limited —nuclear wars will be hastened if the open advocacy by the White House and Pentagon of nuclear superiority, first-strike forces, and first-use threats continues to meet either a positive or a passive response. What Carter sought with his draft registration, what Reagan now seeks with his trillion-dollar-plus arms build-up, what some NATO leaders have intended by pressing the "token" deployment of Pershing and cruise missiles to Europe, are active expressions of consent and commitment from their publics, the nuclear hostages in Europe and America. It is what the Reverend Jim Jones wanted with his suicide drills in Guyana.

Jones called the practice sessions "White Nights", rehearsing his followers in the gestures of sacrificing their children and themselves, training them to react passively to his message (in the recurrent tones of every American president and every other leader of a nuclear weapons state since 1945): "Trust me. This time it's only a drill. *I* will decide...when the time has come for us to meet together on the other side; the time for the cyanide." That time finally came for Jones and his followers in mid-November 1978, just weeks before the NATO governments announced in December their decision, prepared in secret with no prior public discussion, to accept in the name of their citizens the stationing of U.S.-controlled Pershing and cruise missiles on European territory.

But in Europe, now, public consent to these preparations and rehearsals for "omnicide" is beginning to be denied. In many parts of West Europe, in fact, more broadly than in the United States as yet, an active movement of education and protest is well past the stage of beginnings. Reacting in particular to the December 1979 decision, in Holland, Norway, Britain, West Germany, to a lesser extent Denmark and Belgium, public movements are already approaching what is required—a movement of protest and resistance on the scale of that which blocked Nixon from escalating in 1969—to restrain their national leaderships from following the catastrophic overall course proclaimed by the U.S. administration.

As a participant in such projects as the teach-ins and demonstrations of the Mobilization for Survival, the Continental Walk for Disarmament and Social Justice, civil disobedience at Wall Street, the Pentagon, the Department of Energy, Rocky Flats Nuclear Production Facility, and the University of California (designer of all U.S. nuclear warheads), I can testify to the existence of a variegated and growing movement against the nuclear arms race in the United States, which also includes campaigns of civil disobedience organized by Jonah House and by the Pacific Life Community, broad-based regional protests against the MX basing plans in Utah and Nevada, massive non-compliance with draft registration. Yet it is my impression from several visits that West Europe is at this moment the focal point for effective resistance to official American-led nuclear policies, and that the current movement there is potentially an important source of energy and inspiration for Americans. Which is to say that the movement in Europe deserves close attention in America, and the essays in

E.P. Thompson's and Dan Smith's *Protest and Survive* are a good place to start.

The emphasis in *Protest and Survive* on unilateral measures of disarmament and on nuclear-free zones in England and West Europe has little counterpart in the U.S. movement, except for the regional anti-MX activities, and (like the latter) may at first glance seem parochial or unrealistically limited in scope to American readers: perhaps easily circumvented by national leaderships simply by changing the basing modes—putting the cruise missiles out to sea or among more compliant nationals, putting the MX missiles into Minuteman silos—without any fundamental change in the policy or its risks.

Actually, the differences in tactical focus reflect mainly different backgrounds, different national roles within the NATO alliance, a European perspective that is simply unfamiliar to most Americans, but that is important to come to understand. The immediate aims of END (European Nuclear Disarmament) in fact, logically *complement* objectives that have received more attention in the United States, such as a superpower freeze (a bilateral halt to the testing, production, and deployment of all new nuclear weapons and vehicles), bilateral no-first-use commitments, and a sharp reduction in superpower stockpiles, leading toward the general abolition of nuclear weapons. For example, to reject the deployment of neutron warheads and Pershing and cruise missiles and to demand the removal of the U.S. and Soviet nuclear weapons that now exist in West and East Europe, as END does, can be understood not only as part of the freeze demand but as calling for the effective implementation of a no-first-use commitment, since none of these forward-based weapons have much function other than first-use. What is more, the impulse to rid one's own neighborhood of the poisoned bait is a natural and appropriate basis for mobilization, if it comes to be understood within a framework of broader objectives and global concern.

We all live in Guyana now, there is no place to run to. From Utah to Norway to east of the Urals, we must take our stand where we live, and act to protect our home and our family: the earth and all living beings. The slogan of the Dutch Interchurch Council (IKV)—"Rid the earth of nuclear weapons; let it begin in Holland"—can inspire the commitments of individuals and communities in the superpowers and other countries of the world: "Let it begin here, now, with us."

As this is being written (July 1981) more than a thousand citizens of Europe (including delegations from East Germany and

Yugoslavia) are on the road, walking from Copenhagen to Paris on a March for Peace, with the theme: "A Nuclear-free Europe, from Poland to Portugal". The symbolism of the action, launched by three women from Norway and scheduled to arrive in Paris on August 6, seems just right; without relying on jet fuel, it is moving across national boundaries, at the steady pace of humans walking, together, in contact with the earth. As they proceed, holding rallies and teach-ins at each night's stop, others are joining the march: many of them, no doubt, from among the million Dutch citizens who petitioned and demonstrated against the neutron bomb in 1978 and the million West Germans who have petitioned (the Krefelder Appel) and demonstrated against the stationing of cruise and Pershing missiles this spring of 1981.

Like Americans resisting "symbolic" draft registration or sitting on railroad tracks at Rocky Flats, these European marchers are saying with their presence on the road what the mothers and fathers at Jonestown waited too long to say, what they should have said when the cyanide shipments first arrived or at the first rehearsals for murder and suicide: "No! Not our children! This is craziness; we won't be part of it." It is none too soon to be saying this to the President/Prime Minister/Chairman Jim Jones's of the world; nor is it, yet, too late. It is mutiny time in Jonestown: the revolt of the hostages.

Notes

1. Gregg Herken, *The Winning Weapon* (New York: Knopf, 1980), pp. 256-74.

...the important feature of the bombers—to British strategy—was that it worked—or at least many Americans believed it worked. By the end of July (1948) the absence of any Soviet military countermoves to the airlift that had effectively broken the blockade of Berlin was attributed in substantial part to the deterrent effect of the "atomic-capable" bombers within range of Russian cities. [p. 260]

Even Marshall—who throughout the year had been concerned that the United States not "provoke" the Russians into military action—now expressed optimism for the future. His change in attitude had been partly motivated, he confided to Forrestal, by his belief that "the Soviets are beginning to realize for the first time that the United States would really use the atomic bomb against them in the event of war." [p. 274]

2. Press Conference, November 30, 1950. Also Truman's memoirs, *Years of Trial and Hope*, Vol. II (New York: Signet, 1965), pp. 450-51. Dean Acheson, *Present at the Creation* (New York: W.W. Norton, 1969, pp. 472-85. (See note 14.)
3. Eisenhower's memoirs, *Mandate for Change*, Volume I (New York: Doubleday, 1963), pp 178-81.

In the light of my unwillingness to accept the status quo, several other moves were considered in the event that the Chinese Communists refused to accede to an armistice in a reasonable time. These possibilities differed in detail, but in order to back up any of them, we had to face several facts.

First, it was obvious that if we were to go over to a major offensive, the war would have to be expanded outside of Korea— with strikes against the supporting Chinese airfields in Manchuria, a blockade of the Chinese coast, and similar measures... Finally, to keep the attack from becoming overly costly, it was clear that we would have to use atomic weapons... One possibility was to let the Communist authorities understand that, in the absence of satisfactory progress, we intended to move decisively without inhibition in our use of weapons, and would no longer be responsible for confining hostilities to the Korean Peninsula. We would not be limited by any world-wide gentleman's agreement. In India and in the Formosa Straits area, and at the truce negotiations at Panmunjom, we dropped the word, discreetly, of our intention. We felt quite sure it would reach Soviet and Chinese Communist ears.

See also, Alexander L. George and Richard Smoke, *Deterrence in American Foreign Policy* (New York: Columbia University Press, 1974), pp. 237-41.
According to Sherman Adams, Eisenhower's White House chief of staff (Firsthand Report, pp. 48-49).:

Long afterward, talking one day with Eisenhower about the events that led up finally to the truce with Korea, I asked him what it was that brought the Communists into line. "Danger of an atomic war," he said without hesitation. "We told them we could not hold to a limited war any longer if the Communists welched on a treaty of truce. They didn't want a full-scale war or an atomic attack. That kept them under some control."

In the above passage of his memoirs, Eisenhower also mentions: "Meanwhile, General Mark Clark (who had succeeded Ridgway as United Nations commander) began to suspect that the Communists were building up forces in the Kaesong 'sanctuary' area. He requested permission to launch an attack in the event he became convinced that a Communist attack there was pending. This authority I thought unwise to delegate at that time" (p. 181). But recently declassified minutes of the National Security Council meeting on February 11, 1953, to which this refers, record a noteworthy exchange at this point, omitted from the memoirs:

[The President] then expressed the view that we should consider
the use of tactical atomic weapons on the Kaesong area (an area
of approximately twenty-eight square miles, which was according
to Clark, "now chock full of troops and material", which provided
a good target for this type of weapon. In any case, the President
added, we could not go on the way we were indefinitely.

General Bradley thought it desirable to begin talking with our
allies regarding an end of the sanctuary, but thought it unwise to
broach the subject yet of possible use of atomic weapons.

Secretary Dulles discussed the moral problem and the inhibitions
on the use of the A-bomb, and Soviet success to date in setting
atomic weapons apart from all other weapons as being in a special
category. It was his opinion that we should try to break down this
false distinction.

The President added that we should certainly start on diplomatic
negotiations with our allies. To him, it seemed that our self-respect
and theirs was involved, and if they objected to the use of atomic
weapons we might well ask them to supply three or more divisions
needed to drive the Communists back, in lieu of use of atomic
weapons. In conclusion, however, the President ruled against any
discussion with our allies of military plans or weapons of attack.

The corresponding discussion in Eisenhower's memoirs does raise the
subject of allied attitudes (and perhaps, implicitly, those of the American
public as well) in remarks that seem highly pertinent to a number of the
essays that follow:

If we decided upon a major, new type of offensive, the present
policies would have to be changed and the new ones agreed to by
our allies. Foremost would be the proposed use of atomic weapons.
In this respect American views have always differed somewhat from
those of some of our allies. For the British, for example, the use
of atomic weapons in war at that time would have been a decision
of the gravest kind. My feeling was then, and still remains, that
it would be impossible for the United States to maintain the military
commitments which it now sustains around the world (without
turning into a garrison state) did we not possess atomic weapons
and the will to use them when necessary. But an American decision
to use them at that time would have created strong disruptive
feelings between ourselves and our allies. However, if an all-out
offensive should be highly successful, I felt that the rifts so caused
could, in time, be repaired.

Of course, there were other problems, not the least of which
would be the possibility of the Soviet Union entering the war. In
nuclear warfare the Chinese Communists would have been able
to do little. But we knew that the Soviets had atomic weapons in
quantity, and estimated that they would soon explode a hydrogen
device. Of all the Asian targets which might be subjected to Soviet
bombing, I was most concerned about the unprotected cities of
Japan. [p. 180]

4. Prime Minister Bidault in the film *Hearts and Minds*, and in Roscoe Drummond and Gaston Coblentz, *Duel at the Brink* (New York: Doubleday, 1960), pp. 121-22. Also see, Richard Nixon's memoirs, *RN* (New York: Grosset & Dunlap, 1978), pp. 150-55.

As he told Drummond and Coblentz, Bidault understood Dulles, on two separate occasions, to have offered him the use of American atomic bombs by French forces in the Indochina war.

By Bidault's account, offers were made before the fall of Dienbienphu; prior, that is, to the Geneva Conference. According to Bidault, both offers were made to him personally by Dulles in Paris.

The first is recalled by Bidault as an offer of one or more atomic bombs to be dropped on Communist Chinese territory near the Indochina border in a countermove against the Chinese supply lines to the Vietminh Communists. The second is recalled as an offer of two atomic bombs against the Vietminh forces at Dienbienphu.

Bidault, by his account, declined both offers. He told Dulles that it would be impossible to predict where the use of nuclear weapons against Red China would end, that it could lead to Russian intervention and a world-wide holocaust. In the case of the second offer, he considered the French and Vietminh forces to be by then too closely engaged at Dienbienphu to permit the use of atomic weapons.

5. Barry M. Blechman and Stephen S. Kaplan, *Force Without War* (Washington: Brookings Institution, 1978), pp. 238, 256.
6. Morton H. Halperin, *The 1958 Taiwan Straits Crisis: A Documented History* (formerly Top Secret), RAND Corporation Research Memorandum RM-4900-ISA, December 1966.
7. Blechman and Kaplan, *Force Without War*, pp. 343-439.
8. R.F. Kennedy, *Thirteen Days* (New York: W.W. Norton, 1971). (See note 14.)
9. Blechman and Kaplan, pp. 47-49, with a table listing nineteen such incidents between November 1946, and the worldwide SAC alert of October 1973.
10. Herbert Schyandler, *The Unmaking of a President* (Princeton: Princeton University Press, 1977), pp. 86-91. Also see, General Westmoreland's memoirs, *A Soldier Reports* (New York: Doubleday, 1976), p. 338.

Because the region around Khe Sanh was virtually uninhabited, civilian casualties would be minimal. If Washington officials were so intent on "sending a message" to Hanoi, surely small tactical nuclear weapons would be a way to tell Hanoi something, as two atomic bombs had spoken convincingly to Japanese officials during World War II and the threat of atomic bombs induced the North Koreans to accept meaningful negotiations during the Korean War. It could be that use of a few small tactical nuclear weapons in Vietnam—or even the threat of them—might have quickly brought the war there to an end.

Or as General Nathan Twining, U.S. air force chief of staff at the time of Dienbienphu and later elevated by Eisenhower to be chairman of the Joint Chiefs of Staff, recollected in tranquility:

> I still think it would have been a good idea (to have taken) three small tactical A-bombs—it's a fairly isolated area, Dienbienphu—no great town around there, only Communists and their supplies. You could take all day to drop the bomb, make sure you put it in the right place. No opposition. And clean those Commies out of there and the band could play the Marseillaise and the French could march out of Dienbienphu in fine shape. And those Commies would say, "Well, those guys might do this again to us. We'd better be careful." And we might not have had this problem we're facing in Vietnam now if we'd dropped those small A-weapons. [Dulles Oral History Project, Princeton; cited in Carl Solberg, *Riding High* (New York: Mason & Lipscomb, 1973), p. 230]

11. H.R. Haldeman's memoirs, *The End of Power* (New York: Times Books, 1978), pp. 81-85, 97-98; and Richard M. Nixon's memoirs, *RN*, pp. 393-414; and personal interviews with Roger Morris and Eqbal Ahmad.

Haldeman's account:

> When Nixon spoke of his desire to be a peacemaker, he was not just delivering words his listeners wanted to hear. Nixon not only *wanted* to end the Vietnam War, he was absolutely convinced he *would* end it in his first year. I remember during the campaign, walking along a beach, he once said, "I'm the one man in this country who can do it, Bob...."
>
> He saw a parallel in the action President Eisenhower had taken to end another war. When Eisenhower arrived in the White House, the Korean War was stalemated. Eisenhower ended the impasse in a hurry. He secretly got word to the Chinese that he would drop nuclear bombs on North Korea unless a truce was signed immediately. In a few weeks, the Chinese called for a truce and the Korean War ended.
>
> In the 1950s Eisenhower's military background had convinced the Communists that he was sincere in his threat. Nixon didn't have that background, but he believe his hardline anti-Communist rhetoric of twenty years would serve to convince the North Vietnamese equally as well that he really meant to do what he said. He expected to utilize the same principle of a threat of excessive force. He would combine that threat with more generous offers of financial aid to the North Vietnamese than they had ever received before. And with this combination of a strong warning plus unprecedented generosity, he was certain he could force the North Vietnamese—at long last—into legitimate peace negotiations.
>
> The threat was the key, and Nixon coined a phrase for his theory which I'm sure will bring smiles of delight to Nixon-haters everywhere. We were walking along a foggy beach after a long day

of speechwriting. He said, "I call it the Madman Theory, Bob. I want the North Vietnamese to believe I've reached the point where I might do *anything* to stop the war. We'll just slip the word to them that, for God's sake, you know Nixon is obsessed about Communism. We can't restrain him when he's angry—and he has his hand on the nuclear button—and Ho Chi Minh himself will be in Paris in two days begging for peace."

As it turned out, it wasn't Bill Rogers, future Secretary of State, who slipped the word to the North Vietnamese, but a brilliant, impulsive, witty gentleman with an engaging German accent— Henry Kissinger. [pp. 82-83]

12. References in text.
13. References in text.
14. Eisenhower's self-appointed concern (see note 3) about retaliation against "the unprotected cities of Japan" (which were, and are, of course, neither more nor less unprotected against nuclear attack than every other city in the world) if he should carry out his nuclear threats against China in 1953 would have been equally appropriate in connection with his offer of nuclear weapons for use in Indochina in 1954 and his plans for use over Quemoy in 1958. But his concern not only failed to preclude the threats and serious preparations; it did not lead him to alert the Japanese or others including close allies, to the danger he perceived himself as imposing on them.

Immediately after Truman's announcement of U.S. consideration of nuclear weapons in Korea, December 1950, British Prime Minister Atlee flew to Washington, wishing, in Acheson's words, "Britain to be admitted to some participation with us in any future decision to use nuclear weapons," specifically an agreement "that neither of us would use these weapons without prior consultation with the other." (*Present at the Creation*, pp. 478, 484). Like other U.S. allies, Britain failed to get any such assurance, then or later.

The main effect of Atlee's "scurrying across the ocean" in response to Truman's "unfortunate" candor at his press conference (Acheson's words, in an account contemptuously patronizing of the British leader) was to make later presidents more circumspect with their nuclear threats, usually cutting out U.S. allies and the American public from knowledge of them.

Even the Cuban Missile Crisis is only a partial exception to this. In an account unique for its vividness and its authority, Robert Kennedy reports an episode in that crisis when the Navy was preparing to force a Russian submarine to the surface, a few minutes which

> were the time of gravest concern for the President. Was the world on the brink of a holocaust? Was it an error? A mistake? Was there something further that should have been done? Or not done? His hand went up to his face and covered his mouth. He opened and closed his fist. His face seemed drawn, his eyes pained, almost gray. We stared at each other across the table. For a few fleeting seconds, it was almost as though no one else was there and he was

no longer the President.

Inexplicably, I thought of when he was ill and almost died; when he lost his child; when we learned that our oldest brother had been killed; of personal times of strain and hurt. The voices droned on, but I didn't seem to hear anything until I heard the President say: "Isn't there some way we can avoid having our first exchange with a Russian submarine—almost anything but that?" "No, there's too much danger to our ships. There is no alternative," said McNamara. "Our commanders have been instructed to avoid hostilities if at all possible, but this is what we must be prepared for, and this is what we must expect."

We had come to the time of final decision. "We must expect that they will close down Berlin—make the final preparations for that," the President said. I felt that we were on the edge of a precipice with no way off. . .One thousand miles away in the vast expanse of the Atlantic Ocean the final decisions were going to be made in the next few minutes. President Kennedy had initiated the course of events, but he no longer had control over them. [*Thirteen Days*, p. 48]

Minutes later a messenger brought in a report that Russian ships approaching the blockade line had stopped dead in the water, and Kennedy then cancelled the intercept orders. But three days later, the Executive Committee of the NSC with the president presiding was considering an imminent U.S. air strike and invasion.

The NATO countries were supporting our position and recommending that the U.S. be firm, but, President Kennedy said, they did not realize the full implications for them. If we carried out an air strike against Cuba and the Soviet Union answered by attacking (U.S. Jupiter intermediate-range missiles—comparable to Pershing IIs—stationed in) Turkey, all NATO was going to be involved. Then, immediately, the president would have to decide whether he would use nuclear weapons against the Soviet Union, and all mankind would be threatened. . .We had to be aware that we were deciding, the president was deciding, for the U.S., the Soviet Union, Turkey, and really for all mankind. . .[*Ibid*, pp. 74, 77; final dots in original]

Later that evening, alone with Robert Kennedy, the president

talked about the miscalculations that lead to war. War is rarely intentional. The Russians don't wish to fight any more than we do. They do not want to war with us nor we with them. And yet if events continue as they have in the, last several days, that struggle—which no one wishes, which will accomplish nothing—will engulf and destroy all mankind. . .It was not only for Americans that he was concerned, or primarily the older generation of any land. The thought that disturbed him the most, and that made the prospect of war much more fearful than it would otherwise have been, was the specter of the death of the children of this country and all the world—the young people who had no role, who had no say, who knew nothing even of the confrontation, but whose lives would be snuffed out like everyone else's. They would never have a chance to make a decision, to vote in an election, to run for office, to lead a revolution, to determine their own destinies. [Ibid., p. 84-85.]

These reflections had (only) the effect of leading President Kennedy to send his brother to convey an explicit, secret, forty-eight-hour ultimatum to Krushchev through Ambassador Dobrynin, rather than simply to attack two days later without warning. According to Theodore Sorenson, "[T]he odds that the Soviets [sic] would go all the way to war," President Kennedy later said, "seemed to him then 'somewhere between one out of three and even.' " [*Kennedy* (New York: Harper & Row, 1965), p. 705].

Noam Chomsky

Patterns of Intervention

At the UN General Assembly session on disarmament in June 1982, a rather significant address was delivered by the (Christian) Representative of the government of Lebanon, Mr. Ghassan Tueni. Naturally, it received virtually no notice in the American press (it appeared in the *New Outlook*, Tel Aviv). What Ambassador Tueni said bears directly on the topic of this conference, and on the specific topic that I have been asked to discuss.

Mr. Tueni began by asking to be excused if the representative of Lebanon had "no words on universal disarmament, save the pious prayers that it should happen soon enough for his country to survive," a country that was then being, "martyred and crucified." "The atomic holocaust of tomorrow," he said, "becomes a problematic danger, remote and almost unreal, to those who are living an actual holocaust: the holocaust of their mother earth, of men, women, and children physically destroyed along with the cities they built and loved." He was, incidentally, speaking on June 22, before the cruel siege of Beirut and the indiscriminate bombing of heavily populated civilian areas that reached its peak in late July and August.

Mr. Tueni asked that the General Assembly not "be diverted by abstract testimonies for peace. . . Concerned as we all are with the necessity of halting the race towards the atomic holocaust of tomorrow, let us remember the no less apocalyptic realities of today." The representative of the country that was then officially being "liberated" from PLO tyranny by Israel may, perhaps, be excused for a certain degree of hyperbole.

The Lebanese Ambassador also made the important point that "the war in Lebanon was becoming a danger not to Lebanon

alone, but to others as well, and probably to the entire world."
The last point is quite accurate. The world came uncomfortably
close to nuclear war this summer. The U.S. and Soviet fleets were
present in force in the Eastern Mediterranean. The war ended—
temporarily at least—with heavy Israeli artillery in a position to
shell Damascus, as Defense Minister Sharon pointedly observed.
If the fighting between Israel and Syria had escalated a notch or
two higher, the U.S.S.R. might have made some move in defense
of its Syrian ally, a step that surely would have brought about
direct U.S. military involvement and possibly a superpower
confrontation.

Furthermore, as Assistant Secretary of Defense Richard Perle
revealed a few days ago, Israeli jets attacked and killed 11 Russians
who were inspecting a downed Israeli reconnaisance plane to
prevent them from obtaining secret electronic equipment. The
Russian Embassy was shelled during the Israeli bombardment of
Beirut, and parts of the Embassy were occupied by the Israeli army
that invaded West Beirut, a gratuitous act of defiance in the course
of the conquest of a city that was virtually undefended after the
PLO had withdrawn to save it from total obliteration.

All of this was passed over calmly here, because we take it for
granted that the U.S.S.R. will back down in any confrontation—
outside of Eastern Europe, at least. Luckily for the world, this
expectation once again turned out to be correct. But this should
not prevent us from perceiving the seriousness of the provocation.
Suppose that the situation had been reversed. Suppose that a
Cuban army had invaded Costa Rica or Guatemala, purposely
killing 11 American advisers, shelling the U.S. Embassy and
occupying it in the course of conquering the capital city. How
would the U.S. have reacted? Of course, the question is academic;
at the first appearance of a Cuban soldier we would have bombed
Havana or perhaps even Moscow. But as we interpret the rules
of the game, the Russians are expected to accept passively affronts
that the U.S. would never tolerate for a moment. And so far, they
have, or we would not be here to discuss the matter today.

The Lebanese war is a typical example of the circumstances that
will sooner or later lead to a final nuclear war. It is highly unlikely
that this war will break out in Europe. Emphasis on such
possibilities should be understood as a facet of the Cold War
propaganda system, which typically seeks to disguise issues of
intervention in terms of great power conflict. But it is not at all
unlikely that the superpowers will come into conflict, and nuclear
conflict, when some Third World conflagration blazes out of
control. Possible examples are all too numerous. The U.S. has

been carrying out large-scale naval maneuvers in the Caribbean for over a year, obviously aimed at Cuba, Grenada, Nicaragua and El Salvador (perhaps later Guatemala). It has also been attempting to inflame the Honduras-Nicaragua border. If the U.S. moves on to a blockade, as it may unless prevented by public protest, then Russian ships may be intercepted, and as the Secretary of the Navy recently pointed out, this will almost certainly lead to a global confrontation, possibly nuclear war. Or to take another part of the world, consider Southeast Asia. The Chinese invasion of Vietnam in 1979, surely with at least tacit American support, might have led to a Soviet reaction and a superpower confrontation. The chances of something similar being repeated are not small, with the U.S. supporting the Pol Pot forces (via China and Thailand) as part of its policy of "bleeding Vietnam"—an extraordinary example of sadism, considering the legacy of American crimes in Indochina. Many other examples come to mind, though none are so dangerous as the Middle East.

From these considerations, it follows that a prime concern for those who want to do something to avert nuclear war must be to try to reduce the tensions and conflicts that will, sooner or later, serve as the trigger for such a war. Since U.S. intervention has often been a factor in maintaining or exacerbating such tensions and conflict, there is a great deal that we can do here to lessen or possibly eliminate them. There could be no greater contribution to world peace and to the diminishing prospects for human survival—quite apart from the significance for the local victims. It is exactly at this point that the concerns of the disarmament movement coincide, in the clearest way, with those of people committed to reversing the U.S. policy of maintaining its peculiar form of "order", which in practice often means violence and repression, in much of the world.

The Middle East, again, is a crucial example. Claudia Wright commented that the U.S. is creating a system reminiscent of the Ottoman Empire in the Middle East, with the seat of power in Washington rather than Istanbul and with Israeli troops serving as the janissaries, maintaining order as, in effect, an American mercenary force. Just two days ago, the Senate Appropriations Committee voted to increase American aid to Israel, already phenomenal in scale, beyond the increase already proposed by the Reagan Administration, in recognition of Israel's achievements in rapidly extending settlement and oppression in the occupied territories and destroying much of Lebanon—specifically, virtually demolishing organized Palestinian society—in one of the more savage and cowardly military operations of recent history. Both the Administration and the Senate Committee have now expressed their conviction that these achievements merit a still greater American subsidy, though they differ on just how large a reward should be offered. Israeli officials bitterly condemned the attempt by the Administration to limit the reward, arguing that this amounted to a policy of "appeasement" of the Arabs reminiscent of Munich, and that it "clearly violated" the U.S. pledge not to link aid to Israel with political issues, a display of quite astonishing gall; to Israel and its "supporters" here it is the bounden duty of the American taxpayer to finance Israel's military adventures and its settlements in the occupied territories.

It is quite clear that U.S. payments to Israel through a variety of means (including tax-free contributions, a subsidy thereby imposed on the American taxpayer) have reflected Israel's perceived role as a "strategic asset", ensuring American dominance in the region. With this aim, the U.S. has molded Israel into the world's fourth largest military power, doing what it could—which was a great deal—to further the transformation of Israel into a militarized state, a kind of Sparta, completely dependent on the U.S. for survival and serving the interests of American power: primarily, the perceived need to control or destroy indigenous radical nationalist forces. In conformity to these ends, the U.S. has consistently blocked all efforts to solve the Arab-Israeli conflict by peaceful means in a manner that would recognize the national rights of Israelis and Palestinians. The U.S. has, in fact, headed the rejectionist camp for many years, standing virtually alone, alongside its Israeli client, in opposition to an international consensus that has long included the PLO and most of the Arab states. This version of history will no doubt sound completely absurd to a literate (i.e., successfully brainwashed) American audience. However, it has the merit of being true, and easily documented. But the facts are little known here, thanks to the contributions of the press and the intellectual community to what has sometimes been called "historical engineering"— redesigning the facts of history in the interests of established power, a noble contribution of the intelligentsia in many lands. In the past 15 years, the U.S. has generously funded Israel's steps toward integration of the occupied territories, first under the Labor Alignment, then, on a rapidly increasing scale, under Begin's Likud coalition. And more recently, the U.S. has subsidized Israel's aggression in Lebanon since 1978, as it still does, with American liberalism well in the lead.

It has been virtually an axiom of U.S. foreign policy since World War II that the stupendous energy reserves of the Middle East must remain under effective American control, or at least, that other powers gain no privileged access to them. Concern over the flow of petrodollars is a more recent variant of the same commitment. The first major U.S. intervention after World War II was at the periphery of this region and was motivated in part, by concern over a possible threat to U.S. control over Middle East oil. I am referring, of course, to the U.S. counterinsurgency campaign in Greece in the late 1940's, under the farcical Truman Doctrine, which committed the U.S. "to support free people who are resisting attempted subjugation by armed minorities or by outside pressures." A February 1948 CIA study observed that a victory for the Greek guerillas would endanger U.S. control over Middle East oil, 40% of known world reserves, through the familiar domino effect. Similar concerns were repeatedly expressed by high-level government officials.

The U.S. counterinsurgency effort in Greece was no small affair. In the civil war that followed, 160,000 Greeks were killed, 800,000 were made refugees, tens of thousands became permanent exiles and tens of thousands more were sent to concentration camps on prison islands where they were subjected to torture, political execution, or if lucky, only reeducation, all under the enthusiastic supervision of the American mission. The history is illuminating. The British army had entered Greece after the Nazis had withdrawn, and turned to suppressing the anti-Nazi resistance and restoring the rule of Nazi collaborators and Greek Royalists. When Britain, in its weakened postwar state, proved unequal to the task, the U.S. took over under the Truman Doctrine, in the manner just described, attempting—and finally succeeding—to crush the former anti-Nazi resistance and to place in power its favorites, such as King Paul and Queen Frederika, both of whom had been leading lights in the fascist youth movements, meanwhile destroying the unions, controlling elections, etc., with an impact on Greece that was devastating for many years. Here, this was presented as a defense of Greece against the Russians—whose sole role, as far as was known then or now, was to try to call off the Greek guerillas, in recognition of the fact that this area, peripheral to the oil-rich Middle East, was American turf. The appeal to the alleged Russian threat to "scare Hell out of the country" (to use Senator Vandenberg's famous words) worked like a dream, yielding a lesson well-learned and applied with close to 100% regularity in later years, including today.

The counterinsurgency campaign in Greece set the pattern for future interventions, but in other respects as well, it illustrated systematic behavior of the forces that liberated much of the world from the fascist conquests. The vision of the future world held by the resistance forces was often quite different from that of the liberators. This is clear enough in the case of the territories conquered by the Red Army, and since held in an iron grip. The systematic behavior of the western allies, in this regard, has been less studied, apart from a few contributions, such as the pioneering work of Gabriel and Joyce Kolko, which has been consigned to oblivion because it suffers from the grave defects of significant insight and massive documentation. Particular cases are studied in specialized treatments of one or another area, but the pattern, which is quite systematic, rarely emerges.

In fact, in much of the world the allied armies restored the rule of fascist collaborators and removed or destroyed the structures of the resistance, as in Greece. The U.S. liberated French North Africa in 1942, installing in power Admiral Jean Darlan, the author of Vichy's anti-Semitic laws and a leading Nazi collaborator. "As much as Goering or Goebbels, historian Stephen Amborse writes, "Darlan was the antithesis of the principles the Allies said they were struggling to establish." As American troops liberated southern Italy, they installed in power the regime of fascist Marshall Badoglio. The Italian resistance liberated much of northern Italy, received the thanks of the American army as it arrived, and was then sent packing. Greece we have already discussed. In Asia, much the same was true, in Thailand, the Philippines, South Korea, and elsewhere.

In the case of official enemies, we have no difficulty discerning a systematic pattern of behavior and explaining it in terms of the domestic system of power. Such exercise of rationality is excluded in principle in investigating one's own state, however. It is the domain of "extremists" or "emotional" and "irresponsible" eccentrics. The same is true with regard to the systematic pattern of intervention in post-war years.

From virtually its origins, the CIA was directed to covert activities, including "the support of terrorism around the world" in the words of the document that launched these operations. The record is long and bloody. Some particular cases are reasonably well-known: the restoration of the Shah in Iran, the overthrow of a democratic government in Guatemala in 1954, the invasion of the Dominican Republic in 1965, and others. Guatemala was converted to a literal hell-on-earth, with periodic infusions of

American assistance, particularly in the counterinsurgency campaigns of the 1960's under the liberal Democratic administrations, which placed in power the murderous regimes that have tortured the country since, most recently, through the agency of Israel, when Congress blocked direct U.S. government assistance. Cuba was invaded, and after the invasion failed, subjected to a "secret war" of terrorism; since Cuba was the primary victim of terrorism in the world, it is natural, as any student of Orwell would expect, that it is generally regarded here as one of the centers of world terrorism. Then there is the case of Indochina, quickly forgotten here: 2 million dead, 3 countries ravaged, including—perhaps the most obscene example—northern Laos, where a defenseless peasant society was subjected to merciless bombardment with hardly even a pretense of any military purpose. U.S. firepower quite possibly exceeded the total expended on all sides in all previous human history.

In official U.S. history (scholarship, the schools, the media), there is no such event as the U.S. invasion of South Vietnam, later U.S. aggression in all of Indochina, just as official Party history in the U.S.S.R. records no such event as the Russian invasion of Afghanistan. In both cases, the simple truth has disappeared into a convenient memory hole, and what remains is the "defense" of South Vietnam (Afghanistan) from terrorist bands controlled by the superpower enemy. In the U.S., indeed much of the West, the mainstream intelligentsia, liberal to conservative, do not even comprehend what might be meant by reference to the U.S. attack on the peasant society of South Vietnam (80% of the population when direct U.S. aggression began under Kennedy in 1962, after years of terrorism and violence by the U.S. client regime), one of the more notable successes of 20th century indoctrination.

A crucial event of modern history took place in 1961, when the Kennedy Administration changed the mission of the Latin American military (virtually an adjunct of the Pentagon) from "hemispheric defense" to "internal security", i.e., war against the domestic population. This led to what the quasi-governmental Linowitz Commission later called a "plague of repression", without precedent in the bloody history of the continent, as Nazi-like thugs took over country after country, with regular U.S. support. The Latin American scholar Lars Schoultz concluded from a study of American "human rights" policies that U.S. aid "has tended to flow disproportionately to Latin American governments which torture their citizens," "to the hemisphere's relatively egregious violators of fundamental human rights," quite uncorrelated with need, though there was some change in Latin America under the impact of the Congressional human rights programs of the 1970's. This was one aspect of the dread "Vietnam syndrome", a malady that has now been largely overcome, at least in elite circles—where, in fact, only few had been afflicted. Much the same has been true throughout a large part of the world. For extensive evidence on this matter, one may turn to Edward Herman's recent book *The Real Terror*, which also contains a detailed analysis of the mechanisms by which the facts are concealed in the media.

It is, incidentally, an interesting exercise to compare Herman's study to Claire Sterling's book *The Terror Network*. The two books differ in a number of respects. Herman's is factual, extensively documented, carefully reasoned; it demonstrates the central role of the United States in global terrorism. Sterling's is in large measure a compendium of innuendo and fantasy, lacking serious documentation, verging on the ludicrous in its reasoning and with barely a pretense of serious analysis; it places the blame for terrorism on official enemies, the U.S.S.R., Cuba, the PLO, etc. It therefore follows, as night follows day, that Sterling's book is widely known and much respected, while Herman's is ignored or dismissed.

The reasons for the systematic pattern of U.S. intervention in the post-World War II period are not difficult to discern. During World War II, top-level planners recognized that the war would end with the U.S. in a position of global dominance with few if any historical precedents. In fact, by 1950 the U.S. produced about 50% of world output. They developed the concept of a "Grand Area", a global domain including at a minimum the Western hemisphere, the former British Empire, and the Far East, which would be subordinated to the needs of the American economy—or more precisely, the needs of those who own and manage it. This was to be only the nucleus of a still grander system, with indefinite bounds. Given the commitment to this concept—rational in essence, whatever one's moral judgement—it is not difficult to explain the systematic pattern of intervention, subversion and aggression, sometimes through the medium of client states, Israel being the prime example in recent years but hardly the only one. Consider, for example, the Indonesian example of Timor, which led to the death of perhaps one or two hundred thousand people thanks to ample U.S. diplomatic and military support (primarily under the Human Rights Administration) and to a highly efficient press cover-up, which still continues. One will search in vain for analysis of the U.S. responsibility for this tragedy in the mainstream media, with very rare exceptions.

Naturally, this entire topic is under a strict taboo in responsible scholarship and the press—though, as noted, it is permissible on occasion to discuss specific examples, in isolation, as long as they are interpreted in terms of tragic irony, American innocence, idealism gone astray, excessive moralism, or, perhaps, the machinations of certain evil men (say, Richard Nixon, who was expelled from the body politic for such misdeeds as constructing an "enemies list" that included people with power and influence). The study of systematic U.S. behavior cannot be told, and its sources in the distribution of domestic power cannot be investigated. Those who defy the rules are not sent to concentration camps in free society, but they are successfully marginalized, ignored, dismissed as "angry" or "emotional", or as "pamphleteers" (Gabriel Kolko, according to the *New York Times Book Review*), or sometimes condemned for a "double standard" or "lack of even-handedness" when they compare U.S. behavior in the Third World to the behavior of the U.S.S.R., another aspect of the comic antics of the responsible intelligentsia.

These systematic American policies have led to death and suffering on a vast scale, and they are one major factor contributing to tensions and conflicts that repeatedly have come close to setting off the superpower conflict towards which we are steadily advancing.

Talk given at Deadly Connection Conference, 4 December 1982.

Paul F. Walker

The (Il)logic of Nuclear War Fighting

Heady talk of fighting, winning, "prevailing," and surviving a nuclear war is making the rounds in Washington these days. The President describes how "limited" a tactical nuclear war might be in Germany; the Secretary of Defense describes the need for regaining a "margin of safety" in nuclear weapons, in order to allow for "flexibility" of operations; and the Committee on the Present Danger—which has some five dozen members serving in the Reagan Administration—talks of the need for "preparations" during the current "prewar period."

Unfortunately, such talk cannot simply be dismissed as rhetoric. The weapons being developed today—MX, B-1, Trident, cruise—are all intended for nuclear war-fighting scenarios rather than deterrence. In Hegelian fashion, nuclear deterrence theory has been stood on its head. The MAD (mutual assured destruction) theory is that we need nuclear weapons to discourage, or deter, the enemy from launching an attack. But this administration argues that we must have nuclear weapons that provide "maximum flexibility of use"—weapons that could be used to fight a nuclear war—so that, should the need arise, technical limitations would not limit the utility of the weapons.

How have we moved so far from the original goals of deterrence? And what does this mean for nuclear sufficiency? Just how much is enough when we speak of nuclear weapons?

To answer these questions, we must examine several factors: cold-war politics, interservice rivalries, the evolution of nuclear doctrine, and most important, the technological momentum of nuclear weapons systems.

Technical Development in Nuclear Weapons

The nuclear weapons of 1945 were heavy, difficult to deliver, and inaccurate. The bomb dropped on Nagasaki, in fact, was considerably off target. Furthermore, by the end of that summer the U.S. had exploded its total nuclear arsenal at Alamogordo, Hiroshima and Nagasaki. These weapons were bulky and inefficient: Little Boy, which killed some 100,000 people at Hiroshima, weighed 9000 pounds, and Fat Man was 1000 pounds heavier. Each 600 to 700 pounds of bomb weight provided one kiloton of nuclear explosive, making the bombs so heavy that planners worried whether the B-29s carrying the weapons would be able to fly safely.

Since 1945, nuclear weapons and their delivery systems have become quite sophisticated. For example, the new air-launched cruise missile (ALCM) weighing 200 pounds with a 200- to 300-kiloton warhead in its nose, has for each pound of weight a kiloton or more of nuclear explosive. And while Little Boy and Fat Man exploded where they were dropped, an ALCM can fly another 1500 miles because of its air-breathing propulsion system.

More important than yield-to-weight ratios are the increasing accuracy and destructiveness of nuclear weapons. A nuclear warhead's accuracy is measured by the radius within which 50% or more of the targeted warheads will land, a figure known as "circular error probable," or CEP. While Fat Man's CEP was one mile or more, the MX has an estimated 300-foot accuracy. Cruise missiles, although much slower traveling than ballistic missiles, have a radar system that guides them as they approach their target, guaranteeing that they will be even more accurate. Soviet weapons, although less accurate than most U.S. systems, now have CEPs of 900 feet or less.

Furthermore, once they hit their targets, today's nuclear weapons would be far more destructive than the bombs of 1945—by a factor of at least sixty. For example, Little Boy immediately destroyed over four square miles; one MX missile, with ten 350-kiloton warheads, could destroy some 250 square miles around ground zero.

Combine greater accuracy and more destructiveness in both Soviet and American nuclear weapons, and what do you have? Counterforce targeting potential, or the ability to strike hardened targets such as buried missile silos and command posts. When deployed in the thousands, such counterforce technology drives both sides to nuclear-war-fighting doctrines: thinking and planning about nuclear war as though it could be won.

Changes in Nuclear Doctrine

Just after World War II, the U.S. nuclear warheads carried by European-based B-29 bombers covered one hundred or fewer targets in the Soviet Union. As the number of weapons increased, so did the number of targets. By the mid-1950s the number was in the low hundreds, and by the early 1960s there were about a thousand. Although "limited" nuclear scenarios —plans for local back-and-forth nuclear battles—had been debated in studies by the Department of Defense and military contractors since the late 1940s, the first "single integrated operational plan" (or SIOP) for nuclear targeting, written in 1960, relied on firing everything at once. The idea was that, with the threat of that response, the Soviets would not attack. Deterrence reigned supreme.

When faced, however, with a request for 10,000 land-based missiles from the Strategic Air Command in the early 1960's, Secretary of Defense Robert McNamara sought to determine just how much was enough for deterrence. His analysis, shown in Figure 1, illustrated in cold cost-benefit analysis that attacking with any more than 400 megatons would do little more than bounce more rubble. McNamara's analysis, based on Soviet

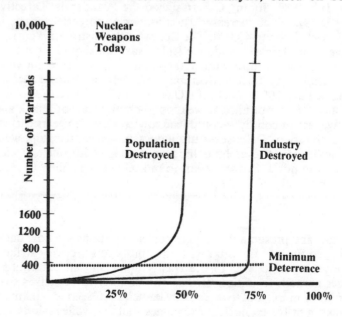

Figure 1: McNamara's "Minimum Deterrence"

demographic and industrial data, still holds true today. According to the theory of deterrence, in order to deter the Soviet Union from nuclear attack, the U.S. must keep a minimum of 400 warheads and house them so they could survive a nuclear attack and still strike back.

Rivalries

Despite this analysis, by the time McNamara left office, rivalry for influence among the different branches of the military had driven the number of warheads and bombs deployed up to 4000. But by the early 1970's, even that was not enough. The Department of Defense wanted a new generation of nuclear weapons systems—and in order to get them, they needed a new argument. Enter nuclear war-fighting doctrine in the guise of "flexible response." National Security Decision Memorandum (NSDM) 242, signed by President Nixon in 1974, offered three reasons for nuclear weapons: deterrence, selected nuclear operations, and the ability to cripple the Soviet Union to prevent quick recovery from holocaust. The doctrine of nuclear war-fighting had actually eclipsed deterrence.

In July 1980, Jimmy Carter signed the Presidential Directive 59 (PD 59), which increased the number of potential targets in the Soviet Union to 40,000. The Reagan Administration's current "Five-Year Defense Guidance" plan says we should have U.S. forces capable of hitting those targets in as many different ways as possible. As former Secretary of Defense Harold Brown explained in a 1980 speech, the U.S. seeks to convince the Soviets "that no . . . use of nuclear weapons—on any scale of attack and at any stage of conflict—could lead to victory." Ten years earlier, the Secretary of Defense would have said we wanted to prevent the Soviets from ever launching an attack. With nuclear war-fighting in mind, Brown began to talk about the ability to meet different levels of attack.

Politics

U.S. (and presumably Soviet) nuclear weapons are now being deployed for war-fighting, with the ability to selectively strike a wide variety of targets in the enemy homeland and in military forces abroad; to initiate strikes and counter-force strikes over months or more; and to selectively launch first, second, and more attacks in tit-for-tat nuclear exchanges—all this while maintaining command, control, and communications with the military and government. In other words, nuclear weapons are being treated as though they were any other kind of weapon.

Such war planning is based on ten highly questionable assumptions.

Nuclear war is likely to be "limited," with escalation carefully controlled. However, most war games involving the use of tactical nuclear weapons would quickly expand into all-out nuclear war. Once the nuclear threshold is broken, it is extremely doubtful that the war can be controlled.

The command structure can survive. The command structure— the President, Secretary of Defense, et al.—must be available to direct and end such a war. Yet war-fighting doctrine places a premium on "decapitation", or destroying the enemy's leaders. Given how vulnerable command centers—the White House, the Pentagon, the Strategic Air Command headquarters in Omaha, and the North American Air Defense Command (NORAD) underneath Cheyenne Mountain, Colorado—are to nuclear attack, most would be destroyed in the first few minutes of a nuclear war.

Destruction of one's homeland can be limited, largely through civil defense. The effectiveness of civil defense is highly dubious. At the very least, 25 million or more Americans and a similar number of Soviets would die in a "limited" nuclear war—and even after that, half or more of both countries would be blanketed by fallout.

The remaining balance between U.S. and Soviet nuclear forces will have military or political significance. Figure 2 shows which country is expected to be "ahead" in numbers of weapons after each country has attacked the other with nuclear weapons. The

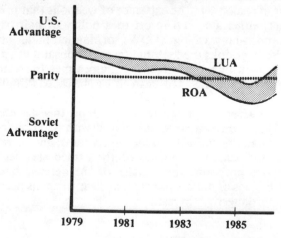

Figure 2: War-Fighting Analysis

pertinent question here: how relevant are nuclear weapons balances when neither country is a functioning entity? **Quick recovery of the socioeconomic fabric of a country is possible.** The most optimistic war-fighters talk of recovery in months, though most analyses indicate that a decade or more would be required. Full recovery is very unlikely, and perhaps impossible. **The country that recovers first could dominate world politics.** This assumption overlooks the long-term devastation, both physical and psychological, wrought by nuclear war, and naively projects prewar politics into a postwar world. **The options of a nuclear war-fighting capability improve deterrence.** Such options—the ability to hit not just civilian and industrial but also military and political targets—predictably mislead military planners to believe they can limit damage. This belief encourages planners to recommend selective use of nuclear weapons rather than to discourage their use. **War-fighting options are needed to overcome U.S. reluctance to use nuclear weapons.** Nuclear war planners argue that without a wide range of options for targeting and firing nuclear weapons, military commanders and political leaders would be "self-deterred" from resorting to nuclear weapons during a war. This astonishing line of reasoning turns nuclear deterrence on its head, failing to recognize that the point is to prevent, not to encourage, the firing of nuclear bombs. **First-strike, preemptive weapons would limit damage and are not destabilizing.** It is true that if the U.S. were to strike the U.S.S.R. first, destroying, say, 1000 ICBMs, then those weapons would not be available to explode over the U.S. But this rationale neglects that in response to the existence of weapons that present such a threat, either side can resort to a policy of hair-trigger response—launch-on-warning (LOW) or launch-under-attack (LUA). It also overlooks the fact that several thousand warheads would still remain in Soviet arsenals, many times the amount necessary to shatter the U.S. This scarcely can be called "limiting" damage. **The US can afford as much as $500 billion this decade for another 15-20,000 nuclear weapons.** Faced with $200 billion in annual deficits, major cutbacks in social programs, and increased competition both among branches of the armed services and among weapons programs for a share of the defense budget, hundreds of billions of dollars for more nuclear weapons becomes a dubious and dangerous investment.

These ten assumptions are most dangerous for three major reasons. 1) They place a premium on striking first in a crisis: the "use them or lose them" mentality takes over. 2) They encourage the use of nuclear weapons earlier in a conflict, blurring the distinction between conventional and nuclear war. 3) They make an almost infinite demand for more and more sophisticated nuclear weapons, because if the primary objective of nuclear weapons plans is to be able to hit up to 40,000 targets in as many permutations as possible, and to stay "ahead" at any phase in any theoretical nuclear war, the current inventory of 10,000 long-range warheads is far from enough. Indeed, the illogic of nuclear war-fighting could demand more than 100,000 nuclear weapons.

The current nuclear war-fighting plans of the U.S. and the U.S.S.R. are real and dangerous. If allowed to continue, they open the door to a never-ending arms race, encourage a continuing fascination with Robert Lifton's "nuclearism", and may well delude us into thinking that nuclear war can be not just survived, but won.

Talk given at the Deadly Connection conference, 4 December 1982.

Tony Polumba

First Strike: Shield for Intervention

As a peace activist, I am aware of how important it is that more Americans join the effort to achieve nuclear disarmament. For this reason it is critically important that the disarmament movement continually provide the information and analysis that will inform and empower people in our common interest. I do not mean to reduce this struggle for nuclear disarmament to a duel of words and ideas. The forces we confront are powerful, and the strategies we use must vary. However, public education that provides the information and analysis that fosters a public sentiment for peace are essential to any effective strategy.

In recent years the efforts of disarmament organizations across the country, particularly the Campaign for a Nuclear Weapons Freeze, have been enormously successful in alerting millions of Americans to the dangers of nuclear war. Our neighbors deeply desire peace and a future uninhibited by the constant specter of nuclear annihilation. Discussions about nuclear war and nuclear weapons are now common in churches, union halls, classrooms, medical centers, and family living rooms. The public knows enough about nuclear war to understand that the United States should not start a nuclear war, and that once started, a nuclear war can probably not be contained. We deserve a moment of self-congratulation for the effort that has led to this state of public awareness. However, this achievement has a darker side.

We might also be applauded by Ronald Reagan and company for our educational successes. The public's knowledge and fear of nuclear war have been used by administration officials as a basis for explaining the value of "star wars." Stressing the "defensive" nature of this system and the higher morality inherent in targetting the enemy's weapons, not its people, and holding out the hope that nuclear weapons (and therefore nuclear war) can soon be obsolete, the president wants the American people's support for spending two hundred to five hundred billion dollars to crowd the heavens with nuclear weapons.

While the struggle for nuclear disarmament is not simply a battle for hearts and minds, it is important that we do our best to provide the facts and analysis that will lead people beyond a fear of nuclear war to an understanding of why nuclear war. It is important to understand *why* nuclear war is a real possibility in the 1980s.

Many of the articles in this book address the question by exploring the relationship between U.S. nuclear weapons policy and U.S. intervention. Here we focus on the nuclear weapons policy that is the foundation for U.S. intervention in the nuclear age: first-strike policy. It will be necessary to review both military and strategic terminology and to review the history of U.S. nuclear weapons policy. This review will demonstrate the following:

> The United States has always targetted Soviet military sites (both conventional and nuclear).

> The policy of mutually assured destruction was never the intended policy of U.S. military planners.

> U.S. strategic planners have continually searched for a means to make nuclear weapons usable in battle.

> U.S. planners have viewed nuclear weapons as usable components in the "utility of military force to achieve foreign policy goals."[1]

What We have been Told

Most Americans believe that the United States maintains a nuclear arsenal only to protect our country against a nuclear attack by an enemy—the Soviet Union. They believe that we would not use these weapons first, but would launch them only in response to an attack. The military language for this policy is "deterrence." The United States, most people believe, deters an attack by the Soviet Union by possessing a nuclear arsenal capable of delivering an overwhelming retaliatory attack against civilian and industrial targets. This conventional notion of deterrence has been referred to as "finite deterrence."

Many, including disarmament activists, believe that the doctrine of "finite deterrence" has guided U.S. nuclear weapons development since 1945. A historical review of U.S. nuclear policy reveals a very different story. It is a story that nuclear disarmament activists must learn if we are to understand fully the nuclear arms race and the present course of U.S. nuclear policy. Before looking at this history, it would help to define a few important terms and clarify their use.

Finite deterrence refers to a policy of deterring a nuclear attack by threatening to destroy the enemy in a retaliatory attack. The characteristics of finite deterrence are these: The policy is defensive and reactive. It requires a nuclear arsenal that is powerful, but not necessarily accurate. The nuclear arsenal's targets are the enemy's urban and industrial centers. The nuclear arsenal must be relatively invulnerable to enemy attack. Finally, finite deterrence requires a finite number of nuclear warheads and delivery systems. (The actual number is determined by calculating what would be needed to destroy Soviet cities and industrial centers after the United States has absorbed an attack by the Soviets.)

Counterforce can refer to both a targetting plan and a policy. As a targetting plan, it means targetting our nuclear weapons at the enemy's military forces, in the belief that our nuclear weapons can destroy these military targets. Counterforce refers to the strategy of targetting the military forces that the enemy would use in a nuclear attack. While this may include both "soft" and "hard" targets, the primary targets are hardened missile silos and command and control centers. Nuclear weapons that can destroy the enemy's hardened nuclear targets are referred to as weapons with "counterforce capability." A counterforce policy is generally associated with a nation's intention to fight nuclear war. It assumes that a nuclear war can be limited (though possibly lasting weeks or months) to a series of reciprocal counterforce strikes. It also assumes that at a certain point one side will "prevail" and that the other will "give in" when it is unable to respond, except with a suicidal counter city attack.

The characteristics of a counterforce policy are the following: The policy may be considered offensive and coercive or defensive and retaliatory. It places a premium on nuclear weapons that are *accurate* and *reliable*. The targets of these highly accurate and reliable missiles are military targets, primarily hardened nuclear targets. The policy requires reliable and consistent communication between U.S. military and political leaders, between U.S. political leaders and Soviet political leaders, and most importantly, between U.S. military commanders and U.S. nuclear forces. The number of weapons needed is related to the number of enemy targets that would be used in a nuclear attack against the United States. Note, the total number must take into consideration the fact that two nuclear warheads are aimed at every nuclear target to ensure its destruction. Further, a certain number of weapons are considered to be in "reserve" (they do not play a role in a counterforce attack) in order to deter a last ditch counter city attack by the "defeated" enemy.

Counterforce policy can, in theory, have a deterrent effect. The enemy may be deterred from initiating a full-scale strategic attack or a limited counterforce attack, *if* they believe their remaining nuclear weapons can be destroyed in a retaliatory "second strike counterforce" attack. The Pentagon argues that it needs new counterforce nuclear weapons, like the MX and Trident II missiles, in order to threaten the Soviets with a "second strike counterforce" attack and thus deter the Soviets from initiating an attack on our nuclear arsenal.

First strike can refer both to the *capability* of a nuclear arsenal and to a nuclear policy. It refers first to a nuclear arsenal that is capable of inflicting a "disarming nuclear attack, leaving the enemy *unable to retaliate.*" First strike should not be confused with the term "first use" which refers to any initial use of nuclear weapons (tactical, intermediate, or strategic) in a limited or exhaustive attack. A nation is pursuing a first-strike policy when it perceives a situation in which it would be the first to use nuclear weapons because it believes it holds the ultimate source of victory—the ability to deliver a disarming first strike.

The characteristics of a first strike policy are the following: The policy is offensive and coercive. It places a premium on accurate and reliable nuclear weapons. It requires a reliable anti-ballistic-missile defense system, it requires reliable and consistent communication between U.S. military and political leaders, between U.S. and Soviet political leaders, and most importantly between U.S. military commanders and U.S. nuclear forces. The targets are both conventional and nuclear forces. The number of weapons needed is related to the number of enemy targets that would be used in a nuclear attack against the United States.

The characteristics of counterforce (and therefore "second-strike counterforce") are very similar to the characteristics of a first-strike policy. However, counterforce does not necessarily mean first strike. Robert Aldridge, a military analyst, explains: "Counterforce is not necessarily equated with first-strike because there are degrees of counterforce. The ability to destroy bomber bases... would require counterforce weapons or counterforce targetting. But destroying a bomber base does not constitute a disarming first-strike because silo-based and submarine-based missiles would be certain to retaliate."[2]

Historical Review

There were no nuclear weapons on earth after the bombings of Hiroshima and Nagasaki. The United States quickly changed that situation and became the only nation which had both nuclear bombs and the means (B-29 bombers) to deliver them. In 1949 the Soviets tested their first atomic bomb, and the United States' nuclear weapons monopoly ended. However, through the late 1940s and early 1950s, the ability to fight and to win a nuclear war was militarily and technologically possible. The U.S. maintained a vast superiority in deliverable atomic bombs. Their purpose was not to deter the Soviet Union from attacking the United States with the few atomic bombs it had, but to defend Europe from a possible Soviet invasion and to "contain" Soviet *political* and military initiatives in general.

In the early 1950s the U.S. B-29s were targetted against approximately one hundred Soviet sites. According to a 1950 National Security Council Memorandum (No. 68), it was U.S. policy to initiate a "global war of annihilation" if our interests were placed in jeopardy. The air force referred to this policy as the "Sunday Punch", a massive siege attack on as many Soviet targets as possible, providing the optimal method of "killing a nation."[3]

In 1953 Secretary of State John Foster Dulles officially made "massive retaliation" U.S. policy. The United States would answer any Soviet *conventional* or nuclear attack on the U.S. or our allies with a massive nuclear attack. The fear of a massive retaliatory attack was to deter the Soviets from initiating military actions in our sphere of influence. Given most Americans' understanding of deterrence, one might assume the targets of a massive retaliatory attack would be civilian targets. However, U.S. counterforce targetting during the mid-1950s was revealed in congressional testimony in 1979 by General David C. Jones and in a February 1955 Weapons System Evaluation Report (WSEG—Report No. 12).

With an estimated advantage of five thousand U.S. nuclear weapons against only three hundred for the Soviets, we can understand how, in 1953 and 1954, both Soviet cities and military sites could be targetted. General Curtis LeMay, commander of the Strategic Air Command in 1957, summarized the real meaning of massive retaliation when he said, "If I see that the Russians are amassing their planes for an attack, I'm going to knock the shit out of them before they get off the ground."[4] It was clear that during the initial stages of Soviet nuclear weapons development, the U.S. used its nuclear superiority not simply to threaten unacceptable damage on the Soviets in a retaliatory attack, but to threaten to defeat the Soviets by destroying all military targets that could be used in a retaliatory nuclear attack. The desire to "win" was not dampened by the realization that even a small number of Soviet nuclear weapons could leave millions of Americans dead and injured. In 1956 Paul Nitze argued that it was still possible to win a nuclear war, if "win" is defined as being in a relatively better position than your enemy after the war.[5]

Other military planners felt differently. While the doctrine of massive retaliation and deterrence remained the official policy through the 1950s, some military theorists realized that growing Soviet capability would create a situation in which massive retaliation, even with counterforce targetting, would be a suicidal strategy for the United States. In 1957 Henry Kissinger, believing that nuclear weapons could be used in U.S. military strategy, entertained the idea of "fighting a limited nuclear war" to allow the use of nuclear weapons without the consequences of thermonuclear war.[6]

In the early years of the Kennedy administration, a strategy of "damage limitation" or "no-cities" warfare was considered. This strategy called for preventing damage to U.S. cities (from Soviet nuclear weapons) by trying to control a nuclear war. Neither side would target the other's cities, and if a nuclear exchange took place, the United States would target the remaining Soviet nuclear weapons, hoping to deter their use against U.S. cities. Secretary of Defense Robert McNamara proposed this first explicitly counterforce strategy in early 1962 when he said, "A major mission of the strategic retaliatory forces is to deter war by their capability to destroy the enemy's war-making capability."[7] He repeated this theme the following month, stating, "We may be able to use our retaliatory forces to limit damage done to ourselves and our cities, by knocking out the enemy's bases before he has time to launch his second salvos...."[8] These statements followed the Secretary's orders to review SIOP (Single Integrated Operational Plan), the U.S. targetting plans for nuclear war, prepared in 1960. Approved in January 1962, the new SIOP contained many counterforce targets including Soviet missiles, bomber bases, submarine tenders, air defenses to protect cities, and command and control systems. By adopting a counterforce/no-cities option, Secretary McNamara was accepting the principles that nuclear weapons could be used in a limited nuclear war and that the United States must be in a position to bring the war to a conclusion on terms favorable to Washington. However, McNamara was soon questioning the feasibility of counterforce given the nuclear balance of the time and the destructive capabilities of the Soviet nuclear arsenal. His doubts were supported by the results of a 1964 top secret study, entitled "Damage Limiting." In sum, the study "suggested that even with a very good U.S. counterforce strike—supplemented by air, anti-ballistic missiles and civilian defense—the Soviets, in a retaliatory strike, could inflict tremendous damage."[9] McNamara may have also been influenced by the study's conclusion that a counterforce attack, given the destructive capacity of U.S. weapons and the number and location of Soviet targets, would produce significant "collateral damage" to Soviet cities. Soviet leaders would thus assume a counterforce attack was a counter-city attack and issue a retaliatory attack against U.S. cities and industrial centers.

The counterforce/no-cities option was replaced by the more familiar policy of assured destruction. (When both sides have the capability, it is considered to be "mutually assured destruction" or MAD) At that time (1964) MAD meant "the United States had enough nuclear weapons that following a Soviet first strike, it could still kill one fourth of the Soviet population and one half of its industry."[10] How many nuclear weapons would be needed? The equivalent of four hundred one-megaton bombs. McNamara later stated that each leg of the U.S. triad—ground, sea, and air—should have the equivalent of four hundred megatons. To many, this doctrine appeared to be the "perfect" answer. Neither the United States nor the Soviet Union would dare to strike first; they knew that each had a "secure and invulnerable second strike capability."

This fragile, but possibly workable policy to control the nuclear arms race was not pursued by U.S. political and military leaders. Throughout the late 1960s and early 1970s, U.S. weapons policy revealed a preoccupation with counterforce capability. This is illustrated by the Pentagon's targetting policy in the 1960s. In a mid-1970 government report, former Deputy Assistant Secretary of Defense Henry Rowan recalled, "Most of our planned targets were military forces."[11] Fred Kaplan, a military analyst, when referring to this period, wrote, "assured destruction became the *declaratory* strategy, the *actual* strategy—as reflected in the targetting plan of SAC (Strategic Air Command)—remained predominantly counterforce."[12] However, MAD was soon to be a strategic fact as opposed to a strategic policy. By 1967 the U.S. arsenal included 1,054 intercontinental ballistic missiles and 41 Polaris submarines with submarine-launched ballistic missiles

(SLBMs). The Soviets were, however, engaged in a major effort to increase the number of their ICBMs and were adding to their arsenal of SLBMs.

The U.S. was slowly but steadily losing its nuclear superiority and therefore its counterforce edge. Since counterforce required targetting the enemy's nuclear forces, the more ICBMs the Soviets built, the more nuclear warheads the U.S. needed to destroy them. The more the Soviets hardened their missile silos, the more accurate U.S. missiles needed to be to destroy these targets. In response to this dilemma, the United States accelerated the nuclear arms race by introducing MIRVs (Multiple Individually-targetted Reentry Vehicles), making it possible for a *single* missile to carry more than one warhead. One missile would be capable of destroying more than one Soviet silo. In addition, the U.S. improved the accuracy of its missiles with new inertial guidance systems.

As we entered the 1970s, the requirements of counterforce were beyond the capabilities of the U.S. nuclear arsenal, notwithstanding the increased number of accurate warheads due to MIRVed missiles.

Mutually assured destruction then was not the result of rational agreement to maintain a limited number of invulnerable nuclear weapons, but the result of the inability of U.S. nuclear weapons technology to maintain a counterforce edge as a result of the increased number of Soviet hardened missile silos. One should note that it made little difference at this time whether Soviet ICBMs were able to destroy hardened U.S. silos or only soft military targets and urban centers. A U.S. counterforce policy required all these weapons to be targetted. This could be achieved only by building more highly accurate silo-busting nuclear warheads and an array of other counterforce nuclear weapons. Thus, development of the Trident missile, the B-1 bomber, the MX missile and the sea-launched cruise missile began in 1972. A year later work on the air-launched cruise missile began.

Meanwhile, the Nixon administration, under Secretaries of Defense Melvin Laird and James Schlesinger, moved U.S. strategic arms policy further in the direction of counterforce policy. Following the signing of SALT I in May 1972, Secretary Laird went to Congress requesting that nine strategic programs be accelerated. Congress refused this and other requests by the Nixon administration to initiate new nuclear weapons programs and to improve the accuracy of others.

Throughout his first term, Richard Nixon urged moves away from the policy of assured destruction toward a policy of flexibility. In 1970 he asked, "Should the concept of assured destruction be narrowly defined and should it be the only measure of our ability to deter the variety of threats we might face?"[13] In 1971 he answered his own question when he stated in his annual foreign policy report to Congress, "Given the range of possible political military situations which could conceivably confront us, our strategic policy should not be based solely on a capability of inflicting urban and industrial damage presumed to be beyond the level an adversary would accept."[14]

Secretary of Defense Schlesinger, like Nixon, strongly advocated a *public* change in U.S. nuclear policy. Like his predecessors, he believed in using nuclear weapons. However, if a U.S. counterforce attack could not be distinguished from a massive attack on Soviet cities because of the sheer number of U.S. counterforce weapons that would be fired, there was a risk that the Soviets would order a full-scale retaliatory attack against U.S. cities.

Schlesinger's answer to this problem was to call for a policy of "selectivity and flexibility." The United States should have a strategic policy that allowed for selective targetting, including "military targets, whether silos or other military targets...."[15] Further, the level of response should be "tailored" to the initial Soviet provocation. Thus a policy of selectivity and flexibility could, in theory, allow the United States to control a nuclear war and avoid destruction of the civilian population. Through limited nuclear attacks on selected targets, the U.S. could coerce the Soviets and force them to end the conflict on U.S. terms. Schlesinger summarized his approach in March 1974 during Senate testimony when he said, "Many people believe that in all likelihood it (a war) must go all the way, but there is some possibility that nuclear war could be constrained at a lower level."[16] Now more openly than ever, U.S. strategy included the possible use of nuclear weapons in a limited war ending in a "victory" for the U.S. The doctrine of selectivity and flexibility required, as Secretary Schlesinger explained, programs to improve missile accuracy or "improved hard kill capacity." This approach was seconded and the ante raised by Defense Secretary Donald Rumsfield who, in his Fiscal Year 1978 Report, requested "more than limited kill capacity."[17]

"Countervailing strategy" was the name given to the nuclear policy pursued by Secretary of Defense Harold Brown. Brown's strategy called for both countercity and counterforce capability, which could be limited or massive, depending on what was considered necessary. The targets of the limited or massive response included a range of options from Soviet cities to ICBMs. The President "would be able to orchestrate a nuclear attack very precisely."[18]

Given the trend from the early 1970's, the announcement by President Carter of Presidential Directive 59 in July of 1980 came as no surprise. Richard Burt, then national security correspondent for the *New York Times*, summarized PD-59 as a strategy that "requires American forces to be able to undertake precise limited nuclear strikes against military facilities in the Soviet Union, including missile bases and troop concentrations...(and) to develop the capacity to threaten Soviet political leaders in their underground shelters in time of war."[19] In the light of this description, Secretary of Defense Brown's statement on April 20, 1980 reveals the hidden history of U.S. nuclear weapons development: "PD-59 is *not* a new strategic doctrine; it is *not* a radical departure from U.S. strategic policy over the past decade or so. It *is*, in fact, a refinement, a codification of previous statements of our strategic policy."[20] While PD-59 may be a codification of the counterforce strategies of the past, it was also the public acknowledgement of U.S. intentions to fight a protracted nuclear war. Further, and most importantly, it was the first public statement of a policy that requires U.S. capability to destroy Soviet hardened targets, a key element of first strike policy. As we shall see, the strategy of limited nuclear war inherent in PD-59 and the trend toward achieving a disarming first strike are being accelerated by the Reagan administration.

It would be useful to summarize the consistent trends in U.S. nuclear policy, before reviewing the "contributions" of the Reagan Administration:

Mutually Assured Destruction. MAD was never U.S. policy, if one defines it as "pure deterrence." It existed from roughly 1970 on as a technological reality as opposed to a policy.

Weapons Development and Improvement. There has been an unabated drive to develop new weapons (and improve existing weapons) that will allow the U.S. to destroy Soviet strategic and tactical nuclear targets.

Counterforce Targetting. U.S. strategists, beginning in the 1950s, selected targets with the intention of destroying the Soviet Union's military forces (conventional and nuclear).

Counterforce Strategy. While receiving varying emphasis, the goal of destroying the enemy's nuclear forces, of limiting its retaliatory capability, and of putting it in the position in which a retaliatory response would spark a devastating second strike, has been constant through the nuclear age. This strategy implies fighting a limited nuclear war with the U.S. emerging as the "winner."

Using Nuclear Weapons. Military planners and political leaders have accepted the inherently limited options in the stated policy of mutually assured destruction and have continually called for flexibility in the use of nuclear weapons.

Finally, the implications of a counterforce policy can be understood as either an attempt to acquire a second strike counterforce capability or a disarming first-strike capability. Robert Aldridge writes, "The counterforce capability to destroy hard targets during limited nuclear exchanges is indistinguishable from that needed to launch a knockout nuclear attack against Russia."[21] It would be naive to believe the Soviets do not know this and, given the history of the arms race, to believe that they view the U.S. purpose as only acquiring second-strike counterforce capability. The policies of the Reagan administration have, at the very least, added to the Soviets' scepticism.

The Reagan Nuclear Strategy

If anyone still believed that the U.S. is committed to the doctrine of mutually assured destruction, listening to the Reagan administration would surely resolve any remaining doubts. This administration has made it clear that the U.S. must "regain nuclear superiority," acquire a "nuclear warfighting capability," and be in a position to win a nuclear war.

The Reagan administration is determined to achieve the goal of superiority. The Republican National Committee Platform of 1980 committed the administration "to close the gap with the Soviets and ultimately reach the position of military superiority that the American people demand." Deputy Secretary of Defense Frank Carlucci put it clearly when he said, "I think we need to have a counterforce capability. Over and above that, I think we need to have a warfighting capability."[22] Finally, Secretary of Defense Caspar Weinberger explained our intentions should nuclear war occur: "We set out to...achieve...U.S. capabilities to prevail should deterrence fail."[23]

In May 1982 Weinberger's "Defense Guidance" outlined the Pentagon's plans to fight a protracted nuclear war. While there is some disagreement whether this nuclear policy is anything more than an extension of those of previous administrations, there is agreement that the Reagan administration intends to build the capability to fight nuclear wars that range from limited use through a protracted conflict to an all out attack.[24]

"Nuclear superiority" at a time when both the U.S. and the U.S.S.R. are capable of destroying each other with thousands of deliverable nuclear warheads? "Warfighting", when millions of Americans would be killed, our economy devastated, and the ecosystem destroyed if only a small percentage of the Soviet arsenal reached the U.S.? What would be necessary to fight and to win a nuclear war? How do you achieve nuclear superiority? The Reagan administration has provided us with the answer to all these questions: develop the capability to administer a disarming first-strike, and let it be known that this capability will be used if the U.S. is perceived to be losing a limited or protracted nuclear war. These are the conclusions one reaches after reviewing Pentagon statements, Defense Guidance Reports, and the military hardware listed in the Pentagon's budgets from 1982 to the present.

The capability necessary to issue a disarming first strike includes: weaponry able to destroy Soviet hard nuclear ICBMs and command and control centers, and critical targets such as warning systems and bomber bases; antisubmarine warfare systems that allow for locating, tracking, and destroying Soviet submarines; an active ballistic missile defense (BMD) system capable of destroying, in flight, any Soviet missiles that might escape; and a passive civilian defense program to protect U.S. citizens in case a Soviet missile manages to evade the BMD system and to explode over the U.S.

Since the Reagan administration announced its plans to spend more than $222 billion on nuclear weapons and related technology, it has made every effort to acquire the necessary components of a first strike policy. While many of the needed programs were initiated by previous administrations, the Reagan administration has demonstrated wholehearted support for these initiatives and has accelerated the process of procurement at every level. The MX, Pershing II, Trident, and Cruise missiles are the best known examples of this program.

The *MX missile*, recently dubbed the "Peacekeeper" by President Reagan, has been in development since 1972. Though the present administration has abandoned the Carter administration's basing plans, it has been relentless in its efforts to gain congressional approval for funding for one hundred missiles. Each missile will carry ten warheads, each with the explosive power of 350 kilotons (more than twenty-four times the explosive power of the bomb dropped on Hiroshima). The MX will not only be one of the most powerful missiles, it will be one of the most accurate, placing its warheads within four hundred feet of their targets. It is theoretically capable of destroying all hardened targets, including ICBM silos, superhard control centers, and hard leadership bunkers.[25] The Reagan administration wants one hundred MX missiles and has scheduled deployment for 1986.

The *Pershing II* missile is an intermediate range ballistic missile with an estimated range of fifteen hundred kilometers. Speed and accuracy are the Pershing II's distinguishing characteristics. It is designed to reach the Soviet Union within six-to-ten minutes, to explode within one hundred feet of its target and to destroy Soviet military installations and command, control, and communication centers. The 1979 announcement that the U.S. was planning to deploy 108 Pershing II launchers in West Germany was met with resistance by the German peace movement. Although millions voiced their opposition to these weapons, the first Pershing IIs were deployed in December 1983 and the Soviet Union was confronted with powerful counterforce weapons based only minutes away. The Pershing II is an example of a missile with a moderate yield, ten-to-twenty kilotons, yet still capable of destroying hardened targets. This is due to the extreme accuracy of the missile, which is provided by a radar guidance system that matches "photographs" of the target site with information stored in the warhead's computer.

Cruise missiles can be air, ground, or sea-launched. They are, in essence, pilotless subsonic jet planes which, because of their inertial guidance systems, are able to change direction and alter altitudes in flight. The *air-launched cruise missile* (ALCM) is deployed on the B-52G bombers at air bases across the United States. There are plans for future deployment on the B-1B and B-52H bombers. The Reagan administration has accelerated the production schedule for the ALCM with the hope of having 3,418 deployed by 1987. The counterforce capability of the ALCM is greater than all present ICBMs. It can deliver its two-hundred-kiloton warhead within three hundred feet of its target.

The *ground-launched cruise missile* (GLCM) is also extremely accurate and capable of destroying Soviet hardened targets. GLCMs were deployed in Italy, Great Britain, and West Germany in December of 1979, and there are plans for deployment in Belgium and the Netherlands. With a range of fifteen hundred miles and a warhead yield of two hundred kilotons, they pose a serious threat to the Soviet Union. It was the decision to deploy the 464 GLCMs and the Pershing II missiles that led to the Soviet Union's withdrawal from the Intermediate Nuclear Forces negotiations in Geneva.

The *sea-launched cruise missile* (SLCM) is considered by some to be the most destabilizing new weapons system. It can travel twenty-five hundred kilometers and deliver its two-hundred-kiloton nuclear warhead close enough to the target to be considered a counterforce weapon. SLCMs are already deployed on surface vessels; there are plans to deploy others on submarines. Because of its small size and its dual capability (it can carry either conventional or nuclear warheads), the SLCM poses a major verification problem. The Reagan administration initially requested 384 missiles, but plans to deploy four thousand by early 1990. While it is unlikely that cruise missiles would be used in an initial disarming first strike, Pentagon officials have assigned all three types of cruise missiles key roles in its nuclear warfighting strategy.

The *Trident II missile*, when deployed on the Trident submarine in 1989, will give the sea leg of the U.S. triad counterforce capability. The Trident submarine is the largest submarine ever built by the U.S. and will be armed with twenty-four missiles, as compared to the sixteen carried on Poseidon and Polaris submarines. The Trident II missile will carry between ten and seventeen nuclear warheads with a yield of seventy-five-to-one hundred kilotons. The missile can travel four thousand miles and drop its warhead within four hundred feet of its target. The weapon's accuracy will "give sea-based strategic forces the capability to attack *any* Soviet target: [it] represents a quantum jump in U.S. *offensive* nuclear capability."[26] The estimated costs for the development and production of the Trident II program is twenty billion dollars.

Together, the MX, Trident, Pershing and cruise missiles represent a major step toward acquiring the capability of destroying all Soviet land- and air-based nuclear weapons capable of reaching the United States and all hardened command and control centers necessary to conduct such a nuclear attack.

The ability to detect, track, and destroy Soviet submarines at sea has been considered among the most formidable obstacles to achieving a disarming first strike capability. However, some military analysts believe the U.S. is well within reach of the capability "to locate and track every Soviet missile launching submarine in the ocean."[27]

The U.S. relies on a combination of escort and open-ocean sensors to detect and to locate Soviet submarines. Research is

underway on the possible use of infrared sensors on spacecraft
as an improved means to track these submarines. Methods of
destroying enemy submarines, once they are located, include an
array of torpedoes, depth charges, and antisubmarine rockets.
The present nuclear armed rockets are the submarine-launched
SUBROC and the surface-ship-launched ASROC. By the late
1980s and the early 1990s, these will be replaced by weapons with
greater range and kill probability, the vertical launched ASROC
or ASROC (VLA) and the ASW Standoff Weapons or ASCSOW.
The Reagan administration has requested development funds for
the ASCSOW in fiscal years 1982, 1983, and 1984 totalling more
than ten million dollars.[28]

Ballistic Missile Defense, Antisatellite Warfare, and Civilian Defense

The final component of a disarming first-strike capability
involves "defensive" systems able to destroy any incoming Soviet
missiles and to protect U.S. citizens if a Soviet missile does reach
its U.S. target. Ballistic missile defense testing and development
was severely limited by the 1972 ABM Treaty. However, research
on BMD (ballistic missile defense) continues to be conducted by
the U.S. army.

President Reagan's March 1983 speech outlining the Strategic
Defense Initiative (SDI) or "Star Wars" made public the U.S.
intention of accelerating this research effort. Initial projections
call for a three-tier, space-based, anti-ballistic-missile system
utilizing advanced technology such as laser and particle beam
weapons. While the complete SDI proposal faces enormous
scientific, technological, and economic constraints, portions of
the necessary technology are being developed through ongoing
U.S. research for antisatellite weapons. *Anti-satellite weapons*
(ASATs) are not banned by the 1972 ABM Treaty, though
achieving the capability to destroy Soviet satellites would further
destabilize the nuclear arms race. Satellites are used by both the
U.S. and the U.S.S.R. for communications and more importantly,
for early detection of an enemy nuclear attack.

The U.S. is presently testing an antisatellite weapon, the
miniature homing intercept vehicle, which is scheduled for
deployment in 1987. In addition, research is moving forward on
a new generation of ASATs involving high powered lasers. The
technology for ASAT development closely parallels what is needed
for the terminal phase of a ballistic missile defensive system, the
most technologically achievable portion of the three-tiered SDI.

Research and testing for the BMD are thus progressing as a by-product of the unrestricted antisatellite program. If the U.S. achieves a successful ballistic missile defense, the Soviets will likely increase their efforts to acquire a system with similar capabilities and/or to increase the number of nuclear warheads it can launch to overwhelm the defense system's capabilities.

The Reagan administration has become famous (or infamous) for its belief that a civilian defense program not only is possible but is a necessary element in U.S. strategic nuclear planning. In fiscal year 1982 the Department of Defense request included more than $130 million for the Federal Emergency Management Administration (FEMA), the agency responsible for civilian defense. This is a thirteen percent increase from fiscal year 1981. Crisis relocation and blast-shelter programs have been roundly criticized as unworkable and deceptive. Dr. Robert J. Lifton has said, "The shelters are fine except for three things: getting to them, staying in them, and getting out of them. It is a dangerous illusion to tell the American public that shelters will protect them."[29]

Though the crisis relocation program has ostensibly been eliminated, Pentagon officials believe it is valuable as indicated by the statement of T.K. Jones, undersecretary of defense, "Everybody's going to make it if there are enough shovels to go around.... Dig a hole, cover it with a couple of doors and then throw three feet of dirt on top. It's the dirt that does it."[30] While this statement may represent the sentiments of the Reagan administration, other officials have made it clear that the purpose of civilian defense is to dispel the idea that nuclear war must end in total destruction. FEMA Public Affairs Director James Holton summed it up when he stated, "We don't believe the planet is doomed if there is an attack. We don't accept the belief that there will be absolute devastation."[31]

An array of offensive, counterforce-capable nuclear weapons; development of new and better antisubmarine warfare programs; research, development, and testing of ASAT and BMD systems; and funding for civilian defense—are the major assets in the effort to achieve a first strike capability. How does it all fit together? Former Secretary of Defense Donald Rumsfeld might have unknowingly provided us with the answer when he described the concept of "damage limitation": "The most ambitious (damage limiting) strategy dictates a first strike capability against the enemy's strategic offensive forces which seeks to destroy as much of his megatonnage as possible before it can be brought into play. An enemy's residual retaliation, assumed to be directed against urban-industrial targets, would be blunted still further by a combination of active and passive defenses, including ASW, ABM's, antibomber defenses, civil defense, stockpiles of food and other essentials, and even the dispersal and hardening of essential industry."³² The Reagan administration has moved forward in the research, testing, development, production, and deployment of the major elements necessary to carry out the scenario described by the former secretary of defense.

First Strike and Nuclear Warfighting

In spite of the technical and strategic doubts about the feasibility of ever launching a disarming first strike, the U.S. is intent on achieving this capability. Why? It is necessary to understand that the U.S. strategists do not wish to use a disarming first strike as the *initiating* act of nuclear war. The confusion is caused by the word "first" in the term "first strike." It is true that the nation with the capability of preventing a retaliatory attack could issue a disabling first strike *before* the enemy fired its missiles, but it does not necessarily follow that the *initial* use of nuclear weapons would be in the form of a first strike attack as it has been defined here.

The advantage of possessing the capability to issue a disarming first strike lies in the *threat* of its use—a threat which makes it possible to use nuclear weapons in a limited regional conflict or in a protracted nuclear war between the superpowers. The capability of launching a first strike is a nation's "trump card." Such an analogy implies a game that involves bluffs or threats, where the holders of the trump card are assured a victory whether they are forced to use it or not.

The "game" that military strategists are playing is a game of nuclear warfighting, that is, using nuclear weapons (tactical, intermediate, and strategic) in conflict. They play this game because the trump card that assures victory is the capability of issuing, if needed, a disarming first strike. The larger game, of course, is the game of international politics, and military and political leaders are well trained in using military force to win a hand in this game. The first strike capability allows them to *use nuclear military force* in the game—a desire that is as old as the weapons themselves.

Military strategists recognize the critical role of "perception" when one is using nuclear force. They know that for the threat of a first strike to serve its purpose, the enemy must recognize it as a *credible threat.* According to the logic of "the game," the U.S. must continue to develop the weaponry and the technology that indicate it is determined to obtain the trump card—the threat of a first strike—and is prepared to play the card to assure "victory" in nuclear war. Colin S. Gray, a State Department consultant, made this point when he said, "The U.S. should plan to defeat the Soviet Union and to do so at a cost that would not prohibit U.S. recovery....A combination of counterforce offensive targetting, civil defense, and ballistic missile and air defense should hold U.S. casualties to approximately 20 million, which would render U.S. strategic threats more credible."[33] If the other player believes that you have the trump card and that you are willing to play it, then you are in a position to up the ante when you are challenged by your opponent. Your hope is that you do not need to up the ante, that your opponent will realize that any escalation will be matched and result in defeat. If this is recognized, your opponent will likely back down, throwing in his chips, saving face, and minimizing losses.

The game of international politics with nuclear force is played with a range of options allowing response to moves by one's opponent. The options must take into consideration the region in which the conflict is located, the nuclear forces of the opponent, the opponent's interests in other regions (and their military strength or weakness in those areas), and most importantly, the prize that is a stake in the region where the conflict is located. The options selected must consider all of these factors at *every point in the conflict*; the best option at one level of conflict might not be the best option at a different level.

U.S. nuclear weapons development is greatly influenced by these concepts. U.S. weapons are designed to implement a particular option in this "game" of nuclear escalation. Some are capable of being used for more than one option. The MX missile is designed to be used when a disarming first strike is needed against the Soviets. Sea-launched cruise missiles may be used against selected Soviet military forces (nuclear and conventional) located outside of the Soviet Union or against Third World nations. The Pershing II may be used in either a "surgical strike" against selected nuclear targets in the Soviet Union to match (and up the ante on) an escalation of the conflict by the Soviets, or in a disarming first strike against the Soviets.

U.S. military planners are working daily to create scenarios that involve the use of nuclear weapons to achieve foreign policy goals. If military power is viewed as essential to the pursuit of our nation's political and economic well-being, and if nuclear weapons are viewed as "indispensable and central components" of military power, it follows that U.S. military strategists have designed a variety of nuclear warfighting scenarios to assure our "military and economic well-being."[34] For example, a U.S.-Soviet confrontation in the oil-rich Middle East might begin as a conventional conflict and quickly escalate to a conflict involving tactical nuclear weapons. If the U.S. felt the need to escalate the conflict in order to assure victory, using counterforce-capable SLCMs to attack Soviet forces in and around the region, the Soviets might respond with an attack by their intermediate range nuclear weapons. The U.S. could counter by firing ground-launched cruise missiles stationed in Italy at Soviet forces in the Middle East, and by threatening the destruction with Pershing II missiles of selected nuclear forces (hardened command and control centers) in the Soviet Union. Either response would expand the conflict to another region of the world, one where the GLCM and the Pershing II missiles give the U.S. a nuclear advantage. Victory might be at hand for the U.S. if the Soviets perceived that any further escalation on their part would force the U.S. to play its trump card, that is, a disarming first strike, leaving the Soviet Union unable to retaliate. If this happened, Soviet cities and industrial centers would be vulnerable to a second-strike attack by the U.S. from air-launched cruise missiles (on B-52s) or non-counterforce-capable nuclear weapons that remained in the nuclear arsenal. U.S. nuclear silos (and in theory U.S. citizens) would be protected from any Soviet missile that was fired by an "active" ballistic missile defense and a "passive" civilian defense program.

Discussion of scenarios like the one presented above are not unusual among U.S. military strategists. The role of the desired U.S. first strike capability, from the new generation of counterforce weapons to the resurgent efforts to obtain a ballistic missile defense system, play a key role in these scenarios. The use of nuclear weapons (and the willingness to fight nuclear war) in the game of international politics is thus directly linked to a U.S. first-strike capability.

What does this unsettling analysis mean for people working for peace and nuclear disarmament? How can we translate the technical jargon and the arcane military strategies so that they are meaningful to our neighbors, friends, and co-workers? Should we even try? Would it not be better to continue to conduct educational campaigns that focus only on the very real danger of nuclear war? The answer to the latter question is both "yes" and "no." We must continue to educate the public about the dangers of nuclear war, but we must also provide the information and the analysis that explain why the nuclear holocaust is close at hand, why "deterrence" is not protecting us. We must find ways to talk about first strike policy, about the offensive nature of new weapons systems, and about military scenarios in which nuclear warfighting plays a key role. Most importantly, we must begin to develop campaigns and strategies that offer concrete ways to oppose and to change the first strike and nuclear warfighting policies of the United States.

Unless we begin this difficult but critical task, our past educational efforts may work against nuclear disarmament and support nuclear war policies and new weapons development that will escalate the arms race and bring us closer to the nuclear holocaust we have worked so hard to avert.

Notes

1. Allan Krass and Dan Smith, "Fallacies in Deterrence and Warfighting Strategies," in *Search for Sanity—The Politics of Nuclear Weapons and Disarmament*, ed. Paul Josephs and Simon Rosenblum (Boston: South End Press, 1984), p. 28.
2. Robert C. Aldridge, *FIRST STRIKE! The Pentagon's Strategy for Nuclear War* (Boston: South End Press, 1983), p. 25.
3. Fred Kaplan, "Interservice Rivalry and the Arms Race," in Paul Josephs and Simon Rosenblum, eds., *Search for Sanity*, p. 55.
4. Fred Kaplan, *The Wizards of Armageddon* (New York: Simon and Schuster, 1983), p.143.
5. Christopher Paine, "Reaganomics, or How to 'Prevail' " in Josephs and Rosenblum, eds., *Search for Sanity*, p. 8.
6. Jerry Elmer, "Limited Nuclear War: America's Counterforce Strategy" (Philadelphia: American Friends Service Committee, 1983), p. 2.
7. House Appropriations Committee, *Department of Defense Appropriations*, Hearing, January 1962, Part 2, pp. 249-50.
8. Desmond Ball, *Deja Vu: The Return to Counterforce in the Nixon Administration* (California Seminar on Arms Control and Foreign Policy, December 1974), p. 14.
9. Kaplan, "Interservice Rivalry," p. 59.
10. Ibid., p. 59.
11. Paine, "Reaganomics," p. 9.
12. Kaplan, "Interservice Rivalry," p. 59.
13. President Nixon to Congress, 9 February 1972, *U.S. Foreign Policy for the 1970s: A New Strategy for Peace*, p. 122.
14. President Nixon to Congress, 9 February 1972, *U.S. Foreign Policy for the 1970s*, p. 22.
15. Address by Defense Secretary James R. Schlesinger at the Overseas Writers Association luncheon in Washington, D.C. on 10 January 1974.
16. Elmer, "Limited Nuclear War," p. 4.

17. Stephen Daggett, *The New Generation of Nuclear Weapons* (Washington, D.C.: Institute for Policy Studies, 1979), p. 5.
18. Ibid.
19. Paine, "Reaganomics," p. 10.
20. U.S. Air Force *Selected Statements*, 1 September 1980, p. 46. His emphasis.
21. Aldridge, *FIRST STRIKE!*, p. 36.
22. The Defense Monitor, *Preparing for Nuclear War: President Reagan's Program* (Washington, D.C.: Center for Defense Information, 1982), p. 2.
23. Ibid.
24. Ibid.
25. Thomas B. Cochran, William M. Arkin and Milton M. Hoenig, *U.S. Nuclear Forces and Capabilities Volume I* (Cambridge: Ballinger Publishing Company, 1984), p. 120.
26. Ibid., p. 144. My emphasis.
27. Aldridge, *FIRST STRIKE!*, p. 163.
28. For further information on U.S. nuclear weapons arsenal, consult Christopher Chant and Ian Hogg, *Nuclear War in the 1980's?* (New York: Harper and Row Publishers, 1983).
29. Subcommittee of the Committee on Government Operations, *FEMA Oversight: Will U.S. Nuclear Attack Evacuation Plans Work?*, U.S. House of Representatives, 22 April 1982, pp. 87 and 90.
30. Robert Scheer, *With Enough Shovels: Reagan, Bush and Nuclear War* (New York: Random House, 1982), pp. 18 and 138.
31. Bernard Weinraub, "Civil Defense Agency: Trying to Do Something," *New York Times*, 8 April 1982.
32. Aldridge, *FIRST STRIKE!*, p. 36.
33. Michio Kaku, "Wasting Space: Countdown to a First Strike," in Josephs and Rosenblum, eds., *Search for Sanity*, p. 159.
34. Krass and Smith, "Fallacies in Deterrence," p.28.

The author wishes to acknowledge the assistance of Sheila Walsh, freelance editor and graphic artist, and Carl Connetta, a member of the South End Press collective.

THE

Part III
The Eroding Firebreak

DEADLY
CONNECTION

Michael T. Klare

Conventional Arms, Military Doctrine, and Nuclear War: The Vanishing Firebreak

Ever since the onset of the Nuclear Age in 1945, military theorists have recognized the existence of a nuclear "firebreak"—a conspicuous breach in the ladder of escalation dividing the most intense and violent state of non-nuclear, "conventional" conflict from the outbreak of nuclear war. By its very existence, the firebreak confirms that there is a fundamental, qualitative difference between the most destructive forms of conventional conflict and the catastrophic potential of thermonuclear war. However violent a conflict on the conventional side of the firebreak, it cannot threaten human survival; once the firebreak is crossed, however, there can be no such assurances.[1] As noted by former Deputy Assistant Secretary of Defense Alain C. Enthoven in an influential 1963 speech at Loyola University of Los Angeles, nuclear weapons are not simply high explosives writ large. Their destructive power makes them a completely new kind of military force which must be understood in new ways. In the first known use of the "firebreak" term, Enthoven went on to say that "there is and will remain an important distinction, a 'firebreak' if you like, between nuclear and non-nuclear war, a recognizable qualitative distinction that both combatants can recognize and agree upon if they want to agree upon one." [2]

At its most basic level, therefore, the firebreak represents an appreciation of the special nature of nuclear war and, as such, acts as a psychological deterrent to escalation. By emphasizing the qualitative difference between conventional and nuclear warfare, it underscores the extraordinary political, moral, and military risks a government assumes when it crosses that breach. As suggested by Enthoven, however, the concept represents more than a perceptual distinction: by constituting a sharp *discontinuity* in the process of escalation, it provides a sort of "maneuvering space" within which warring parties can establish (through formal negotiations or tacit agreement) concrete limits on the scale of hostilities. Indeed, given the growing power of nuclear weapons and the escalatory pressures inevitably generated by their use, the conventional/nuclear firebreak offers the only obvious interlude for such negotiations short of all-out nuclear combat. Future adversaries "will have a very powerful incentive to agree upon this distinction," Enthoven explained, "for there does not appear to be another easily recognizable limitation on weapons—no other obvious "firebreak"—all the way up the destructive spectrum to large-scale thermonuclear war."[3]

Preservation of the firebreak is, therefore, an essential barrier against the outbreak of nuclear war. For, should the distinction between conventional and nuclear weapons be erased, there will be no moral or political inhibitions against escalation and the critical "maneuvering space" would disappear. "The 'firebreak' must be absolute," Swedish disarmament expert and Nobel Peace prize laureate Alva Myrdal wrote in her classic study *The Game of Disarmament*. "If the present distinction between nuclear and conventional weapons becomes blurred, it will be impossible...to avoid uncontrollable escalation."[4]

To fully appreciate the significance of the firebreak, it is useful to imagine a "spectrum" of violence, ranging from guerilla war and civil conflict at the lower end to all-out thermonuclear war at the opposite end. Midway across this spectrum is the firebreak, falling between high-intensity conventional war on one side, and so called "limited" or "theater" nuclear war on the other. With the firebreak in place, a conflict can escalate continuously along the conventional side, but cannot escalate beyond this point without a conscious decision to leap the breach and thereby risk global destruction—a decision no leader has chosen to make since the U.S. nuclear monopoly was broken in 1949.[5]

Although scientists have in the past warned of various technological threats to the firebreak, the very real discrepancy in destructive power between conventional and nuclear weapons ensured that the gap remained relatively intact. Recently, however, the development of new types of both conventional and nuclear munitions has begun to erode the firebreak in significant ways. Modern conventional weapons employing new explosives and dispersion techniques are beginning to approach the damage potential of the smallest nuclear devices, while, at the same time, new "third generation" nuclear weapons are being introduced with a damage radius comparable to that of the most powerful conventional munitions. Indeed, many experts believe that it will soon be possible to deploy weapons systems with interchangeable nuclear and conventional warheads. This means, of course, that the firebreak is being eroded from both sides of the conventional/nuclear gap simultaneously. This process is being accelerated, moreover, by the introduction of new military doctrines stressing the deployment of "dual capable" combat forces that are trained and equipped to fight with both nuclear and conventional armaments.

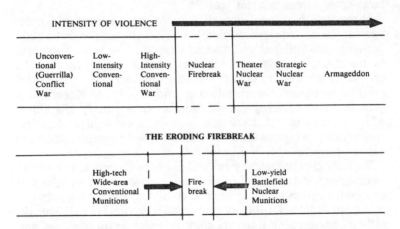

Clearly, the erosion of the nuclear firebreak has profound implications for world peace and security. As conventional weapons become more destructive, it will become possible to escalate conventional conflicts to increased levels of violence, approximating those anticipated from a limited nuclear conflict; and if, once such levels are reached, tactical nuclear munitions are perceived as being essentially interchangeable with the most powerful conventional arms, the inhibitions against going that "one step further" and substituting nuclear for conventional arms are likely to disappear. As Julian Perry Robinson of Sussex University's Science Policy Research Unit observed at a recent Pugwash Conference, "If the destructiveness of the one (class of munitions) in fact overlaps with that of the other, the threshold becomes merely symbolic. How strong and how permanent a bulwark against nuclear war can such an abstraction be?"[6]

Unfortunately, Robinson's question has gone largely unanswered. In recognition of the frightening potential of the new generation of intercontinental nuclear missiles and Eurostrategic nuclear arms, national leaders and arms control specialists on both sides of the Atlantic have accorded highest priority to negotiating new limits on weapons of these types. These efforts at the upper end of the spectrum of violence are critically important; they have, however, had the unintended effect of diverting attention from equally threatening trends at the midpoint of the spectrum—where the conventional and nuclear sides of the firebreak are moving ever closer together. Because eradication of that gap will increase the nuclear risk—no matter how much progress is made at the arms-limitation talks in Geneva—it is essential that we identify and evaluate the threats to the firebreak and consider any new steps that may be needed to ensure its continued survival.

To facilitate our discussion of the firebreak issue, let us again consider the spectrum of violence. So long as the gap remains intact, a conventional conflict can escalate up to the firebreak under its own momentum, but cannot proceed further without a clearcut decision to move across the breach into the perilous realm of nuclear combat. If, however, conventional war can escalate to significantly *higher* levels of violence, and/or if nuclear war could be fought at relatively *lower* levels of violence, the firebreak would be narrowed and it would become that much easier to cross the breach. This is the danger we face today, as weapons developments and doctrinal innovations whittle away at the firebreak. To best appreciate this danger, let us examine each of these developments in turn:

**Conventional Weapons are Becoming
More Like Tactical Nuclear Munitions
in their Capacity to Saturate Large Areas.**

In the past, military scientists in the United States, Europe, and the Soviet Union have developed new generations of conventional munitions with greater range, accuracy, and destructive potential than anything available previously. These weapons combine advanced guidance and target-detection systems with new explosive technologies to produce munitions capable of engaging targets with great precision, and of saturating very large areas. Many of these weapons, in fact, approximate the destructive power of small nuclear weapons. As noted by Senator Sam Nunn in a May 13, 1982 report to Congress, "long-range conventional weapons are now being developed that begin to approach the destructive potential of small-yield (two to three kiloton) battlefield nuclear weapons."[7]

Weapons of the type cited by Nunn are being developed under
the Pentagon's "Assault Breaker" program, designed to produce
conventional arms capable of destroying enemy bases and attack
formations deep inside Warsaw Pact territory. As now envisioned,
the Assault Breaker system (also known as the Joint Tactical
Missile System program, or JTACMS) will be composed of a
short-range missile (Lance and Patriot are likely candidates) that
will break open over the battlefield and spew out hundreds of
terminally-guided submunitions (TGSM's) that will seek out and
engage individual targets in the area. Different TGSM's are being
designed for attacks on vehicles, fortifications, and personnel,
so that each missile can be individually loaded for a particular
array of targets. By dispersing the submunitions in a uniform
pattern, the missile can ensure blanket coverage of sizable areas—
as much as one square kilometer, or approximately the same area
destroyed by a one-kiloton neutron bomb[8] (see illustration).
Indeed, West German Defense Minister Manfred Woerner has
suggested that "the effectiveness of these (conventional) weapons
enters a dimension that heretofore was limited to nuclear
weapons."[9]

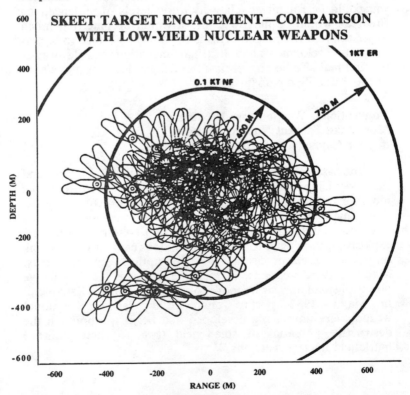

SKEET TARGET ENGAGEMENT—COMPARISON
WITH LOW-YIELD NUCLEAR WEAPONS

Many strategists suggest that deployment of these "near-nuclear," conventional weapons will strengthen deterrence and "raise the nuclear threshold" by enhancing NATO's capacity to repel a conventional Warsaw Pact attack with conventional weapons. "If NATO had those (improved conventional) capabilities," NATO Commander-in-Chief General Bernard W. Rogers told the Association of the U.S. Army in October 1982, "then the aggressor—should he attack conventionally and his attack be frustrated—would be forced either to withdraw or make the agonizing decision to be the first to escalate to nuclear weapons —(a situation in which) I do not believe Soviet leaders would attack."[10] This, indeed, is the basis upon which many security analysts, including some who have endorsed a "no first use" nuclear policy, support the development of high-tech conventional weapons.[11] But other analysts have disputed this thesis, arguing that the deployment of such weapons by the West will almost inevitably be followed by similar actions in the East—thereby forcing NATO to *increase* rather than decrease its reliance on the nuclear deterrent, and ensuring that any wars that do occur will be fought at such levels of violence that the introduction of nuclear weapons would become a near-certainty. "I question whether the development (of more powerful conventional weapons) will raise the nuclear threshold," military theorist Col. Trevor N. Dupuy observed in a recent issue of *Armed Forces Journal*. "I suspect...that the more effective and destructive conventional weapons have become, the inhibitions on using nuclear weapons are lowered correspondingly."[12]

Certainly, introduction of high-tech, wide-area conventional arms will produce a new and more lethal battlefield where anything that moves or gives off heat or sound will be targettable by precision-guided munitions (PGM's) with near-100% effectiveness. "The environment of future warfare is likely to differ greatly from any we have known in the past," the Pentagon noted in its "Defense Guidance" document for Fiscal 1984-88. "Combat against Soviet (and) Soviet-supplied forces will be of higher intensity and longer duration, with weapons of much greater accuracy and possibly higher rates of fire and mobility."[13] Such a battlefield will obviously be highly violent and destructive—and, in the view of many experts, will be more likely to witness the introduction of nuclear weapons than present battlefields, where the firebreak between nuclear and conventional forces remains intact. As suggested by J.P. Robinson, "May it not be the case that, as more and more of the militarily valued effects available from nuclear weapons come to be provided by a variety of non-nuclear means, a non-nuclear battlefield may come closer and closer to resembling a nuclear one, even to the point where it would seem to make no great practical difference to initiate nuclear war?"[14]

This danger could become particularly critical in the area of naval warfare, where the introduction of high-tech conventional weapons is occurring at an especially rapid pace. With the extension of the U.S.-Soviet military rivalry to the high seas, and the growing use of naval "platforms" for both strategic warfare and power projection, both superpowers are arming their warships with large numbers of high-tech conventional arms and tactical nuclear munitions (nuclear depth charges, torpedoes, anti-ship missiles, anti-aircraft missiles, and land-attack missiles). As of March 1983, an estimated 247 U.S. surface ships and submarines were armed with nuclear munitions, and it is assumed that a large number of Soviet warships are similarly equipped.[15] At the same time, naval vessels are becoming increasingly vulnerable to attack by precision-guided conventional munitions, such as the Exocet missile used by the Argentinians to sink the British destroyer HMS Sheffield during the Falklands conflict of 1982.[16] And because warships from both superpowers' fleets often intermingle during exercises and contingency operations, it is not hard to imagine how a future confrontation at sea could escalate rapidly across the firebreak once major vessels came under attack by modern conventional weapons.

The risk of nuclear escalation may be further enhanced by the fact that many of the proposed delivery systems for the new conventional weapons, such as the Lance, Patriot, and Tomahawk missiles, are also intended to carry nuclear warheads. Their use in battle, therefore, could prompt an enemy to order a nuclear strike in the belief that he was being attacked with nuclear rather than conventional weapons. "The firing of a cruise missile armed with a conventional warhead may send an ambiguous signal to the Soviets," Bradley Graham noted in *The Washington Post*. "Though intended to postpone a nuclear engagement, the missile could be mistaken by the Soviets for one carrying a nuclear warhead, which could result in the nuclear escalation that NATO had intended to avoid."[17]

Nuclear Weapons are Becoming More Like Conventional Weapons in their Capacity to Destroy Discrete Targets.

Just as military scientists are being encouraged to "think big" and to produce conventional weapons with near-nuclear damage potentials, nuclear engineers are being encouraged to "think small" in order to produce nuclear munitions with "near-conventional" damage radii. According to recent congressional testimony, scientists at the Energy Department's Los Alamos and Lawrence Livermore Laboratories are developing a new generation of nuclear munitions with highly-controlled blast, radiation, and heat effects. These weapons, often described as "third generation" nuclear arms to distinguish them from the earliest fission and fusion devices (the "first generation") and the compact, high-yield warheads of current nuclear weapons (the "second generation") could theoretically be used in attacks on discrete military targets without producing widespread "collateral damage" to surrounding structures and populations. Some of these new weapons are intended for use as "defensive" weapons in space—i.e., to disable incoming enemy missiles in the event of an actual shooting war—while others, such as the enhanced radiation (ER) or "neutron" warhead, are intended for use as "battlefield" weapons on earth—i.e., for attacks on enemy aircraft, tank formations, and other front-line combat systems.[18]

To be militarily effective in this second role, such battlefield munitions would have to produce relatively confined blast or radiation effects; they would, in other words, have to produce a damage radius not much greater than that of the most powerful conventional weapons. Indeed, U.S. strategists have long advocated the development of battlefield nuclear arms with "near-conventional" damage radii for deployment in Western Europe, to replace the 6,000 or so first- and second-generation tactical nuclear munitions now stockpiled there. Because these older munitions would undoubtedly produce immense collateral damage if ever employed, NATO officials may hesitate to use them in a crisis, and thus they are considered by some analysts to be a less effective deterrent against Soviet conventional attack; the third-generation weapons, on the other hand, are considered a more effective deterrent because they would produce less collateral damage and thus their use would be more likely to gain NATO approval.[19] As suggested by former NATO Commander-in-Chief G. Andrew J. Goodpaster in testimony before the Military Applications Subcommittee of the Joint Atomic Energy Committee, "Achievable new weapons of lower yields and of greater accuracy could increase military effectiveness while reducing possible collateral damage, thereby increasing their utility as well as *the acceptability in NATO planning for employment in the NATO countries* and the adjacent areas in which they would most likely be used."[20]

In accordance with this perspective, the United States has already commenced production of two ER warheads, the W70-3 for the Lance battlefield missile and the W79-1 for the Army/Marine Corps 8-inch howitzer. (These warheads are currently stockpiled in the United States, but could be deployed in Europe if approval is granted by the prospective host nation.) Other third-generation munitions, with equivalent or smaller radii of destruction, are now under development at the Lawrence Livermore and Los Alamos laboratories.[21]

While the introduction of these weapons has been welcomed by some U.S. officials as an important contribution to deterrence, many analysts have argued that it could *enhance* the risk of nuclear war by eroding the difference between nuclear and conventional arms, and thus increasing the temptation to "go nuclear" in a future high-intensity conflict. If such low-yield weapons "became standard equipment," Alva Myrdal wrote in *The Game of Disarmament*, "this would blur the distinction between nuclear and conventional weapons, making escalation across the firebreak more likely."[22]

The Adoption of New Military Doctrines Stressing Offensive Action by "Dual Capable" (Nuclear/Conventional) Combat Forces.

In response to the development of new weapons technologies and the continued buildup of Soviet conventional capabilities, U.S. and NATO strategists have developed new combat doctrines stressing offensive thrusts into enemy territory by "dual capable" (i.e., both conventionally and nuclear armed) forces. This approach, incorporated both into the U.S. Army's AirLand Battle Concept (ABC) and NATO's so-called "Strike Deep" strategy, is intended to cripple Warsaw Pact attacks by exposing the enemy's rear-area forces and installations to attack by high-tech conventional arms and battlefield nuclear munitions. By "extending the battlefield and integrating conventional, nuclear, chemical, and electronic means," an Army concept paper notes, "the ABC envisions a battlefield where the enemy is attacked to the full depth of his formations, and where early initiative of offensive action" will "bring about the conclusion of battle on our terms."[23]

For many strategists, adoption of the AirLand and Strike Deep doctrines represents a long-overdue modernization of U.S. combat doctrine. But while this effort has produced considerable enthusiasm in military circles, several aspects of the AirLand and

Strike Deep concepts have produced concern elsewhere. Two features of these doctrines, in particular, cause alarm: their emphasis on fielding "dual capable" formations able to use conventional and nuclear weapons interchangeably, and their emphasis on offensive strikes deep within enemy territory.

Normally, U.S. pronouncements on military policy are devoid of any reference to the nuts and bolts of nuclear combat, but the ABC position paper (TRADOC pamphlet 525-5) is conspicuous for its advocacy of the integration of nuclear and conventional capabilities on the battlefield. Since the Warsaw Pact can bring numerically larger forces to bear in future conflicts, "systems designed to defeat enemy assault elements, to disrupt follow-on forces and to seize the initiative by attack must be able to deliver conventional and/or nuclear fires throughout the spectrum of the battle (and) throughout the depth of the battlefield." This requires, the paper further notes, that Army combat systems be "dual capable, with sufficient range, accuracy, and lethality to hold enemy follow-on echelons at risk in peacetime and to successfully attack them in wartime."[24] This emphasis on the integration of nuclear and conventional capabilities has disturbed some U.S. legislators, who fear that it will help blur the distinction between nuclear and conventional weapons, and increase the Army's reliance on battlefield nuclear weapons. These concerns were voiced publicly in July 1982, when Army officials told a group of U.S. Representatives at a classified briefing on the AirLand Concept that they were seeking "pre-clearance" for the use of tactical nuclear weapons in the Central European battlefield of the future. Rep. Norman W. Dicks, who attended the briefing, told reporters that he was "stunned" by the presentation, which stressed the need for pre-clearance so that field commanders could use their nuclear arms at the very start of a conflict, without waiting further for presidential authorization.[25]

Concern over the nuclear dimension of the AirLand Concept has been reinforced by worries about the offensive aspects of the doctrine. Arguing that NATO defenses will crumble if the Warsaw Pact can use its "second echelon" forces to exploit any breakthrough achieved by the initial wave of attacking forces, the AirLand doctrine calls for counterstrikes against these rear-area forces at the very onset of the battle, while they are still far behind the front lines. To overcome a Warsaw Pact assault without giving up territory, the ABC paper declares, "The defense must...begin well forward and proceed aggressively from there to destroy enemy assault echelons and at the same time to slow, disrupt, break up, disperse, or destroy follow-on echelons in order to quickly seize the initiative and go on the offensive."[26] While possibly sound from a tactical point of view, this "hair-trigger" approach could lead to U.S. conventional and (possibly) nuclear thrusts into Warsaw Pact territory at the very outbreak of hostilities, before NATO officials could assess the nature and intensity of the attack, and thereupon adopt a collective response. "This comes very close to calling for pre-emptive strikes," was how John Mearsheimer of Harvard University's Center for Science and International Affairs characterized the new doctrine.[27]

Offensive operations of this sort—even if conducted initially with conventional arms—are considered particularly perilous by some U.S. analysts because they would endanger Soviet *strategic* installations in Eastern Europe (early-warning radars, command and control facilities, air-defense systems, and so forth), and thus risk an immediate nuclear response. Arguing that any Western attack on vital Soviet strategic facilities would trigger an extreme reaction, Barry Posen of Harvard wrote in *International Security* that "strike deep" operations would "unleash enormous, and possibly uncontrollable escalatory pressures despite the preferences of American or Soviet policy-makers."[28]

Clearly, each of the three developments described above represents a significant threat to the firebreak in its own right; when combined, the threat is very grave indeed. By blurring the distinction between conventional and nuclear munitions, the new arms technologies are progressively erasing the psychological barriers to escalation along with the critical "maneuvering space" within which restraints can be negotiated; by stressing deep offensive strikes by dual-capable forces, moreover, the new military doctrines threaten to further accelerate the escalatory process. It appears, in fact, that the technological and doctrinal trends are reinforcing one another to systematically erode the nuclear firebreak—suggesting that future wars are likely to harbor an ever-increasing risk of escalation across the spectrum of violence into the nightmare realm of nuclear annihilation.

If this analysis proves accurate, it is obvious that the arms control and disarmament community will have to develop a new approach to the prevention of nuclear war. Efforts to reduce the world's stockpiles of nuclear munitions will have to be accompanied by efforts to safeguard the firebreak against further erosion. Because this barrier is being assaulted from three directions—conventional arms technology, nuclear technology, and military doctrine—so must the defense of the firebreak entail three components: restraints on the introduction of near-nuclear conventional weapons; restraints on the introduction of near-conventional nuclear weapons; and restraints on the deployment of offensively-oriented dual-capable combat forces. Needless to say, such expansion of the already crowded arms-control agenda will not be easy to achieve. So long as any nuclear weapons remain in existence, however, we will not be safe from annihilation unless we also ensure that non-nuclear wars do not leap across the firebreak and precipitate a global conflagration.

Notes

1. The author first addressed the issue of the firebreak in "The Conventional Weapons Fallacy," *The Nation* (April 9, 1983), pp. 438-444; and "Leaping the Firebreak," *The Progressive* (September 1983), pp. 31-33.
2. Alain C. Enthoven, American Deterrent Policy, in Henry Kissinger, ed. *Problems of National Security* (New York: Praeger, 1965), pp. 123-124.
3. Ibid, p. 124.
4. Alva Myrdal, *The Game of Disarmament* (New York: Pantheon, 1976), p. 48.
5. For further discussion of the firebreak concept, see Bernard Brodie, *Strategy in the Missile Age* (Princeton, NJ: Princeton University Press, 1959), esp. pp. 103-111; Herman Kahn, *On Escalation* (New York: Praeger, 1965), esp. pp. 94-133; and Thomas C. Schelling, *The Strategy of Conflict* (Cambridge, Mass.: Harvard University Press, 1960), esp. pp. 257-266.
6. J. Perry Robinson, "Neutron Bomb and Conventional Weapons of Mass Destruction," *Bulletin of the Atomic Scientists* (March 1978), p. 43.
7. Senator Sam Nunn, "NATO: Can the Alliance Be Saved?" Report to the Committee on Armed Services, U.S. Senate, Washington, D.C., GPO 1982, p. 6.
8. For an introduction to these systems, see Benjamin F. Schemmer, "Defend Forward, But Strike Deep," *Armed Forces Journal* (November 1982), pp. 50-68; and Mark Hewish, The Assault Breaker Program, *International Defense Review,* (September 1982) pp. 1207-1211.
9. "NATO's New Conventional Option," *The Wall Street Journal,* November 19, 1982.
10. Gen. Bernard W. Rogers, "Enhancing Deterrence—Raising the Nuclear Threshold," *NATO Review* (February 1983), p. 8.
11. See *No First Use: A Report by the Union of Concerned Scientists* (Cambridge, MA, 1983).
12. Trevor N. Dupuy, "Why Deep Strike *Won't* Work," *Armed Forces Journal* (January 1983), p. 57.
13. Cited in *The New York Times*, May 30, 1982.

14. Julian Perry Robinson, "Quasi-Nuclear Weapons," Report to Pugwash Syposium, London, December 10-12, 1980.
15. Thomas B. Cochran, William M. Arkin, and Milton M. Hoenig, *Nuclear Weapons Databook*, Vol. I, *U.S. Nuclear Forces and Capabilities* (Cambridge, Mass.: Ballinger, 1983), pp. 244-278.
16. For discussion, see Paul Walker, "Smart Weapons in Naval Warfare," *Scientific American* (May 1983), pp. 53-61.
17. *The Washington Post*, November 2, 1982.
18. See article by Judith Miller in *The New York Times*, October 29, 1982.
19. For elaboration of this argument, see W.S. Bennett, R.R. Sandoval, and R.G. Shreffler, "A Credible Nuclear-Emphasis Defense for NATO," *Orbis* (Summer 1973), pp. 463-479.
20. Quoted in *The New York Times*, January 27, 1974.
21. Cochran, Arkin, and Hoenig, *Nuclear Weapons Databook*, pp. 29-30, 72-73, and 77-78.
22. Myrdal, *The Game of Disarmament*, pp. 47-48.
23. U.S. Army, Training and Doctrine Command, *The AirLand Battle and Corps 86* (Ft. Belvoir, Va., 1981), p. 2.
24. Ibid., p. 7.
25. *The Washington Post*, July 21, 1982.
26. *The AirLand Battle*, p. 6.
27. Quoted in *U.S. News & World Report* (September 20, 1982), p. 59.
28. Barry R. Posen, "Inadvertent Nuclear War?" *International Security* (Fall 1982), p. 28.

Reprinted from *Thought* magazine, April 1984.

Christopher Paine

On the Beach: The Rapid Deployment Force and the Nuclear Arms Race

There are two kinds of beaches in U.S. defense planning. The first is the shoreline that U.S. marines typically storm in a real or rehearsed military intervention. The second belongs to the domain of the nuclear strategists. When their "limited" nuclear war games go astray, simulating escalation into all-out thermonuclear war, the strategists privately label this outcome a "beach," after the title of Nevil Shute's popular novel of nuclear apocalypse, *On the Beach*. In this era, when two military superpowers envelope the globe with the reach of their nuclear weapons, the question inevitable arises: is it possible for the Rapid Deployment Force to storm the beaches of the Persian Gulf without leaving all of us on the beach of nuclear annihilation?

This metaphor of the beach encapsulates the two dimensions of the current U.S. military buildup—"rapid" intervention capability, aimed chiefly at the Middle East, and the Soviet-U.S. nuclear arms race. The links between the two are considerable, though they are not generally perceived by opponents of present U.S. policy. Most U.S. citizens look at the nuclear "balance" and see only growing stockpiles of morally inconceivable destructiveness. In the eyes of high-level policy makers, though, the shift since the late 1960s towards a rough nuclear balance, from the previous condition of clear U.S. superiority, coincides with increasing instability in key strategic regions of the world. "Western Europe, our Asian allies and the United States have sharply increased their dependence on raw materials from other parts of the world at the very time that these areas have become increasingly vulnerable to hostile action", wrote Defense Secretary Caspar Weinberger in his FY 1983 Annual Report to the Congress.[1] This perceived threat lies behind the decisions of the

Carter and Reagan administrations to build a Rapid Deployment
Force for intervention. The strategic calculations surrounding U.S.
planning for military intervention abroad are, in turn, a major
driving force in the nuclear arms buildup.

General David C. Jones, then Chairman of the Joint Chiefs
of Staff, argued for the MX missile in these terms in 1979.
"Because the mission of our strategic forces extends beyond
merely deterring an attack on our cities to encompass U.S.
interests and allied forces overseas," he told *Air Force Magazine*,
"there could be a reversal of the Cuban situation (the missile crisis
of 1962) where (the Soviets) might have a strategic advantage
combined with a local conventional force advantage." In such
a situation, the U.S. might have to back down regardless of the
stakes. In order to forestall this possibility, Jones argued for
increased "strategic force modernization", with the "silo-killing"
MX as the top priority. The Soviet Union's conventional force
superiority in key regions like the Middle East (Southwest Asia,
or SWA, in Pentagon parlance), could only be offset by heightened
Soviet fear of U.S. escalation. "The focus must be on this nation
having the capability actually to fight a sustained nuclear war,"
Jones concluded, "including all the ingredients that entails."[2]

More recently, top Reagan Administration policy makers have
explicitly linked up U.S. nuclear strategy with intervention
capabilities directed at the Middle East. "Our FY 1983-87
programs place increased emphasis on our ability to project forces
into Southwest Asia," Weinberger stated in his annual report.[3]
At another point in the same report, he wrote: "For the region
of the Persian Gulf, in particular, our strategy is based on the
concept that the prospect of combat with the U.S. and other
friendly forces, coupled with the prospect that we might carry the
war to other arenas, is the most effective deterrent to Soviet
aggression."[4]

U.S. ability to "carry the war to other arenas" is questionable,
officials assert. According to John Lehman, Secretary of the
Navy, the current period is one in which "American decision
makers must operate in an environment in which, if escalation
is taken to the ultimate level, they know the United States would
not prevail...Much of the world, wherein lies the vital interests
of the United States and its allies, is now for the first time outside
of the nuclear umbrella." Even in the event of a Soviet military
move against the Persian Gulf, Lehman claims, "it would be
unthinkable during this period for us to contemplate escalation
to the nuclear level."[5]

The RDF: A "Portable Dienbienphu"

Strategic "parity" with the Soviet Union, and the consequent decline in the effectiveness of U.S. threats to employ nuclear weapons, has been one factor behind the concept of a rapid deployment force. At one level, the Rapid Deployment Force represents a reorganization of existing conventional forces, making such forces available for "power projection" in the Middle East region.

It would be a mistake, however, to see the RDF concept as an alternative to a strategy built on nuclear escalation. Rather, it represents a key ingredient in an overall strategy that rests more than ever on a doctrine of first use of nuclear weapons. This is true at several levels. First, the availability of a Rapid Deployment Force will make it much easier for the U.S. to intervene militarily in a situation it might otherwise have had to resolve by political or diplomatic means. It thus makes it more rather than less likely that Washington's interventionary impulse will translate into armed action. Such interventions represent the most likely first steps of a confrontation that could quickly acquire a nuclear dimension. Second, the RDF is composed of existing armed units which are themselves already "integrated" and "dual-capable": that is, equipped with tactical nuclear as well as non-nuclear weapons. Third, the RDF is designed as a "tripwire"—to signal U.S. determination to escalate to nuclear weapons as much as to cope directly with opposing conventional forces. The RDF can serve as a sort of "doomsday device" which an opponent dares attack only at the risk of triggering a mutually destructive war.

The RDF is first of all a frame of mind, a piece of the ideological setting which encourages the projection of U.S. forces abroad, whether in the form of small groups of military advisers armed with rifles and grenade launchers, or B-52 bombers loaded with more explosive power than was expended in all of World War II. Along with "forward bases" in Europe and elsewhere, a navy of more than a dozen carrier battle groups, and long-range airlift, the RDF is part of a capability to project military power on a global basis in order to maintain what Eugene Rostow calls "world public order". Rostow, an influential figure in the campaign to revive militarism in the U.S. political establishment, and now director of the State Department's Arms Control and Disarmament Agency, recently testified that "adequate military strength deployed in key areas around the world" was essential for maintaining "a progressive and integrated capitalist world economy which serves the interests of the industrialized and developing nations alike, and those of the Communist nations as well.''[6] In President Reagan's words, "We have to be so strong that no other nation on earth will dare violate the peace.''[7]

In some parts of the globe, though, U.S. forces cannot be "projected" with impunity. In Europe and the Middle East in particular, the Soviet Union is able to pose a countervailing power on the basis of its conventional military strength and geographic proximity. Some U.S. strategists recognize that the Soviet Union may not be the primary threat to U.S. interests in the Third World. Former Secretary of Defense Harold Brown, in his fiscal 1981 "posture statement", warned that turbulence stemming from "the explosive disparity between wealth and hunger" could "almost equal in severity the military threat from the Soviet Union''.[8] For the Reagan Administration, this seems to be a distinction without a difference. As Eugene Rostow explained to the First Committee of the 36th U.N. General Assembly, "What the Soviet Union does is to exploit and manipulate regional turbulences in the interest of enlarging its own sphere of dominance.''[9] For President Reagan, the analysis is even less complicated. "There is an evil influence throughout the world," he told an Israel Bonds meeting in 1978. "In every one of the far-flung trouble spots, dig deep enough and you'll find the Soviet Union stirring a witches' brew, furthering its own imperialistic ambitions. If the Soviet Union would simply go home, much of the bloodshed in the world today would cease.''[10] During a campaign interview in June 1980, Reagan reiterated that "the Soviet Union underlies all the unrest that is going on. If they weren't engaged in this game of dominoes, there wouldn't be any hotspots in the world.''[11]

In the world outlook of the president and his key advisers, then, U.S. strategic interests are considered irreducible, while all threats to those interests essentially emanate from the Soviet Union. Sole reliance on conventional forces in Europe or the Middle East could lead to military defeat or, at best, accommodation—i.e., appeasement. A strategy of deterring all major challenges to U.S. global interests by conventional forces anywhere in the world would bankrupt the Western alliance it is supposed to defend. The question of relative military expenditures is already a matter of bitter dispute between the U.S. and its major allies. Moreover, there remains the possibility that the Soviet Union might resort, however irrationally, to its nuclear deterrent in such a situation. For these reasons, U.S. planners have consistently rejected an exclusively conventional force posture. Whatever the arguments over the years about the proper size and composition of U.S. conventional forces, these have always been in the context of an "integrated" posture of conventional and nuclear forces.[12]

The essence of this strategy is for the United States to maintain the initiative for escalating any conflict to the nuclear level, if necessary—to deter challenges if possible and do battle with those challenges that do occur. Eugene Rostow has defined deterrence in so many words: "to confront Soviet expansion through the use of aggression with the prospect of unacceptable risk, to which they have always responded with prudence."[13] Ronald Reagan, during his presidential campaign, responded to a question about possible Soviet intervention in the Persian Gulf in similar terms:

> If it thinks this will cause a confrontation—this is going to give them a pause. They're not going to move too swiftly because they don't want the world blown up—they want the world. And they'd like to take it piecemeal, a chunk at a time, until finally they might have the power to give us a choice of surrender or die. But we still have going for us the fact that they don't want to make that kind of move until their superiority is so unquestioned that there is no risk to their homeland.[14]

In his first press conference as Commander in Chief of the U.S. military machine, Reagan was asked if the U.S. could prevent militarily any Soviet move to cut off Persian Gulf oil. "Well, no," he replied, but went on to repeat his call for a U.S. military "presence" in the region:

> What is meant by a presence is that we're there enough to know and for the Soviets to know that if they made a reckless move they would be risking confrontation with the United States.

"Wouldn't that be an empty threat?" a reporter asked.

> Well, it's not. You just don't plant a flag in the ground and walk away and leave it. There would be Americans there...we're doing that right now with the Navy in the Indian Ocean. But I think we need a ground presence also...It's based on the assumption—and I think a correct assumption—the Soviet Union is not ready to take on that confrontation which could become World War III...They're going to have to take that into their computations.[15]

In other words, any Soviet attack on an American expeditionary force would become the occasion for Washington's first use of nuclear weapons. It is precisely this possibility that prompted

Daniel Ellsberg to label the RDF as "a portable Dienbienphu," referring to the besieged French fortress in Vietnam in 1954, which might have been "saved" only by the threat or actual use of nuclear weapons.* "Perhaps its major function would be as an instrument of real and visible commitment to the possible first use of nuclear weapons by the United States."[16]

The RDF: "D" is for "Dual-Capable"

The RDF is not a new or special conventional force. It is an aggregation of elements already existing in the four services. As such, it comes equipped with its share of weapons systems that are "dual-capable"—i.e. able to deliver both nuclear and conventional warheads. The RDF has at its disposal some portion of the roughly 17,000 tactical nuclear warheads that are part of the entire U.S. force structure.

Such interchangeability is essential both in terms of cost and available manpower, according to the Army's Major-General Louis Wagner. "We use the same troops and we have the same cannons available to do the nuclear and conventional job," he told the House Armed Services Committee in March 1980. "We want to provide for contingency forces. This is very important today, and if we have dual-capable forces, particularly in our 155 (mm) and 8-inch artillery, all of the units that would be in the rapid deploying forces can have these things made available to them so that they will have dual capability."[17] President Reagan has no reservations in this regard. "I consider the neutron warhead conventional," he remarked during the 1980 campaign. "I favor development and deployment of the neutron warhead for U.S. theater forces, including ballistic missiles, cruise missiles, artillery and bombs."[18]

The president believes that escalation to full-scale nuclear war can be contained. "I could see where you could have an exchange of tactical nuclear weapons against troops in the field without bringing either one of the major powers to pushing the button," he remarked in October 1981.[19] Secretary of Defense Weinberger has expressed readiness to use nuclear weapons even against non-nuclear opponents. Asked during his confirmation hearing whether he would have "recommended the use of nuclear weapons in Vietnam," Weinberger responded:

---

*Secretary of State John Foster Dulles reportedly offered Premier George Bidault three tactical nuclear weapons to end the siege, but France declined the offer. —Eds.

It is still possible, I believe, to fight some wars using conventional forces that don't involve nuclear weapons...but I think that if you advise potential opponents in advance that you do not intend to cross certain lines, that you have almost assured another Vietnam...Any time you get into a war the possibility that you will use every weapon available has to be left open.[20]

As if to underscore the nuclear dimension of the RDF, one of its earmarked components is a wing of 28 B-52H strategic bombers, with refueling tankers and reconnaissance planes, from the Strategic Air Command. Dubbed the Strategic Projection Force, it represents "an inexpensive, near-term solution to a national problem," according to SAC head General Richard Ellis in 1980.[21] "SAC aircraft can provide rapid long-range force projection in the conventional and theater nuclear areas," testified Ellis, specifying elsewhere that the SPF "can deliver up to 200 tons of (conventional) explosives per day," as well as a range of thermonuclear gravity bombs. "The force can deploy within 24 hours," claimed Ellis, "and be flying operational missions within 12 hours after landing at a forward operating location."

"A forward operating location" has been the weak link in this plan. When Ellis testified a year later, the U.S. did "not have the bases from which we have fuel or the munitions to take advantage of that capability...We would be ready to go with nowhere to go...One of the more critical things in our conventional capability has been the reduction of our overseas base structure in the last ten years." "B-52s seem to have a stigma that causes a great deal of problems," Ellis added innocently. Ellis spoke hopefully in March 1981 of "the availability of certain bases in the Middle East that I think are too sensitive to get into. We hope to store fuel and munitions there which would enable us to operate."[22] Several months later, during the "Bright Star" war games that followed the assassination of Anwar Sadat, the Pentagon staged a B-52 bombing run from SAC bases in North Dakota to the Egyptian desert. Airfields in and around the region are being constructed or expanded to accommodate B-52s. These include Diego Garcia in the Indian Ocean, and Ras Banas on the Egyptian coast of the Red Sea.* Thamrit, in Oman's Dhofar province,"has one of the longest runways in the world."[23]

---

*Perhaps as many as four of the new military airfields being constructed in Saudi Arabia will be capable of handling B-52s, along with Qena Air Base in Upper Egypt. Iran has one or more airfields which reportedly

The B-52s are practically incidental to the nuclear weapons already within easy reach of the Gulf. The three carrier battle groups stationed in the Indian Ocean and eastern Mediterranean are loaded with hundreds of the following weapons: B-61 light-weight nuclear bombs with four yields ranging from 100 to 500 kilotons (kt); B-57 light-weight nuclear depth charges with four yields ranging to 20 kt; B-43 medium-weight nuclear bombs with at least five yields; W-44 warheads with about one kt yield for ship-launched anti-submarine missiles; W-55 warheads of several kt yields for submarine-launched anti-submarine missiles; and W-45-1 warheads of one kt yield for surface-to-air anti-aircraft missiles.[24] The Lockheed P-3 anti-submarine patrol aircraft now flying out of Diego Garcia and Oman's Masirah Island also carry the B-57 light-weight nuclear depth charge. A new medium-weight high-yield nuclear bomb, the B-83, will replace the B-43 now deployed on the carriers. Terrier anti-aircraft missiles are being equipped with new W-81 low-yield warheads. In 1984, the ships and submarines patrolling the Indian Ocean may begin carrying the 1500 kilometer range Sea-Launched Cruise Missile with W-80 kt warheads.* Cruise missiles based in Sicily will also have the Middle East within their range.

The Marine Corps has been greatly increasing its nuclear potential. The Marine Air-Ground Task Force is another important component of the RDF. Old F-4 Phantom warplanes which were not "certified" for nuclear weapons delivery are now being replaced by F/A-18 Hornets which are nuclear "certified." The non-nuclear AV8-A Harrier vertical take-off and landing close-support aircraft are being replaced by the nuclear-capable AV8-B. Non-nuclear capable 105mm artillery are being replaced by the dual-capable 155mm gun, almost doubling the Marine Corps' nuclear artillery potential.[25] There are some eight types of nuclear capable 155mm guns which can fire roughly 3,300 W-48 low-yield atomic projectiles in the U.S. stockpile. A typical Marine Amphibious Force is also equipped with about a dozen eight-inch howitzers which fire both the older W-33 atomic projectiles and the newer W-79 neutron warhead. Originally conceived for deployment in Europe, 800 of these neutron warheads are being produced initially to stockpile in the U.S. for potential crisis deployment overseas.

---

can receive B-52s. Several of the military bases in Morocco, for which the Reagan Administration negotiated renewed access in the spring of 1982, had been Strategic Air Command bases up through the late 1950s, and are therefore presumably capable of handling B-52s. —Eds.
*As indicated elsewhere in this book, the Sea-Launched Cruise Missiles with nuclear warheads have been deployed. —Eds.

"Escalation Dominance":
What the MX Means to King Fahd

A strategic balance would merely suffice to deter nuclear attacks on U.S. and Soviet home territories "has always been rejected as a totally inadequate standard for nuclear negotiations," according to Arms Control and Disarmament Agency Director Rostow. At his confirmation hearings he told the Senate Foreign Relations Committee that "facing the Soviet strategic arsenal which such a SALT policy would imply, we would be in no position to use conventional or nuclear forces in defense of our interests in Europe, the Far East, the Middle East or elsewhere."[26] More recently, Rostow told the House Foreign Affairs Committee that any new arms control agreement would have to be based on the principle of "true parity" as "allowing each side the equal capacity to deter aggression against its vital interests."[27]

The trick then becomes one of defining the relative scope of U.S. and U.S.S.R. vital interests. Henry Kissinger, whose first book was entitled *Nuclear Weapons and Foreign Policy* and who continues to serve as an informal advisor to the Reagan Administration on Middle East developments, recently proclaimed that "the countries in the Gulf have to understand that we are prepared to protect both their domestic structure and their frontiers; and they need to be given confidence in the means which we will use."[28] Kissinger went on to say, "We must generate a credible capability for rapid support against internal upheaval." U.S. vital interests, by this perspective, include the preservation of the ruling families of the Gulf and Arabian Peninsula. President Reagan said as much in October 1981, when he declared that "Saudi Arabia we will not permit to be an Iran."[29] Most U.S. military planners do not consider Soviet military intervention to be the most plausible serious threat to ruling family longevity in the Gulf. The propensity to see "Soviet subversion" and "Soviet proxies" behind any local upheaval, though, makes it difficult to rule out military measures against local Soviet allies and interests in the area. Indeed, the possibility of such an intervention against Iran must be considered quite high. Soviet concern about developments in Iran, and Moscow's readiness to intervene militarily if necessary to prevent hostile forces from taking control along its southern borders, are matters of record.

There is a very great risk, in other words, of U.S. military intervention leading to confrontation with the Soviet Union which quickly threatens to become nuclear. Prevailing military logic dictates that a threat to begin the process of nuclear escalation must be made "credible" by regional and ultimately intercontinental capacity to destroy preemptively an opponent's nuclear arsenal. Short of this, the goal is to deprive an adversary of all responses that are remotely proportional to the scale of the initial provocation. This forces the adversary to choose between potentially suicidal escalation or retreat. U.S. reliance on a strategy of nuclear first use inevitably produces an intense preoccupation in Washington with the overall balance of preemptive nuclear capabilities at the intercontinental strategic level, and with the nuclear balance in various theaters at different levels of intensity.

This bizarre and apocalyptic vision provides an all-too-plausible linkage between the prospective stability of the House of Saud and the Reagan Administration's decision to produce and deploy the MX missile. This is the real consequence of Secretary Weinberger's admonition that "the possibility that you will use every weapon available has to be left open." Examining the military balance in Southwest Asia, an American military planner can see that the threat to Soviet armored and airborne divisions which might intervene in the Gulf—for example, nuclear armed A-6 attack planes on carriers in the Arabian Sea—is countered by the threat of a Soviet preemptive attack on those carriers with nuclear-armed Backfire bombers and submarines. To make the initial threat credible, the U.S. must be able to deter any Soviet attacks on U.S. forces concentrated in the area. This produces the military need to threaten preemptive destruction of all Soviet airlift bomber bases, command posts and war reserves stocks which could support a Soviet military operation in the Middle East—in effect, a "limited" first strike using missiles and aircraft deployed in Europe, the Indian Ocean and the western Pacific.

But Soviet strategists have the intermediate range SS-20 missiles to pose an equivalent threat to U.S. bases and forces in the Middle East and the approaches to the region. To deter *this* potential escalation, U.S. planners count on Pershing II and other ground-launch missiles to threaten devastation of Soviet early warning and command and control systems, and thus immobilize Soviet ICBMs. The Soviet arsenal would then be vulnerable to the new MX or Trident II missiles, or even to existing Minuteman II and III "silo-busting" warheads. To continue this conflict scenario, the Soviets would have to attack American cities and industries with whichever of their submarines had survived a preemptive missile attack on their bases, or U.S. "hunter-killer" submarines and aircraft. The Soviets would probably not take this step, our strategists tell us, for fear of exposing their own cities to the enormous nuclear destructive potential in remaining U.S. submarines and bombers.

The Soviet general staff, argue U.S. strategists, would consider this chain of events in advance and advise the Soviet leadership that the current strategic balance allowed the U.S. to think it could credibly threaten nuclear escalation. Since this might make it more likely that the U.S. would so escalate, the Soviet Union should not consider, say, intervening in Saudi Arabia to assist the new and beleaguered revolutionary government there and prevent the restoration of the monarchy. (To forestall such an outcome, the Soviet general staff might recommend: upgrading the accuracy of Soviet ICBMs to pose an equivalent threat to the U.S.; developing a new, more accurate submarine-launched ballistic missile; placing new medium-range missiles in Cuba and eastern Siberia; hardening the Soviet command and control systems against electromagnetic pulse disruption. This would simply be a mirror-image of the program outlined by President Reagan in October 1981.)

There are other possible scenarios. For example, the Soviets could aim to destroy U.S. tactical nuclear forces on carriers and forward bases in the Middle East before Washington decides to use them. In this situation, according to one former senior advisor to the Secretary of Defense, the U.S. needs a strategic nuclear force capable of threatening the prompt destruction of all Soviet forces relevant to this Middle East operation while limiting damage to the rest of the U.S.S.R. The Russians, realizing that escalation would only widen the damage to their homeland, would back down and withdraw. Better yet, having made these calculations in advance, they would refrain from any incursion in the first place.[30]

Such scenarios constitute the underlying rationale for new strategic weapons such as the MX and the Pershing II. It is within this particular context of nuclear escalation and first use that the Pentagon views the potential vulnerability of the silo-based Minuteman force as a serious "deficiency" in the U.S. nuclear posture. Many other nuclear forces would survive a Soviet attack on the U.S. But, military planners say, Minuteman vulnerability lessens the credibility of U.S. nuclear threats against the Soviet Union in a crisis involving American "vital interests" overseas. In his 1980 Annual Report, Defense Secretary Harold Brown warned: "No enemy should be left with the illusion that he could disable portions of our nuclear forces—[U.S.]-based or overseas—as a preliminary to attacks in specific theaters with his general purpose forces."[31] According to the proponents of the MX, Soviet leaders presently entertain precisely such illusions. The United States would like to preserve the option of threatening "limited" use of its ICBM force to back up the threat of "limited" attacks with tactical and nuclear forces. The alleged vulnerability of U.S. ICBMs to Soviet ICBMs undermines the credibility of this threat. Without a "survivable" capability for threatening controlled strategic nuclear escalation, according to this line of thinking, "the Soviets can undertake peripheral political and military actions without considering possible nuclear consequences to the same degree that was necessary in the past."[32] Richard Burt, now director of the State Department's Bureau of Politico-Military Affairs, and before that responsible for *New York Times* coverage of such national security issues, believes that "the nuclear balance is the crucial barometer of Soviet willingness to take risks and nurture crisis in trouble spots around the world." According to Burt, the Soviet capacity to destroy "a large fraction of our ICBM force" is one that is "not available to us. In a future crisis, U.S. military capabilities could be paralyzed by such a threat."[33]

This "loss" of American nuclear superiority is in itself a debatable proposition. Far more tenuous is the notion that "parity" leaves the U.S.S.R. "free" to employ its conventional and tactical nuclear forces in specific regions without fear of "controlled" U.S. nuclear attacks on the Soviet Union itself. It is a theory scarcely susceptible to empirical confirmation, but its proponents—who occupy the highest national security positions in the U.S. government—clearly believe it to be the case. They ascribe to it the manifold setbacks to U.S. interests in the Third World over the past decade, from Afghanistan and Angola to Nicaragua and El Salvador. This is despite the fact that the Soviet Union has attempted nothing so "adventurous" as the attempt to place medium-range missiles in Cuba in 1962, when it had no such nuclear parity with the U.S.

What is involved in these calculations is the "mirror-image" projection of U.S. plans and capabilities to the Soviet side, now that the U.S. can no longer fully "dominate" any conceivable escalation scenario. Soviet ability to destroy preemptively the U.S. ICBMs lends credibility to any Soviet threats to defend their conventional forces with limited nuclear attacks. All Soviet "improvements" to their nuclear force, such as hardening missile silos or increasing the number of warheads per missile, only undermine further the credibility of the U.S. preemptive threat. Without the "hard-target kill capability" of the MX and Trident II missiles, U.S. strategists believe that Washington will no longer

be able to credibly threaten nuclear escalation in a crisis. General
Lew Allen, Air Force Chief of Staff, summarized the situation
for the Senate Armed Services Committee:

> The real conclusion one must reach in this closed room is
> that the United States does not face a very serious strategic
> nuclear problem . . . the Soviets' perception of an advantage
> for a preemptive first strike is much higher than it has been
> in the past. And it is at a point, while perhaps not dangerous
> in that it will incite them to a first strike, it nevertheless gives
> them confidence in their nuclear forces. *That confidence
> means that we will find the threshold of nuclear war much
> higher than in the past,* and we will see greater Soviet
> confidence in their ability to be adventuresome and
> provocative to the United States across a broad range of
> areas.[34]

The implication is clear: a high threshold for the initiation of
nuclear violence by the United States is not in the security interest
of the United States. This U.S. inability to threaten seriously
nuclear escalation, by being able to control it through counter-
military preemption, lies behind the Reagan Administration's
misleading call to restore the U.S. "second-strike capacity" and
"margin of safety". With such a restoration, says Reagan's chief
arms negotiator, General Edward Rowny, "we could take certain
slight risks without having those become big risks."[35]

Intervention and the Doctrine of Credibilty

To be effective, U.S. threats to use nuclear weapons must
remain credible even in the face of countervailing Soviet threats.
The task of sustaining this credibility is at one level technical, and
to that extent based on a certain "rational" calculation. At the
primary level, though, it is fundamentally a psychological
campaign of bluff and intimidation. "Modernization" of nuclear
capabilities, improving accuracy and "survivability" (of missiles!)
and reducing undesirable "collateral effects" (such as blast
damage to oil facilities, fallout inflicted on one's own troops)
increases the nominal military utility of these weapons. Military
planners calculate that these "improvements" should heighten
"rational" expectations of an adversary that these weapons would
actually be used to defend U.S. "vital interests" in the Gulf and
around the globe. Continuing modernization is essential to prevent
any "misperception" by opponents or allies that U.S. leaders have
lost their "resolve" to use nuclear weapons.

Defense Secretary Weinberger and other high officials in the present administration argue strenuously that their nuclear war policy represents no radical departure from that of previous administrations since World War II. Weinberger might have in mind documents like the National Security Council Memorandum 68 of April 1950 which asserted that:

> our present weakness would prevent us from offering effective resistance at any of several vital points. The only deterrent we can present to the Kremlin is the evidence we give that we may make any of the critical points which we cannot hold the occasion for a global war of annihilation.[36]

For the 1980s, the most "critical point" has been identified as the Persian Gulf/Arabian Peninsula region. As of January 1, 1983, the nuclear-equipped and nuclear-backed Rapid Deployment Force is formally constituted as a separate "Unified Command for Southwest Asia."* According to the defense secretary's classified *1984-88 Defense Guidance* document:

> It is essential that the Soviet Union be confronted with the prospect of a major conflict should it seek to reach oil resources of the Gulf. Because the Soviets might induce or exploit local political instabilities, their forces could be extended into the area by means other than outright invasion. *Whatever the circumstances*, we should be prepared to introduce American forces directly into the region should it appear that the security of access to Persian Gulf oil is threatened....[37]

Since less than 13 percent of U.S. oil needs, and only five percent of total U.S. energy needs, are supplied from the Persian Gulf,

---

*According to Lt. Gen. Robert Kingston, commander of the RDF, the new command will have "clear authority and responsibility for United States military activity within the region of the Persian Gulf and Southwest Asia." The RDF is expanding rapidly at every level: the Army's contribution of three divisions has been expanded to five, the Air Force's five tactical fighter wings has been doubled to ten, and headquarters has increased from 260 persons in March 1982 to 960 in January 1983. The U.S. Information Agency is sending one official to supervise propaganda efforts. The new commmand will be the first to have a chaplain assigned to its staff, as advisor to some 200 chaplains of the component units. The head chaplain will also "review operational orders as they are carried out to check on their morality," writes *New York Times* reporter Richard Halloran. "We don't want to see any My Lais coming out of this," one official is quoted as saying. Some more Horishimas presumably lie beyond morality. (*New York Times,* September 25, 1982.) —Eds.

the question of access is not related to oil supplies as such. Regimes of any conceivable ideological complexion would continue to face an irrepressible need to produce and market oil for the international market, especially to U.S. allies in Europe and Asia. As for the Soviet "need" for oil supplies from the Gulf, it is quite hypothetical, and in any event their unquestioned need for mammoth imports of grain has not led Moscow to threaten an invasion of Argentina or Saskatchewan. It would appear that the question of "security access" amounts to the preservation of U.S. energy companies' dominance of the processing and global marketing of Persian oil. For this, the U.S. military planners have, in effect, wired up the Saudi throne, and those of other ruling families in the area, to a nuclear tripwire. As long as the United States and the Soviet Union persist in making more "credible" their nuclear warfighting capacities, and as long as the U.S. remains determined to "insert" its "dual-capable" power projection forces into the region, we dare not contemplate the crumbling of decrepit political formations like the Saudi monarchy with anything like the equanimity this process deserves. In its present phase, Washington is promoting the nuclear arms race as the ultimate guarantor of the status-quo.

Notes

1. Caspar W. Weinberger, *Annual Report to the Congress, Fiscal Year 1983* (Washington, 1982), pp. 11-13.
2. Interview with General David C. Jones, *Air Force Magazine*, May 1979, p.26.
3. Weinberger, pp. 101-111.
4. Weinberger, pp. 1-14.
5. John F. Lehman, "The Soviet Strategic Nuclear Advantage and How To Eliminate It," *International Security Review*, Vol.5, No.3 (Fall 1980), pp. 271-286.
6. Prepared statement of Eugene V. Rostow, Committee on Foreign Relations, U.S. Senate, June 22, 1981.
7. Campaign statement in Columbus, Ohio, reported in *New York Times*, June 2, 1980.
8. Cited in Michael T. Klare, "The Brown Doctrine," *The Nation*, March 8, 1980.
9. Address by Rostow to the First Committee of the 36th General Assembly of the United Nations, October 1981.
10. Cited in *The New Republic*, April 15, 1980.
11. Interview with *The Wall Street Journal*, June 3, 1980.
12. For more on the origins and dilemmas of nuclear-conventional "flexible response" doctrines, see the chapter "NATO Strategy and

Forces" in Enthoven and Smith, *How Much is Enough: Shaping the Defense Program 1961-69*, (New York, 1961).

13. Rostow, June 22, 1981.

14. Interview with the *National Journal*, March 8, 1980.

15. *New York Times*, February 3, 1981.

16. See Ellsberg's introduction in E.P. Thompson and Dan Smith, *Protest and Survive*, (New York: Monthly Review Press, 1981).

17. Testimony before the House Armed Services Committee, March 11, 1980, in FY 1981, Part 4, Book 2, pp. 2299-2301.

18. *Boston Globe*, March 30, 1980; January 31 policy statement, *Washington Post*, April 24, 1980.

19. *Washington Post*, October 22, 1981.

20. "Nomination of Caspar Weinberger to be Secretary of Defense," Senate Armed Services Committee, January 6, 1981, p. 45.

21. House Armed Service Committee, *Authorization for FY 1981, Hearings*, Part I, pp. 10-11.

22. Senate Armed Services Committee, *Authorization for FY 1982*, Part 5, p. 2466; Ibid, Part 7, p. 3845.

23. *Time*, October 25, 1982.

24. "Preparing for Nuclear War: President Reagan's Program," *The Defense Monitor*, Vol. X, No. 8, Washington,D.C.: Center for Defense Information, 1982, pp. 12-13.

25. Interview with William Arkin, co-editor, *The Nuclear Weapons Databook,* (Ballinger Press, 1983).

26. "Nomination of Eugene V. Rostow," Senate Foreign Relations Committee, *Hearings*, June 22-23, 1981, p. 11.

27. "Overview of Nuclear Arms Control and Defense Strategy in NATO," *Hearings*, House Foreign Affairs Committee, February 23, March 18-22, 1982 (Washington, D.C.) p. 9.

28. Interview with *The Economist*, November 13, 1982.

29. *New York Times*, October 18, 1981.

30. Interview with senior advisor to the Secretary of Defense, April 1980.

31. Department of Defense *Annual Report*, FY 1980, p. 78.

32. "Strategic Nuclear Forces Report," Introductory Remarks by General Richard H. Ellis before the Senate Armed Services Committee, February 20, 1980, p.3. See also David Gold, Christopher Paine and Gail Shields, *Misguided Expenditure: An Analysis of the Proposed MX Missile System*, Council on Economic Priorities, New York, 1981, pp. 77-89.

33. Richard Burt, statement before the House Armed Services Committee, February 23, 1982.

34. Senate Armed Services Committee, *Authorization for FY 1982, Hearings*, Part 7, pp. 3924-25. Emphasis added.

35. "Nomination of Edward L. Rowny," *Hearings*, Senate Foreign Relations Committee, July 9-10, 1981.

36. *Foreign Relations of the United States, 1950*, Volume 1, National Security Affairs (Washington, D.C.: U.S. Government Printing Office, 1977), p. 264.

37. *New York Times*, September 25, 1982. Emphasis added.

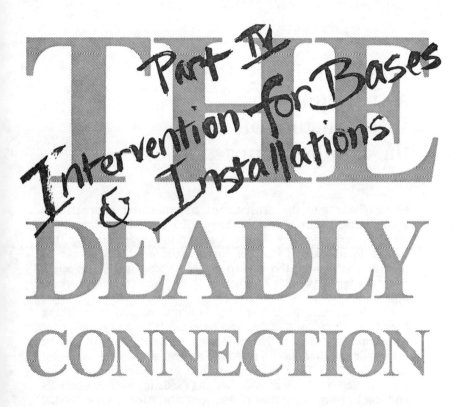

THE
DEADLY
CONNECTION

Part IV
Intervention for Bases
& Installations

Boone Schirmer

Foreign Military Bases and Installations: Infrastructure of the Deadly Connection

Nuclear war and the prospect of national and international annihilation it carries with it throw a harsh and revealing light on U.S. foreign policy. There is a growing understanding that conventional wars of intervention constitute a likely source of nuclear conflict for the United States. Accordingly, there is a sharper edge to popular opposition to an interventionist foreign policy.

In this context, the U.S. policy of acquiring and maintaining foreign military installations and bases takes on a new and more threatening character. These foreign installations provide the infrastructure that make a policy of nuclear warfighting and first strike possible. They provide storage and launching sites for atomic weapons. They provide landing fields for nuclear bombers and nuclear-armed fighter planes and ports for nuclear-armed aircraft carriers, surface ships, and submarines. They provide the control, communications, command, and intelligence (C3I) systems essential to nuclear warfighting and first strike or counterforce capabilities. They serve as jumping off points for interventionary armed forces equipped with tactical nuclear weapons. If nuclear weapons should be opposed, what about the support systems that make their use possible?

U.S. military installations abroad should be questioned for another reason. These bases and installations help make U.S. wars of intervention possible, and these wars in turn can lead to tactical and strategic nuclear conflicts.

The United States is the leading nation in the number and size of its foreign military installations. There are over one thousand significant U.S. military installations throughout the world, forming a nearly continuous chain from South Korea to the North Atlantic.[1] Key links in this chain are bases in Japan, the Philippines, and Australia in the Pacific; Diego Garcia in the Indian Ocean; Greece, Italy, and Spain in the Mediterranean; and West Germany, Great Britain and Iceland in the Atlantic. Some of these, like bases in Cuba, Puerto Rico and the Philippines, date to the turn of the century when imperial expansion exploded in the Spanish-American and Philippine-American Wars. A greater number of the bases, such as those in Greece, Turkey, West Germany, Italy, Spain, Japan, and South Korea, were consolidated in the post-World War II period as the U.S. sought to "contain" the Soviet Union, and in the process, dislodged from positions of influence economic rivals weakened by war. Still others, like the base at Diego Garcia, were built recently as a result of preoccupation with the growth of nationalism in the Middle East and with perceived threats to U.S. control of that area's massive oil resources.

In 1981 approximately five hundred thousand U.S. military personnel were stationed abroad. Many of these were attached to foreign bases and installations. Others were on board U.S. naval vessels in foreign seas.[2]

Forty years after the end of World War II more than three hundred thousand U.S. troops are still in Europe, scattered in six hundred installations in eleven different countries. Since the 1950s these European bases have been saturated with an estimated six thousand tactical nuclear weapons. In 1983 the U.S. added the Pershing II and ground-launched cruise missiles with first-strike capacity to European deployments.

In Asia and the Pacific, important U.S. installations and troop deployments include those in South Korea, with one hundred bases and thirty eight thousand troops, Japan and the Ryukyus with one hundred nineteen bases and forty six thousand troops, and the Philippines with twenty-three installations and fourteen thousand troops.

In South Korea the primary firepower of the U.S. ground troops is nuclear. Nuclear bombs have been stored in the Philippines. In Japan, Australia, and the Philippines, there are important C3I installations. In Guam there is a base for B-52 strategic nuclear bombers. At Kwajalein, in the Marshall Islands, there is a testing facility for long range U.S. missiles. In 1984 the Navy began deploying nuclear-capable Tomahawk sea-launched cruise missiles on its surface ships and attack submarines. These weapons are designed for both tactical and strategic nuclear warfare. Their deployment was seen by Asian observers as having the same implications for them as the deployment of the ground-launched cruise missiles had for the people of Europe.

To understand more fully how U.S. foreign military installations support intervention and nuclear warfighting, it would help to look at one such complex in detail—the U.S. bases in the Philippines. The two largest, Clark Air Field and Subic Naval Base, are among the most important of all U.S. foreign military installations. Together with U.S. bases in Japan, Australia, and Guam, they constitute an essential infrastructure for the U.S. nuclear warfighting capability in the Pacific.

Philippine bases support nuclear warfighting in the following ways. The nuclear-armed aircraft carrier Midway frequently calls at Subic as does the U.S.S. Sterett, a cruiser equipped with nuclear-armed missiles. Because almost one-third of all U.S. naval vessels will be equipped with Tomahawk missiles, the presence of nuclear-armed U.S. ships in Subic will soon become even more common. Subic Bay is also reportedly a storage site for U.S. nuclear weapons. Clark Air Field is the home of the Third Tactical Fighter Wing with its nuclear-capable F4Es. A unit of the Strategic Air Command's communications network is located here as well. In time of war this installation would direct B-52 bombers, from Guam or elsewhere, on nuclear strikes against the Soviet Union.

U.S. military installations in the Philippines have been used as springboards for U.S. wars of intervention on more than one occasion: in China in 1900 to suppress the nationalist uprising of the Boxers; in Korea in the 1950s; and in Indochina in the 1960s and early 1970s.

In 1977 Major General Freddie Poston, U.S. commander at Clark Air Field described the base's role to a United Press International reporter:

> . . . in the war room of Maj. Gen. Freddie Poston, wall maps outline air routes to such points as South Korea, Japan, and the U.S. Navy base at Diego Garcia in the mid-Indian Ocean. Others show airfields in the Middle East and Africa that can be used for Phantoms or aerial tanker planes.
>
> Poston says that in a future Middle East war the United States may find it necessary to use a "back door" air supply route to Israel rather than through the Mediterranean because of a lack of refuelling bases. His pointer follows a red strip up the Red Sea. "From Diego Garcia, it is eight hours flying time to Tel Aviv," he says. The pointer moves toward Africa. "Or, using tanker planes, I can have

Phantoms into some fields in East Africa 12 hours after they
leave here, for example, to cover an evacuation of civilians
in Southern Africa.''. . . Ammunition and supply stockpiles
earmarked   for   Korea   are   located   at   both
locations. . . "During the first 90 days of a Korean war, 9,000
cargo flights would be flown out of Clark," says
Poston. . . . An air base at Subic would add 1,000 tons daily.³

Today, Subic Naval Base is a major source of supply for the
U.S. naval armada that patrols the Indian Ocean and the Persian
Gulf. Should the U.S. decide on military intervention in the
Middle East, a rapid deployment force incursion from the Pacific
would be spearheaded by U.S. Marines stationed in Japan and
trained in the use of tactical nuclear weapons. These would jump
off from Subic Bay for Diego Garcia and the Persian Gulf.

As Poston suggested, Philippine bases would also serve as a
back-up for any future U.S. military intervention on the Korean
peninsula, for which U.S. bases in Japan would serve as the main
source of supply. Nuclear-capable planes from Clark regularly
participate in annual U.S. war exercises over South Korea. In case
of a conflict there, these same aircraft would be used as were
planes from Clark Field during the Korean War.

In 1947 Paul V. McNutt, the U.S. high commissioner for the
Philippines, helped negotiate the original bases agreement with
the newly independent Philippine government. (The Philippines
was a U.S. colony from 1898 to 1946.) After the agreement was
signed, he said, "Defense bases in the Far East. . . now make it
possible for the United States, through business groups, to build
up the economy of the Orient."⁴ Nearly 40 years later, in January
1983, the U.S. commander of Clark Field described the U.S. bases
in the Philippines as serving "to provide the punch to protect our
trade initiatives and economic interests."⁵ In more recent years
nuclear weapons and nuclear weapons systems have been added
to "the punch."

As with other U.S. bases around the world, it is argued that
American bases in the Philippines are necessary to the national
security of the United States. The opposite may be nearer the
truth. These bases undermine the security of the people of the
United States because they promote foreign military interventions
and because they provide key elements in the preparation and
support of nuclear war.

Filipinos are beginning to view the U.S. bases as a threat to
their security as well. A symptom of this is a declaration signed
in December 1984 by twelve outstanding democratic opponents

of President Marcos (including Cory Aquino, wife of the slain senator), which called for the removal of foreign military bases from the Philippines.

U.S. bases in the Philippines make that nation a target for Soviet nuclear attack in case of a nuclear exchange between the Soviet Union and the United States. With the danger to the Southern Hemisphere now projected by nuclear winter theorists, Filipinos have additional reasons for opposing the use of their country as a center for the preparation of nuclear war.

The U.S. bases also have the effect of degrading and demoralizing Philippine social life. Olongapo and Angeles City, urban areas next to Subic and Clark, have become centers of prostitution and drug traffic. Manila, the capital and a port city, is also affected. Early in February 1985 ten thousand nuns and Catholic school girls paraded through Manila's streets denouncing prostitution. Six days later, the U.S.'s aircraft carrier Midway came into the harbor and disgorged five thousand U.S. sailors who poured half of a million dollars into the impoverished city. Mark Fineman of the *Philadelphia Inquirer* reported:

> The restaurants and souvenir shops were packed. The bars were wall-to-wall with sailors. Before the U.S. Navy pulled out of Manila Bay the sailors had also paid about $20 each for thousands of brief dates with those same Filipino prostitutes who had watched the procession of nuns a week before.[6]

Finally, Filipinos see the bases as a source of foreign intervention in their nation's political life—intervention which has had the effect of keeping a violent and repressive dictatorship in power. It is the Filipino perception that Washington supports President Ferdinand Marcos with economic and military aid because he guarantees the U.S. use of the bases. In 1985, at the peak of Marcos's isolation and unpopularity, President Reagan proposed sending Marcos a record-breaking $280 million aid package. It is hard for Filipinos to avoid the conclusion that if they wish to end U.S. intervention in their country's affairs, they will have to rid themselves of the bases.

Bases and Democracy

There is another side to this coin. The longer Marcos, or any other right wing military dictatorship that succeeds him, stays in power with U.S. support, the more Filipinos will feel compelled to turn to armed resistance. Hence, if the present policies of the

Reagan administration toward the Philippines are not soon reversed, the people of the United States may find the fourteen thousand troops now based in the Philippines intervening on the side of repression and militarism in a Philippine civil war. The Philippines is not the only country in which U.S. bases have been hosted by right-wing military dictatorships. Greece of the Colonels' regime, the military regime of Turkey, Spain under Franco, Portugal under Salazar, and the South Korean dictatorship all attest to the fact that U.S. bases have had no difficulty cohabiting with repressive governments.

Speaking in Manila in 1983 at an international conference against foreign military bases sponsored by opponents of the Marcos government, a retired Greek army officer, General George Koumanakos, explained:

> The best way to maintain foreign bases in a country is to keep in power the government which is kindly disposed to them and that will have its base of strength in the same political forces that first made the concession. These political forces are as a rule forces of the right. This means a continuous follow-up by the foreigners and intervention, when they think it necessary, in the internal affairs of the host country in order to secure power in the hands of political forces friendly to foreigners. With this practice, however, political changes are held back and natural social developments are halted causing great harm to the interests of the people and to the program of the country.[7]

General Koumanakos, who fought with the United Nations forces in Korea and was decorated by the U.S. government for bravery, had experienced the U.S.-supported Colonels' regime in his country.

Perhaps one reason that the U.S. foreign military bases and installations have been secure with right-wing dictatorships is that the policy of maintaining foreign bases is inherently undemocratic. At its core lies the denial of the sovereignty of the nation in which the base is located. Bases are a foreign military presence over which the people and the government of the host country do not have ultimate control. As such, these bases serve as an undeniable impediment to complete self-determination. Foreign bases therefore represent a policy that complements governments which deny their people their democratic rights. The relationship is symbiotic. The dictatorship surrenders the country's sovereignty to the foreign power. In return the foreign power gives its support to the government and its repressive and anti-popular policies.

This is not to say that foreign bases cannot exist without dictatorships in the host countries, or that only in such dictatorships do foreign bases have the effect of undermining national sovereignty. U.S. bases have been located in Great Britain, West Germany, and Italy since the end of World War II, but it is only recently that they have been widely opposed.

The connection of nuclear warfighting with military bases is an extension of the anti-democratic policy in extreme form because it brings with it the possibility of annihilation. It is natural that it is around the nuclear issue that opposition to foreign military installations has emerged with the greatest vitality. Opposition to foreign bases has grown within the democratic allies of the United States as these bases have become more prominent in preparations for nuclear war, and as fear of the danger of nuclear war has spread and mobilized public opinion.

It is no accident that Japan, the only country to have experienced nuclear war, and since then a democratic ally of the United States, has been the scene of two very representative international conferences against foreign military bases. These were held in 1981 and 1983 under the leadership of a national peace organization called Gensuikyo. Japan has, perhaps, the most sophisticated and well-organized movement of opposition to foreign military bases. The anti-nuclear weapons movements in Western Europe have also begun to oppose the presence of foreign bases. Most outstanding in this regard have been the women of Greenham Common with their siege of that U.S. base in England. The human chains that have "linked" U.S. bases in West Germany and the opposition to the missile base at Comiso in Sicily have also played important roles in their anti-nuclear movements.

The fact that democratic nations often provide less than congenial environments for foreign military bases is demonstrated by the challenges to basing agreements raised by democratic governments which have recently replaced dictatorships. The democratic government that followed the Colonels' Junta in Greece obtained an agreement from the U.S. that called for the removal of the U.S. bases in 1988. In Spain after Franco and in Portugal after Salazar, anti-nuclear movements have challenged the presence of foreign installations.

Preparations for nuclear war sharpen perceptions of the denial of sovereignty by U.S. bases. This was evident in the reaction to revelations made by William Arkin in February 1985. He reported that the U.S. military had been given presidential authorization to deploy nuclear weapons in eight countries in times of crisis.

These countries included Canada, Iceland, Spain, the Philippines, Puerto Rico (a territory of the U.S.), Bermuda (a British colony), the Azores of Portugal, and the British island of Diego Garcia. None of the governments involved had been officially informed of any U.S. plans or authorization to deploy nuclear weapons on the U.S. bases in their countries.

Complaints about this infringement on national sovereignty were made by Spain (where the lower house of Parliament is unanimously on record against the nuclearization of Spain), by Iceland, and by Canada. In the latter case, retired Rear Admiral Falls, former chief of Canada's defense staff, declared, "The implication is they're saying, 'To hell with you little guys, Icelanders, Bermudans, Canadians, we're going to do it anyway.' "

In the case of Puerto Rico, these contingency plans would violate the Treaty of Tlatelco, the Latin American Nuclear Free Zone Treaty, which the United States signed in 1967.

In reply to the protest of the Icelandic government, U.S. Ambassador Richardson cited the "longstanding U.S. policy neither to confirm nor deny the presence of nuclear weapons anywhere."

As long ago as 1970, the Senate Committee on Security Agreements and Commitments Abroad chaired by Senator Stuart Symington pointed to the "veil of secrecy" hiding U.S. nuclear weapons abroad and added, "Nowhere is this veil of secrecy stronger than in the United States." The committee declared the policy to be unconstitutional. The senators thereby registered the fact that the policy of nuclear secrecy cuts two ways: Abroad it infringes on national sovereignty; at home it undermines the accountability of the military to Congress and to the people.

The gigantic military budget Mr. Reagan forces on the country to finance foreign intervention and nuclear warfighting costs at home. This budget takes from the poor, the children, the elderly, education, public health, and transportation to meet the needs of the administration's military program.

An analysis made by former Pentagon official Earl C. Ravenal offers an idea of what preparations for intervention and nuclear warfighting cost the people of the United States. Assigning probable costs to each of the Pentagon's main contingency areas, Ravenal estimates that out of a $305 billion Reagan military budget for 1985, Europe will absorb $129 billion, Asia $47 billion, and the Rapid Deployment Force $54 billion (about $47 billion of which is for the Persian Gulf).[8] Maintaining five hundred thousand troops and over one thousand military installations in foreign lands accounts for much of this sum, of course. President Reagan has asked Congress to increase the overseas military construction budget by fifty percent to two billion dollars in 1985, to enlarge the U.S. military presence in the Indian Ocean, the Persian Gulf, the Mediterranean and the Caribbean. "Floating bases," the anti-aircraft carriers, contribute substantially to this cost as well. Ravenal notes that the full cost of the forward deployment of an aircraft carrier battle group is over thirteen billion dollars, and U.S. policy posture requires that four or five such battle groups be kept in forward positions.

The advantage of Ravenal's approach to the military budget is that it focuses attention away from the questions of weapons systems and their reform, from questions of elimination of waste, and from other secondary matters. He focuses attention where it belongs: on the policy. It becomes clear that the only way to make significant cuts in the military budget is to put an end to the policies of foreign intervention and nuclear war. In practical terms that means the withdrawal of U.S. troops and installations from foreign soil and *the abolition of nuclear weapons*.

Peace advocates in the United States will not want to urge these demands only on the United States. The nuclear armaments of the Soviet Union, the other leading power, and of other nuclear weapons nations must be eliminated as well. Accordingly, the U.S. government should be encouraged to take a stand in favor of abolition and then all other nuclear nations must be pressed to do the same.

Bases Critical to a First Strike

Policies of nuclear warfighting (as distinct from deterrence) are essentially of two kinds: tactical or limited nuclear war, and first strike—a preemptive nuclear attack on the nuclear capabilities and military command posts of another power. The role of U.S. foreign bases in supporting tactical nuclear war has been described with the Philippines as an example. What must be better understood is that foreign military bases play a major role in building a first-strike capability. There is an asymmetry between the United States and the Soviet Union in this regard.

This ground has been well covered by Owen Wilkes, a New Zealand peace researcher, in a paper he prepared for the 1981 World Conference Against A- and H-bombs held in Japan. In the first place, apart from missile-launching submarines deployed in international waters and (since 1983) SS-20s apparently located in East Germany and Czechoslovakia, all the strategic systems of the Soviet Union are located within the Soviet Union. By contrast, the United States has important components of its strategic infrastructure located on foreign soil, most importantly, C3I systems. Since the U.S. has much greater access to foreign basing facilities than the Soviet Union, U.S. strategic systems are more able to survive, more accurate and more reliable than those of the Soviet Union. As a consequence, they are better suited to first-strike or counterforce use than those of the Soviet Union. It is Wilkes's opinion that if all U.S. foreign facilities were withdrawn or eliminated, its nuclear deterrent capability would not be diminished in any way. U.S. first-strike capability (which is inherently destabilizing) would, however, be sharply reduced. The element of surprise provided by theatre systems and B-52 bombers, and the accuracy of sea-launched ballistic missiles, depend considerably on foreign installations. The C3I infrastructure is largely dependent on foreign installations. Sophisticated C3I is vital to first-strike and counterforce targetting, especially when the targets are elusive and frequently mobile. Loss of C3I infrastructure would not, however, weaken the ability of the U.S. to target cities in a policy of deterrence. U.S. strategic anti-submarine warfare capabilities are vital to a first-strike posture and are highly dependent on foreign facilities.

A Challenge to the Peace Movement

U.S. foreign military bases and installations provide necessary infrastructure for current U.S. policies of military intervention and nuclear warfighting. The peace movement of the United States has developed opposition to nuclear war and to intervention. Intervention could lead to nuclear war, and there is a growing appreciation of this "deadly connection." What must be realized, however, is that foreign military installations are the material embodiment of the "deadly connection." They are the physical integument that binds a policy of foreign intervention to a policy of nuclear war. It is time for the peace movement to develop a campaign around the demand for a withdrawal of foreign bases and military installations; such a demand is central to the campaign against intervention and nuclear war and should be made a part of both campaigns. A campaign against foreign military installations would further synthesize the aims of the U.S. peace movement and give the movement a global scope. It would bring the peace movement face to face with the global military machine of the United States, interventionist and nuclear, in all its complex and interdependent reality.

To bring about the withdrawal of all U.S. military installations, nuclear weapons, and troops from abroad, the U.S. peace movement, even more than it has done so far, must support the peace and anti-nuclear movements in all countries burdened by the U.S. military. U.S. peace activists should support these overseas movements and bring them and their demands more vigorously to the attention of the U.S. public and government. Sustained public sensitivity to these issues has not yet been developed. When President Carter called for a reduction of U.S. troops in Korea, there was little public response, and his proposal was dropped. In the 1984 presidential election campaign, only Jesse Jackson called for the removal of U.S. troops from Europe and U.S. bases from the Philippines. Public interest mounts in the case of particularly sharp manifestations of U.S. interventionist policy, as in Lebanon in 1984 and Central America today, but the U.S. government posture as a whole has been essentially unchallenged since World War II.

Even if it grows spasmodically and irregularly, the international movement of opposition to nuclear weapons and foreign military installations grows continuously over the long run. Consciousness of the danger deepens and spreads. Ronald T. Paul was chief counsel for the Symington Committee of the U.S. Senate that investigated U.S. commitments to the countries in Europe, the Far East, and Africa where U.S. forces were stationed. In a book written in 1970, he described a condition that has today become a prime source of international concern. He wrote, "The United States is a global power and its European allies are only regional powers. This country benefits from its pre-eminence. Possibly the chief benefit is the right to have its finger on the nuclear trigger to the virtual exclusion of its allies."[9]

The people of the allied countries in Europe and in other parts of the world are beginning to find this U.S. privilege too dangerous. They are beginning to want it annulled. This is what the Reagan administration refers to as the growing "nuclear allergy."

The clearest and sharpest expression of this "nuclear allergy" has been the New Zealand government's prohibition of visits to its ports by any warships carrying nuclear weapons. Two small nations in the Pacific, the Solomon Islands and Vanuatu, took this step earlier, but it was New Zealand's actions that caught international attention and brought threats of retaliation from the Reagan administration. The *New York Times* reported a senior administration official as saying, "Unless we hold our allies' feet to the fire over ship visits and nuclear deployment, one will run away and then the next.''

What gives particular urgency to these fears is the fact that Japan, Norway, and Denmark all have banned nuclear weapons from their soil during peacetime. But enforcement of the prohibition has been passive. The ban appears to be regularly violated by the U.S.

The rejection of nuclear weapons is not confined to allies of the United States. Rumania, of the Warsaw Pact, has also barred nuclear weapons from its soil. Commenting on some U.S. reaction to the anti-nuclear position of her own country, Helen Clark, member of the New Zealand Parliament, said, "It would indeed be curious if New Zealand were to be permitted less freedom within a loose partnership like ANZUS than Rumania is within the Warsaw Pact.''

A new stage in the international peace movement, a stage in which governments of countries allied to the U.S. begin to respond actively to the demands of their people for peace and nuclear disarmament, has developed as a result of New Zealand's banning of nuclear weapons. Even before New Zealand's action, Greece had mandated the removal of U.S. bases in the near future, and Prime Minister Papandreou followed with a call for the immediate withdrawal of U.S. nuclear weapons from his country. Following New Zealand's action, the Australian government announced that it would not allow U.S. planes monitoring MX missile tests to operate out of Australia. A month later it was reported that the government of Portugal had approved the draft of a resolution barring nuclear weapons from Portugal, including the Azores, where the U.S. has a base.

If the people of the United States reach out to these popular movements in the many lands opposing intervention, nuclear war, and foreign military installations, there is an opportunity to force a real change in U.S. foreign policy. This would be very much to the advantage of the people of the United States—and of the world.

Notes

1. Material by Owen Wilkes, New Zealand peace researcher, was used in assessing the number and location of U.S. foreign military installations.
2. Information as to the number and disposition of U.S. troops abroad from the *Hearings before the Committee on Armed Services*, United States Senate, 2 February 1982.

3. *Philippine News*, 27 August to 21 September 1977.

4. Quoted in George Marion, *Bases and Empire*, Fairplay Publishers.

5. Quoted in the *Declaration of the First International Conference on General Disarmament, World Peace, and the Removal of All Foreign Military Bases*, Manila, 24-26 October 1983.

6. Mark Fineman, *Philadelphia Inquirer*, 24 February 1985.

7. General George Koumanakos "Foreign Military Bases," (presented at the First International Conference on General Disarmament, World Peace, and the Removal of All Foreign Military Bases, Manila, 24-26 October 1983), 4-5.

8. Earl C. Ravenal, *Defining Defense: the 1985 Military Budget*, (Washington, D.C.: Cato Institute, 1985), 16-17.

9. Roland A. Paul, *American Military Commitments Abroad*, (New Jersey: Rutgers University Press, 1973), 147-48.

Michael Bedford

The Strategic Role of U.S. Deployments in the Pacific and Indian Oceans

I think it is important that the American people understand that U.S. security strategy is based on forward defense, and for us to essentially retreat from those forward defense positions is not in the best interest of the United States. We maintain a forward defense strategy in the Pacific as well as the Atlantic.

Admiral Robert L.J. Long[1]

From Japan and South Korea in Northeast Asia, through Micronesia, Guam, the Philippines, Australia, and the Indian Ocean, to Oman, lie a series of U.S. military bases. Across this nine-thousand-mile arc, the United States has developed a basing structure for the purposes of launching nuclear war against the Soviet Union and of intervening in the Third World.

After the withdrawal of U.S. forces from the mainland of Southeast Asia in 1975, U.S. military policy was focussed on avoiding the commitment of U.S. ground forces in a protracted land war in the Third World. Simultaneously, it sought to contain Soviet influence and military power with a network of bases situated near the U.S.S.R. Friendly and allied nations were to provide the troops for their own national defense while the U.S. would provide materials and possibly air support. This policy change culminated with President Carter's 1977 announcement that U.S. ground forces would be removed from Korea by 1983. The U.S. regional profile was to be greatly reduced.

The year 1979 was a critical turning point for U.S. involvement in Asia and the Middle East. The Soviet Union signed a friendship treaty with the Socialist Republic of Vietnam in November 1978, and full diplomatic relations were established between the United

States and the Peoples Republic of China in January 1979. The Shah of Iran, the mainstay of U.S. influence in the Middle East, fell to a popular Islamic movement, while south of Saudi Arabia, North and South Yemen engaged in violent border conflicts. The U.S. declared a postponement in the withdrawal of American forces from South Korea. China attacked Vietnam in an attempt to force Vietnamese withdrawal from Kampuchea. The attack resulted instead in an expanded Soviet military presence in Cam Ranh Bay and Danang in Vietnam. In December 1979 the Soviets invaded Afghanistan.

With the fall of the Shah of Iran and the subsequent rise of the fundamentalist Islamic movement of Khomeini, the conservative regimes in the Middle East became vulnerable to the new Islamic nationalism, which was viewed as inimical to Western interests. In his 1980 State of the Union Address, President Carter announced the importance of the oil-rich region of the Middle East. "Let our position be absolutely clear: An attempt by any outside force to gain control of the Persian Gulf region will be regarded as an assault on the vital interests of the United States of America, and such assault will be repelled by any means necessary, including military force."

Under President Reagan, this commitment has been reaffirmed and expanded. Secretary of Defense Weinberger remarked in Washington, D.C. in 1981 that "the umbilical cord of the industrialized free world runs through the Strait of Hormuz into the Arabian Gulf and the nations which surround it. That area, Southwest Asia and the Gulf, is and will be the fulcrum of contention for the forseeable future."

In Asia, reports of a growing Soviet military threat were coupled with a call for the rebuilding of U.S. naval power in the Pacific. A secret 1977 presidential review memorandum, entitled "Military Strategy and Force Posture Review" concluded "the overall ability of American and allied forces to prevail against Soviet forces outside of Europe is uncertain...." and U.S. bases in Japan and South Korea are "offset by the difficulty of establishing anti-air and antisubmarine barriers in the face of intense Soviet opposition." Admiral Maurice Weisner, former U.S. Pacific commander in chief, in a statement for the *Far East Economic Review* gave U.S. military forces an "even chance" of defeating Soviet forces but felt the "balance of power was tipping toward the Soviets."[2] A Congressional Budget Office report reached different conclusions, stating "...the United States appears to have forces in East Asia and the Pacific *considerably* [my emphasis] in excess of the needs generated by the Korean contingency...or by the relatively small portion (30%) of the Soviet Navy represented by its Pacific fleet." Secretary of Defense Harold Brown apparently agreed with the Congressional Budget Office report. In the Department of Defense (DOD) annual report of 1978, Brown stated that in the Pacific, "submarine and air threats could be brought under control within an acceptable time." Without national consensus, pressures mounted for a return to a powerful U.S. military presence in the Pacific Basin.

U.S. Deployment—The Arcs of Containment and Intervention

The United States' military policy in the Pacific-Indian Oceans arc is twofold. First, the overseas basing structure provides for the launching of nuclear attack against the Soviet Union. This policy, built upon nuclear-capable bases and the Pacific fleet, places American nuclear forces as close as possible to the Soviet Union. From Japan in the north, to the pivotal Philippine bases and the Indian Ocean, the United States has built launching pads for fighting a nuclear war against the Soviet Union. The second military objective is the maintenance of the supply of natural resources from the oil-rich Middle East and the South Asian-African continents to Western Europe, Japan, and the United States. This objective bolsters the ability of U.S. military forces to ensure Western access to these resources and to protect the sea lines of communication (SLOC) against any external or internal force. This second role of the U.S. basing structure has been largely ignored with the Soviet "menace" receiving primary attention. Yet U.S. military planners see the role of the overseas bases as dual, providing both the launching pads for nuclear war against the Soviet Union and the option of conventional or nuclear attacks against Third World nations. President Reagan, in the request for the Fiscal Year (FY) 1984 budget, made the preparation of U.S. military forces to respond to events in the Third World a top priority. By once again dividing the world into "cold war" camps, the Reagan administration has provided a rationale for a return of U.S. intervention to combat "Soviet surrogates" in the Third World.

Intervention has a new name in the halls of the Pentagon. Called "low-intensity conflicts," the policy calls for the rapid introduction of U.S. conventional forces into Third World nations. Low-intensity conflict covers a wide spectrum of conventional operations—from gaining and protecting territory to influencing Third World political and economic systems. U.S.

policy calls for a military force capable of being deployed quickly and under adverse conditions to protect U.S. interests in the Third World.

The principal conclusion of a military planning report, "Strategic Requirements for the Army for the Year 2000,"[3] was that low-intensity conflicts would be both widespread and frequent in the coming decade. The need for the introduction of a flexible force into the Third World was underscored by Secretary of Defense Weinberger's report for FY 1985 to Congress, which stated that this new priority of U.S. forces "reflects our recognition that low-level conflict...will pose the threat we are most likely to encounter throughout the end of this century." Learning from the Grenada invasion which required seven thousand troops, eleven warships, and scores of transport aircraft, the Pentagon is reshaping the character of U.S. military forces in the Third World.[4] Grenada, with the small armed opposition and being close to the United States, demanded a major operation for U.S. interventionary forces.

In areas further away from the U.S. mainland, strategists have seen the need for a forward basing structure for rapid intervention in the Third World. These bases are designed to provide the logistical support and communication facilities for the introduction of U.S. forces in conflicts where U.S. national interests are seen to be threatened, especially in the Middle East.

Intervention in the Indian Ocean

Secretary of Defense Caspar Weinberger stated before the House Budget Committee in 1981, that "we are, in a very real sense, an island nation. American commerce and industry, access to vital resources, and the sinews of the Western Alliance depend upon our ability to control the seas. We must be able to defeat any military adversary who threatens such access."

While the primary American military objective in Southwest Asia (as stated in the DOD Annual Report to Congress for FY 1985) is to deter Soviet aggression in the unstable Middle East, a second and equally important role is for intervention into the Gulf region.[5] The nations in the Middle East are seen by the Department of Defense as being politically, economically, and socially unstable. Coupled with the threat of a "growing Soviet power projection...," this continues to make, "the Middle East-Southwest Asia region one of the most volatile and potentially dangerous for the U.S. and allied vital interests." In Joint Chiefs of Staff military posture statements, reference is repeatedly made to halting "Soviet or Soviet-surrogate dominance."[6] This coupling of the Soviet military threat with "surrogates" opens the door for the intervention by U.S. military forces to shore up its "unstable" oil-producing allies. In the Joint Chiefs of Staff military posture report of 1982, the purpose of U.S. military presence is identified as the "support of friendly regional governments against hostile states or groups... Whether fed by Soviet intrigue or not, instability may lead to revolution and outside aggression." Former Secretary of State Alexander Haig warned Congress during hearings before the Committee on the Interior and Insular Affairs in 1980, that "as one assesses the recent step-up of Soviet proxy activities in the Third World, then one can only conclude that the era of the 'resource war' has arrived."[7]

Following the fall of the Shah of Iran, the U.S. military planners acknowledged the need for the possible rapid introduction of U.S. ground troops in the Persian Gulf and elsewhere in time of crisis. According to a presidential directive, the U.S. must maintain a "deployment of force of light divisions with strategic mobility independent of overseas bases and logistical support" and "moderate naval and tactical air forces which could be used in the Middle East, Persian Gulf, Korea, and elsewhere." In order to carry out this directive, the Rapid Deployment Joint Task Force (RDJTF) was established in 1980. The RDJTF was to "deny the Soviet Union easy access to SW Asian objectives and for the rapid reaction to other regional contingencies that may have no direct Soviet involvement."[8] In January 1983, President Reagan created the U.S. Central Command, replacing the Rapid Deployment Force with a formal command structure to protect U.S. "interests" in Southwest Asia. The Central Command, the first geographic unified command created in over thirty-five years, includes tactical aircraft for early interdiction of enemy aircraft, the pre-positioning of supplies for early deployment of U.S. forces, joint combat exercises with allies and friends in the region, strengthening of C3I (Command, Control, Communication and Intelligence) capabilities, and the logistical upgrading of U.S. combat readiness.

In a 1976 agreement with Great Britain, the United States acquired rights to develop naval and air facilities at Diego Garcia, part of the Chagos Archipelago lying strategically in the middle of the Indian Ocean. It is three thousand miles from the head of the Persian Gulf. Since the 1976 agreement, the atoll has been transformed into a strategic base for U.S. nuclear-capable forces and a launching pad for U.S. conventional forces. With a

U.S. Forces of CENTOCOM

Army
1 Airborne Division
1 Airmobile/Air Assault Division
1 Mechanized Infantry Division
1 Light Infantry Division
1 Air Cavalry Brigade

Marines
1⅓ Marine Amphibious Forces (usually a reinforced marine division and marine air wing, having three times the number of tactical fighter/attack aircraft as an air force wing)

Air Force
7 Tactical Fighter Wings
2 Strategic Bomber Squadrons

Navy
3 Carrier Battle Groups
1 Surface Action Group
5 Maritime Patrol Air Squadrons

Source: DOD Annual Report to Congress, FY 1985, 2/1/84, p. 212.

lengthened runway of twelve thousand feet, Diego Garcia is capable of handling B-52 bombers, KC-135 air tankers, and all air transport airplanes. In addition, there are hanger facilities for P-3 Orion aircraft which monitor Soviet submarine activity in the ocean. Petroleum storage facilities have been expanded, and the harbor is capable of sheltering an aircraft carrier task force. Diego Garcia also serves as a relay point for the global U.S. military C3I system.

On the island of Masirah, off the coast of Oman and only four hundred miles from the Strait of Hormuz, the U.S. has developed facilities for the "prepositioning" of military supplies for use by U.S. ground and air forces. Three other facilities in Oman are also available to U.S. forces: an airfield at Thamarit, storage facilities at Seeb, and runway usage at the tip of the Strait of Hormuz. The United States also has access to various base facilities in the region. In times of crisis, the former Soviet base at Berbera on the coast of Somalia, airfields in Kenya, Saudi

Arabian ports, and Egyptian and Israeli facilities are to be made available to American forces. To counteract any restrictions placed upon U.S. access to bases in the region, and to avoid embarrassment on the part of the Arab host governments, seventeen U.S. Near-Term Pre-Positioning Force (NTPF) ships are located in the Persian Gulf area. Aboard are supplies and equipment for a heavily mechanized marine amphibious brigade, hospital facilities, and supplies for army and air force units. Eventually there will be enough maritime prepositioning ships to supply three marine amphibious brigades.

The major U.S. *strategic* objective in the Indian Ocean is the deployment of ballistic missile submarines targeted against the Soviet Union. The ocean offers an unprotected Soviet southern flank. While the older Polaris submarines operating out of Guam have a limited operating range and thus can operate for only brief periods in the Indian Ocean, the new Trident submarines, with longer operating ranges and longer range Trident missiles, will make Indian Ocean operations more feasible.[9]

In describing the U.S. policy relating to Soviet involvement in the Middle East, Secretary of Defense Weinberger stated in "the region of the Persian Gulf, in particular, our strategy is based upon the concept that the prospect of combat with the United States and other friendly forces, coupled with the prospect that we might carry the war to other arenas, is the most effective deterrent to Soviet aggression."[10] Laying the political groundwork for potential U.S. military intervention, Weinberger stated that Soviet forces "could be extended into the area by means other than outright invasion. Whatever the circumstances, we should be prepared to introduce American forces directly into the region should it appear that the security of access to Persian Gulf oil is threatened."[11] Clearly, the Reagan administration sees the possibility of intervening in the Middle East under the name of stopping Soviet expansionism.

The Soviet Union has maintained a military presence in the Indian Ocean since 1968, partly in response to the presence of American nuclear submarines stationed on their southern flank. Soviet Foreign Minister Andrei Gromyko wrote in January 1981 in *Izvestiya* that "the policy of deploying and stockpiling American nuclear weapons not far from the Soviet Union's southern borders affects the interests of safeguarding its security and cannot fail to evoke resolute condemnation from the Soviet public." The presence of Soviet naval task forces has increasingly included anti-submarine warfare ships. Soviet activities in the Indian Ocean include anti-carrier maneuvers, intelligence

gathering, and surveillance. Like the West, the Soviet Union seeks
to protect its all-weather sea lanes. The main base for the Fifth
Squadron of the Soviet Pacific Fleet is located in the Dahlak
Archipelago in the Red Sea. Other facilities available for Russian
naval forces are in South Yemen and Ethiopia. The Soviet navy
sought and received use of the Vietnamese base at Cam Ranh Bay
in the wake of the Chinese invasion of Vietnam in 1979. The
former American air base at Danang is also now used by the Soviet
forces. It has been reported that Moscow is pressuring Vietnam
to allow Soviet use of the Kampuchean base at Kompong Son,
near the Straits of Malacca.[12]

The Link between Oceans: U.S. Military Bases
in the Philippines

U.S. objectives in the Western Pacific can best be understood
by recognizing the region as a bridge between the Pacific and
Indian Oceans. The most important U.S. bases in the western
Pacific are in the Philippines. They provide logistical support,
intelligence and communication facilities, and forward
deployment for U.S. nuclear and conventional forces. Strategically
placed, these bases allow the U.S. to control the four
"chokepoint" straits between the Indian and Pacific Oceans, to
provide air support for the Korean peninsula, and to dispatch
naval and air forces to East Africa and the Middle East.

The history of the bases in the Philippines reflects their
importance for U.S. intervention in Asia and the Middle East.
From 1898, when the United States fought the Spanish to replace
their colonial rule over the Philippines, until the present, U.S.
bases there have been used for U.S. intervention. From 1898 to
1907 the U.S. army fought a Filipino nationalist movement with
brutal force to impose American control. When the war ended,
Subic Bay became a training facility for U.S. marines who later
fought in World War I. U.S. expeditionary forces were dispatched
from Subic Bay to China to fight during the Boxer Rebellion.
From 1950 to 1953 both Clark Field and Subic Bay served as the
logistical bases in support of U.S. forces during the Korean War.
In 1958 U.S. naval forces based at Subic Bay were deployed to
the islands of Quemoy and Matsu off the Chinese coast. Subic
Bay and Clark Field provided, from 1965-1975, key logistical
facilities for the U.S. war in Indochina. Subic Bay was also the
staging area for the U.S. rescue mission of the crew of the USS
Mayaguez in Kampuchea in 1975. Seventh Fleet carriers based
in Subic Bay were used as instruments of U.S. foreign policy in

the Indo-Pakistan War in 1971, the 1973 Arab-Israeli War, the oil embargo of 1974, the Kenyan-Ugandan conflict in 1975, the Iranian hostage crisis of 1979, and the war between North and South Yemen the same year.

U.S. bases in the Philippines have several missions supporting introduction of U.S. forces to the Pacific and Indian Oceans. Dr. Larry Niksch, of the Congressional Research Service of the Library of Congress, has written, "in the period following 1978, U.S. officials became increasingly aware of the importance of the bases in supporting the American military presence in the great arc of potential crises from South Korea through South-East Asia to the Persian Gulf, and as a symbol of political and security commitments to friends and allies." The U.S. facilities at Subic Bay and Clark are designed to "aid in personnel training, regional contingency combat situations, intelligence, reconnaissance, and logistical support for air and Seventh Fleet operations in Asia, the South China Sea, and the Indian Ocean."[13] In the event of another Middle East war, U.S. officials have suggested Israel will be supplied via Clark Air Field and Diego Garcia. The U.S. bases in the Philippines would also serve as refueling and resupply bases for U.S. aircraft and forces destined for the Persian Gulf.

Clark Air Field is the largest American air base outside the United States, located about fifty miles north of Manila. This vast complex employs nearly ten thousand servicemen, and another one thousand American civilians. More than thirteen thousand Filipinos work at the base. Clark has runways capable of handling any aircraft in the U.S. air force or navy inventory. In addition, Clark has storage facilities for twenty-five million gallons of oil and petroleum and approximately two hundred thousand square feet of ammunition storage located in four igloos. These igloos contain nuclear and conventional weapons.

Subic Bay has four floating dry docks, large pier and harbor support facilities, oil storage for over one hundred million gallons, 3.8 million cubic feet of ammunition storage (including bunkers containing nuclear weapons) and a naval air station large enough to handle one hundred aircraft. During the Vietnam and Korean Wars, it was not uncommon for as many as ninety ships to be in Subic Bay at any one time.

U.S. Military Objectives in the Pacific

U.S. military forces are placed close to the U.S.S.R. to contain Soviet naval forces. Five straits around Japan permit the Soviet Pacific to reach open ocean from their ports. Japan, called the

U.S. Forces of USCINCPAC

Army
1 Infantry Division (South Korea)
1 Infantry Division (Hawaii)

Marines
1 Marine Division (Okinawa)
1 Marine Division (Hawaii)
1 Marine Division (California)

Air Force
1 Strategic Bomber Squadron (Guam)
10 Tactical Fighter Squadrons
5 Tactical Support Squadrons

Navy
6 Carriers with Air Wings
89 Surface Combatants
2 Amphibious Ships
40 Attack Submarines
12 Maritime Patrol Aircraft Squadrons

Source: DOD Annual Report to Congress, FY 85, 2/1/84, p. 218.

"unsinkable aircraft carrier" by Prime Minister Nakasone, is also viewed as the barrier against the movement of Soviet long-range bombers from Vladivostok to the shipping lanes of the Pacific. Admiral Crowe, the former commander of U.S. naval forces in the Pacific, has stated, "U.S. policy in the Pacific is forward operations, not prevention of fighting. U.S. seeks to have military advantage of U.S.S.R. as close to Soviet territory as possible. When the U.S. navy has 15 carrier battle groups, eight of them will be in the Pacific."[14]

By contrast, the Soviets have only one fleet for both the Indian and Pacific Oceans, while in Europe the Soviets have three fleets. The U.S.S.R. Asian fleet is particularly vulnerable, since Soviet naval bases are completely frozen for long periods of the year. The supply routes from European U.S.S.R. are long, vulnerable and underdeveloped. Vladivostok, the major Russian naval port, is only ten miles from the Chinese border. The former commander of the Pacific Command, Admiral Long, told the Senate Armed

Services Committee that the Soviet submarines pose the principle threat to U.S. naval forces, but added, "we enjoy significant advantage over them in the overall ASW arena."

Soviet military missions in the Pacific are designed to protect the flank of the Soviet Union to secure the launching area of submarine-launched ballistic missiles and to provide limited interdiction. Most of the Soviet military build-up in Northwest Asia, though, is directed at China. A 1984 Pacific Command briefing stated: "The Chinese tie down approximately 90% of all Soviet ground forces in the Far East."[15]

The Second Arc of Containment

Covering an area the size of the continental United States, Micronesia lies in the vast ocean area between Hawaii and the Philippines. Coming under American administration after the Second World War, Micronesia is the only trust territory of the eleven established by the United Nations which still remains under foreign administrative control. Micronesia was also the only trust territory established as a strategic trust territory, giving the United States the right to establish military bases throughout the islands.

Micronesia remains one of the most valuable areas for U.S. nuclear war preparations. It has served as a site for above ground testing of nuclear weapons, testing of U.S. strategic missiles, basing of nuclear-capable B-52s and Trident submarines, and basing of the C3I communications network.

The Department of Defense has four explicit objectives in Micronesia: denying Micronesia to the armed forces of hostile nations, allowing access for U.S. military forces, maintaining unhampered use of the Kwajalein Missile Range (KMR), and ensuring contingency use of Palau.[16] The strategic importance of Micronesia has grown with the continued instability of the Marcos regime in the Philippines and the calls by Philippine nationalists for the removal of U.S. bases. U.S. planners remember that during the Vietnamese War, the U.S. was prohibited from using Clark Air Field for launching B-52 raids. Micronesia is seen as a fallback position.

From the beginning of the nuclear age, Micronesia played an important role in the U.S. nuclear war strategy. The "Enola Gay," the B-29 which dropped "Fat Boy" over Hiroshima, flew from the U.S. air base on Tinian in the Northern Marianas of Micronesia.

From 1946 to 1958 the U.S. performed sixty-six announced nuclear tests on Bikini and Enewetak in the Marshall Islands in

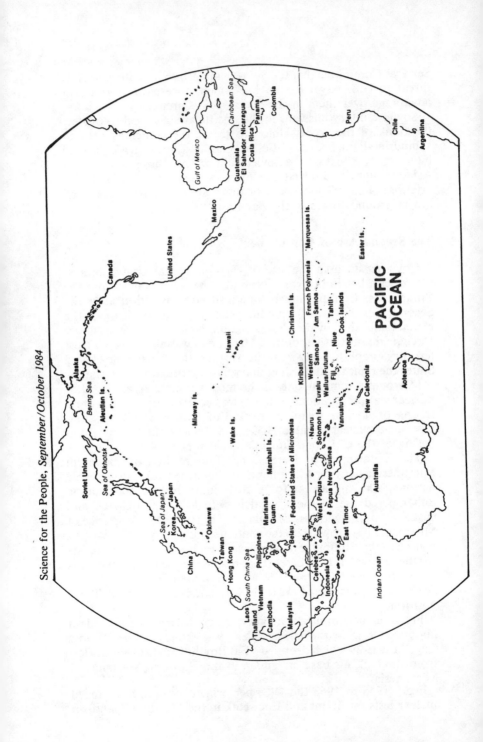

Science for the People, *September/October 1984*

eastern Micronesia. Marshall Islanders were at first "resettled" from their islands to facilitate the tests. But on March 1, 1954, they were exposed to high levels of radioactive ash from *Bravo*, the first hydrogen bomb test. Fallout from the test fell from the sky like snow onto the islands of Rongalap and Rongerik, where the islanders had been resettled. Other tests were conducted on Johnson Island, near Hawaii, and on Christmas Island, where the United States tested a twenty-megaton bomb, the largest of the U.S. warhead experiments. Though all above-ground nuclear testing was halted in 1963, the United States still maintains facilities for atmospheric testing on Johnson Island. If the Partial Test Ban Treaty were ever abrogated, these Defense Nuclear Agency facilities could start testing within a few months.

The Micronesian Islands were militarized in other ways soon after the end of World War II. In 1951 the CIA established secret training bases on Saipan (northern Mariana) for Chiang Kai Shek's nationalist forces who planned a return to the Chinese mainland. In the eastern part of Micronesia, in the Marshall Islands, Kwajalein was developed into a large military installation.

Criticism over the lack of social, political, and economic development of the islands led the Kennedy administration in a 1962 National Security Memorandum, to call for the "movement of Micronesia into permanent relationship with the United States within our political framework." The Solomon Report, prepared under direction of the Kennedy administration, outlined the plans necessary for achieving the political and economic integration of Micronesia into a dependency relationship with the United States. Beginning in 1963 U.S. funding for an educational program (modelled after domestic U.S. programs) and for surplus food distribution grew rapidly. Little money was available, however, for development projects which could contribute to economic self-sufficiency.

During the 1960s, after the end of CIA involvement in Saipan and the conclusion of U.S. nuclear testing in the Marshall Islands, the major U.S. military presence was in the Kwajalein Atoll. First under navy administration, and then in 1964, under army control, the central lagoon of Kwajalein became the primary testing range for succeeding generations of American intercontinental ballistic missiles. In 1960 the residents of Kwajalein Island were resettled on nearby Ebeye. The lagoon of Kwajalein, the largest in the world, was transformed into the "bullseye" for testing Minuteman, Polaris, Poseidon, and MX missiles launched from Vandenberg Air Force Base in southern California.

154 THE DEADLY CONNECTION

Anti-ballistic missile systems (ABM) were also tested at Kwajalein. Starting with the Nike-Zeus system in 1955, through the Spartan and Sprint systems of the 1960s, until the ABM Treaty of 1972, Kwajalein has been the key testing facility for American anti-ballistic missile systems. The Reagan administration has continued research for missile defense under the name of ballistic missile defense (BMD). A heat sensor device in the head of intrecept missiles was successfully tested at Kwajalein on June 10, 1984. According to Owen Wilkes, a New Zealand peace researcher, no other place on the face of the earth may have contributed more to the arms race than Kwajalein.[17]

Kwajalein has, in addition, an important C3I installation. The U.S. C3I network uses satellites and land-based communication and detection stations to provide communication between weapons systems, give accurate navigational positions for military systems, and monitor Soviet satellites and communications. Information generated by the North American Defense Command (NORAD) in Colorado's Cheyenne Mountains is passed to Kwajalein for integration into overall U.S. military strategy. According to *Pacific Command*, NORAD is the operation center for waging nuclear war.[18]

The NORAD network of sensors and monitoring devices spreads across the Pacific. On the Hawaiian islands of Maui and Hawaii, and the U.S. base at Taegu, South Korea are components of the Ground-Based Electro-Optical Deep Space Surveillance System (GEODSS) designed to track objects in the outer reaches of the atmosphere. Additional tracking and communication facilities are found at Pine Gap and Northwest Cape in Australia and on Guam.

Strategic Air Command B-52 bombers and the navy's nuclear submarines depend upon communication links to receive orders to launch a nuclear attack. To ensure the survivability of the communication links, a number of systems have been developed. Very low-frequency (VLF) radio stations transmit orders to submerged nuclear submarines. VLF stations are found in the Pacific at Northwest Cape in Australia, Misawa in Japan, and Oahu, Hawaii. Conventional communication stations are on Guam, in San Miguel in the Philippines, and on Oahu. The Strategic Air Command operates communication stations at Clark Field in the Philippines, Yokota Air Force Base outside Tokyo, and in California.[19]

In 1973 the United States announced plans for the military development of the entire island of Tinian, in the Northern Marianas. Resettlement plans were developed for the population of eight hundred to make way for a naval base and an air base. Opposition to the resettlement plan led to a compromise. In February 1975 the northern Marianas became a commonwealth of the U.S., permitting seventeen thousand acres, or two-thirds of Tinian, to be leased to the U.S. for fifty years, with a renewal option for another fifty years. Tinian Islanders were allowed to remain on the remaining one-third of the island.

Guam, south of Tinian, served as an important base for U.S. air attacks against Indochina during the Vietnam War. Today, a Strategic Air Command (SAC) wing of fourteen B-52 bombers is stationed at Andersen Air Force Base. Nuclear and conventional weapons are stored at Andersen and at the nearby Apra Harbor Naval Base. Recently reequipped B-52 Gs armed with air-launched cruise missiles have been stationed at Andersen.

The islands of Palau lie in the western part of Micronesia. On Palau there are more than two thousand acres of deep-water harbor at Malakal and Bebeldaob. The thirty thousand acres on Bebeldaob are replacing U.S. facilities in the Canal Zone of Panama for jungle, amphibious, and counterinsurgency warfare training. Ponape and Babelthuap also "have land areas in excess of 100 square miles and are suitable for nuclear weapons storage and training areas."[20] While not as suitable as the Philippine bases, Palau, six hundred miles to the east of the Philippines, has repeatedly been mentioned as a possible replacement for Subic Bay.

Palau is the site of the most visible clash between U.S. military plans and the desire of Micronesians to be free of the superpowers' arms race. The Compact of Free Association, developed by the U.S. as a result of the renegotiation of the political relationship between Micronesia and the United States, has been repeatedly rejected by the voters of Palau. Under the provisions of the compact, the United States would have a permanent right to deny any outside power a military presence in Micronesia. Palau has sought to establish independence from the United States, voting for its own constitution which prohibits transit, storage, or deployment of nuclear weapons within its two hundred-mile territorial waters.

The Palauan constitution is unacceptable to the U.S. because of the precedent it establishes in restricting the movement of U.S. military forces around the globe. The U.S. government fears other nations could follow Palau's example and declare nuclear-free zones, which would seriously upset U.S. military deployment plans. As events in New Zealand have shown, the tide against U.S. nuclear war plans in the Pacific is growing. New Zealand joins Palau, Vanuatu, and the Solomon Islands in prohibiting the visits of U.S. nuclear-capable warships. Admiral Long, in 1980, warned about the spread of anti-nuclear sentiments in the Pacific. He told Congress that in negotiations on the political status of Micronesia, the United States must prevent the creation of island nations which could extend territorial sovereignty two hundred miles into the oceans, making Micronesia and other islands off limits to U.S. ships, aircraft, and submarines. He envisioned the possibility that the U.S. might not be able to "get forces from Japan into the Indian Ocean without going back to the coast of South America, and then come around."[21]

Sea-Launched Cruise Missiles

Because the navy constitutes the major portion of U.S. force in the Pacific and Indian Oceans, the planned deployment of the sea-launched cruise missiles (SLCM) is a significant escalation of the arms race. The SLCM is a versatile weapon that can "strike enemy surface ships and shore targets beyond the horizon."[22] The SLCM, known as Tomahawk, is a low-flying torpedo-shaped bomb powered by turbofan engines. The Tomahawk reaches subsonic speeds of 550 miles per hour and carries onboard computers displaying the earth's contour which can place the weapon within one hundred yards of target from a distance of fifteen hundred miles. Targets for the SLCM will be "deep inside enemy territory, currently outside the combat radius of tactical aircraft, point targets of extreme hardness, previously unable to be attacked with a high kill probability...that are so heavily defended as to cause excessively high levels of aircraft attrition."[23]

The Reagan administration plans to deploy 3994 Tomahawks with the dual-use capability of either conventional or nuclear warheads. The conventional SLCM carries a one-thousand-pound warhead, while the nuclear version has a two-hundred-kiloton warhead (with an explosive power fifteen times that of the Hiroshima bomb). According to William Arkin of the Institute for Policy Studies, "by the early 1990's, over 140 ships and submarines will be armed with SLCM. Four recommissioned battleships, 24 cruisers, 37 destroyers and 83 attack submarines will be converted to carry the Tomahawk."[24] The Tomahawks are housed in protective, armored boxes, making it virtually impossible to distinguish between the conventional and nuclear SLCM. The Tomahawk is thus an instrument of U.S. "nuclear blackmail" for intervention in the Third World.

With the acquisition of increasingly sophisticated defensive systems by Third World nations, U.S. military planners see the

ASIA AND INDIAN OCEAN

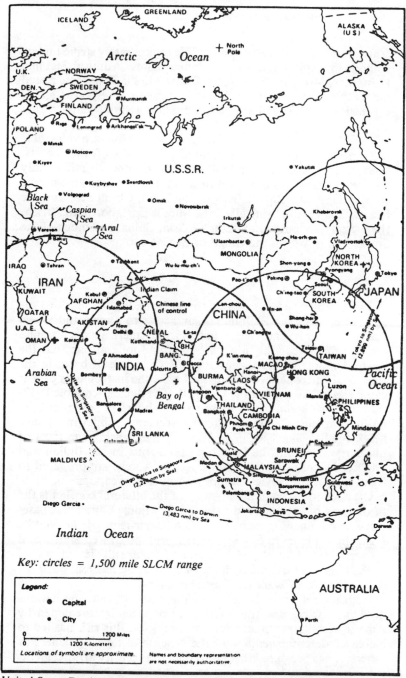

Key: circles = 1,500 mile SLCM range

Legend:
- ● Capital
- • City

0 —————— 1200 Miles
0 —————— 1200 Kilometers

Locations of symbols are approximate.

Names and boundary representation
are not necessarily authoritative.

United States Foreign Policy Objectives and Overseas Military Installations,
Committee on Foreign Relations, United States Senate, 96th Congress, April 1979.

cruise missile as a delivery system able to accurately strike targets without immediate risk to the United States. Admiral Stephen Hostettler, director of the Joint Cruise Missile Program, stated the cruise "can permit a limited, measured response as an expression of U.S. will and determination without jeopardizing aircraft and pilots."[25]

Third World nations, as well as the Soviet Union, are vulnerable to Tomahawk missiles stationed hundreds of miles off their coasts. Since the range of these missiles is fifteen hundred miles, only five cruise-missile ships, stationed in the Mediterranean, the Persian Gulf, the Bay of Bengal, the South China Sea, and the Sea of Japan could bring all of the Middle East, northern Africa, the Indian subcontinent, Southeast Asia, China, and much of the Soviet Union within the range of SLCMs.

Conclusion

The basing of U.S. military forces from Japan, south to the key facilities in the Philippines, and west to Oman and Diego Garcia in the Indian Ocean has placed American nuclear and conventional weapons in a nine-thousand-mile arc around the Soviet Union. Behind this arc lies a second line of bases in the islands of Micronesia. From these bases, the instruments of war can be launched against the U.S.S.R. The nuclear-capable B-52s stationed on Guam, the cruise missiles on board hundreds of U.S. naval warships, and the deadly Trident submarines have heightened tensions with the U.S.S.R., increasing the risks of nuclear war. From the launching platforms in the Indian and Pacific Oceans, American naval and air forces are prepared to fight against the Soviet Union with nuclear weapons.

Often overlooked in the urgency of the bilateral conflict is the second role of U.S. bases in Asia and the Middle East. These bases serve as a launching pad for U.S. intervenfields of the Middle East, the sea lanes to Europe, Japan, and the United States, and the resources of Southeast Asia and Africa are all viewed as vital to the U.S. As former Secretary of State Haig has reminded us, this is the era of wars for these resources.

With the return of U.S. interventionary policies, the nations of Asia, Africa, and the Pacific are once again threatened by American military forces. For some nations, this risk has led to increased defense spending at the expense of development. For others, it has pressured them into bilateral security arrangements with the superpowers.

The integration of nuclear weapons into U.S. overseas forces means that the Third World, like the Soviet Union, is now a potential target for U.S. nuclear strikes. The "greying" of this distinction between conventional and nuclear weapons makes the nations of the developing world "hostage" to U.S. nuclear capabilities. Any U.S. intervention carries the risk of nuclear weapons being used. And, in nations where U.S. bases are located, the presence of American military forces assures they will be a target in a nuclear war between the superpowers. Finally, the fallout from any U.S.-Soviet nuclear war would drift across the Asian and African continents, contaminating life for thousands of years.

U.S. military forces in the Indian and Pacific Oceans have been deployed to assure a peace based upon a strong forward defense. But the presence of these forces has failed to contribute to world security. The Soviet Union is strengthening its military to counteract U.S. military growth. Third World nations are increasingly seeking advanced technological defense systems to protect them from the superpowers. And the threat of nuclear war hangs behind every U.S. policy demand, keeping these countries vulnerable— unless they are willing to call Washington's bluff.

Notes

1. Admiral L.J. Long, *Seapower*, 3 August 1983, 4.
2. Admiral Maurice Weisner, *Far East Economic Review*, May 5, 1978, 25.
3. Dr. Robert H. Kupperman, "Conventional Forces, Unconventional War," *The Sun*, 9 November 1983, sec. A, 15.
4. *Washington Post*, 24 November 1983, sec. A, 22.
5. *Department of Defense, Annual Report to Congress, FY 1985* (Washington, DC: GPO, 1984), 39-40.
6. Joint Chiefs of Staff, *Military Posture, 1984* (Washington, D.C.:GPO, 1983), 25.
7. Secretary of State Alexander Haig, *Testimony before House Committee on Interior and Insular Affairs*, 1980.
8. Joint Chiefs of Staff, *Military Posture* (Washington, DC: GPO, 1982), 55.
9. Dale R. Tahtinen, *Arms in the Indian Ocean: Interests and Challenges* (Washington, DC: American Institute for Public Research, 1977), 20.
10. Department of Defense *Annual Report to Congress, FY 1983* (Washington,DC: GPO, 1982).
11. *New York Times*, 25 September 1982, 1.
12. Chandra Kumar, "The Indian Ocean: Arc of Crisis or Zone of

Peace?," *International Affairs* 60, No. 2, (Spring 1984).

13. W.R. Feeney, *The Pacific Basing System and U.S. Security, U.S. Foreign Policy and Asian-Pacific Security: A Transregional Approach* (Westview Press, 1982).

14. Admiral Crowe, Testimony before the Senate Armed Services Committee, 24 February 1984.

15. *Pacific Area Update*, 17 February 1984, 1-4.

16. Commodore Jack N. Darby, Deputy Director for Politico-Military Affairs, Office of Joint Chiefs of Staff; statement before the Senate Energy and Natural Resources Committee, 24 May 1984.

17. Reported in *An American Lake: Nuclear Peril in the Pacific*, Hayes, Zarsky, and Bello, *Nautilus Research*, forthcoming July 1985. Provides the best research and analysis of U.S. military policies in the Pacific Basin.

18. Ibid.

19. Lenny Seigel, "U.S. Strategic Arms in the Pacific," *Pacific Research* XI, No. 3, (June 1982).

20. Lt. Colonel A.R. Giroux, U.S. Army War College, 1973, Reported in the *Micronesian Support Committee Bulletin* 5, No. 2, (Summer 1980).

21. Admiral Robert Long, Reported in the *Micronesian Support Committee Bulletin* 5, No. 2, (Summer 1980).

22. Department of Defense *Annual Report to Congress, FY 1985* (Washington, DC: GPO, 1984), 141.

23. House Appropriations Committee Hearings on the Department of Defense Budget, FY 1980.

24. William Arkin, "Tomahawks: Ominous New Deployment," *Bulletin of Atomic Scientists* (October 1984), 4.

25. Arkin, "Tomahawks," 5.

THE DEADLY CONNECTION

Part V
Third World Nuclear Triggers

Stuart Schaar

The Dangers of Nuclear Proliferation and War in the Middle East

We are aware, as never before, that big wars often start in remote places.[1] We know that since Hiroshima the United States has threatened to use its strategic nuclear arsenal against the Soviet Union at least 20 times. Fourteen of these threats occurred over Third World countries.[2] We cannot forget that the two major involvements of United States troops in major wars since 1945 took place in Asia, in a divided Korea and Vietnam.

We are also reminded that between 1946 and the mid-1970's the United States, according to Secretary of State George Schultz, intervened militarily to affect policies, preserve allied regimes, and topple adversaries in Africa, Asia and Latin America at least 185 times.[3]

Since President Lyndon Johnson's time, every United States administration has acknowledged that the Middle East is the most likely flashpoint for nuclear war. It is not surprising that the last known nuclear threat took place in 1980 over the Persian Gulf, with President Jimmy Carter warning the Soviet Union to stay out. Also recall that in 1973 we were brought in the Middle East to the stage of DEFCON III—the third step out of five towards Armageddon.

Therefore, to the extent that we acknowledge the deadly connections between big wars and their small beginnings, we have to focus on the Middle East as a potential tinder box of nuclear war. As an historian of the Middle East, I am subdued by the thought that this cradle of civilization may one day become the coffin for civilization.

Of the four most important crisis areas of the world today—the Middle East, Central America, the Koreas and Southern

Africa—the Middle East is the most likely to trigger a nuclear war. There are at least four main reasons for that.

First there is danger of rampant proliferation of nuclear weaponry in the area from Morocco to Pakistan.[4] Israel has close to 100 nuclear devices which can be activated at moment's notice.[5] The Dimona nuclear complex has produced sufficient plutonium to manufacture and stockpile at least one Hiroshima sized bomb (20 kilotons) yearly since 1966.[6] It is widely believed that Pakistan, on the borders of the Middle East, has developed a nuclear capability through technology supplied by the West and China, capital from other Islamic states and through its own efforts. Both Israel and Pakistan have refused to sign the International Non-proliferation Treaty.

Whether or not Pakistan actually exploded a nuclear device in China during 1983 is irrelevant, since the country has developed the capacity to do so and has boasted of its ability to enrich uranium locally to weapons-grade levels.[7] The Pakistan experience shows that any country intent on producing nuclear weapons can muster the resources to do so.

The countries from Morocco to Pakistan are also rich in phosphates which by chemical processes can now be converted into raw uranium.[8] New laser technology, pioneered by Israel, allows the enrichment of the resultant uranium yellow cake to weapons-grade quality. By the 1990's we can expect several Middle Eastern and North African countries to have the technology and raw materials needed to manufacture nuclear weapons.

A nuclear arms race in the Middle East is a terrifying prospect since the region is highly unstable. Because of rapid social changes and disorganic development there, we can expect future conflicts.[9]

As a second point, any future war in the Middle East will be fought initially with the deadliest and most modern advanced conventional weapons in the world's arsenal. The superpowers and other manufacturers of weapons have been pouring large quantities of state-of-the-art weaponry into the region for years, so that unlike what we find in other parts of the Third World, in the Middle East conflicts rage at the highest levels of conventional warfare. If the superpowers were to fight in the Middle East, either over the Persian Gulf or as a result of another Arab-Israeli war, they might feel obliged to employ tactical nuclear weapons at an early stage in order to reduce their casualties.[10] Nuclear armed ships and planes stationed in the Arabian and Mediterranean Seas and the Indian Ocean are ready at a moment's notice to intervene.

In this context, and as a third point, the United States has developed the Central Command (formerly called the Rapid Deployment Force) as a mobile interventionary force. Initially numbering 70,000 under Carter, it will mushroom to a projected 425,000 under Reagan. Its bases and facilities range from Diego Garcia in the Indian Ocean to Somalia and Oman, Sidi Slimane and Kenitra in Morocco and the Azores in the Atlantic Ocean. Present United States strategic doctrine holds that if an internal revolt were to occur in Saudi Arabia—a very unstable desert kingdom with the largest proven oil reserves in the Western alliance system—the Central Command will be sent in to take over and hold the oil fields.

Finally, no conflict of the 44 now raging globally is more susceptible of becoming internationalized than the Arab-Israeli conflict. The Soviet Union shares a 1200 mile border with the Middle East and has large Muslim populations in Central Asia who share cultural affinities with their cousins across the Soviet border. For the Soviet Union, the Middle East is a vital strategic area, their "front yard," and they perceive it as strategically significant for their interests as the United States does Central America and the Caribbean.

Western Europe and Japan also have primary interests in the region through trade relations and their dependence on Middle East oil. Yet the United States, given its special relationship with Israel and certain conservative Arab states, is promoting its own interest while attempting to keep out the other interested powers.

People in this country interested in a peaceful resolution to the Arab-Israeli conflict should push the United States to reach a settlement between Arabs and Israelis in an internationally arranged context, and one acceptable to the parties themselves. The Soviet Union, Western Europe and Japan should be involved in this process, because leaving them out means that there will not be peace. By the same token, neither Israeli nor American interests lie in ignoring Palestinian rights which have been violated.

I am gratified that we are beginning to focus on these issues so vital for our survival. In so doing, we must not be ethnocentric, eurocentric and nucocentric, but have to remember that big wars start in remote places, and that the Middle East may be the Balkans of World War III. The way to stop this from happening is by trying to address the roots of the problem and not by ignoring them.

Notes

1. Eqbal Ahmad, "Flashpoint for Armageddon: The Potential for World War III in the Middle East," *Sojourners*, Vol. 11, No. 8 (September 1982), pp. 12-15 makes this point and places these issues in a wider political context.
2. Barry M. Blechman and Stephen S. Kaplan, *Force Without War: U.S. Armed Forces as a Political Instrument* (Washington, D.C.: The Brookings Institution, 1978), pp. 47-48. They cite 19 incidents of U.S. nuclear diplomacy against the Soviet Union until 1973.
3. "Security and Economic Assistance for FY 1984," statement by Secretary Schultz before the House Foreign Affairs Committee, *Current Policy* No. 454, February 16, 1983 (Washington, D.C.: United States Department of State, Bureau of Public Affairs) p. 2 cites a "study by the Brookings Institution." The study in question is probably the Blechman & Kaplan book cited above. They claim that there were "215 incidents in which the United States employed its armed forces for political purposes between 1946 and 1975..." p. 23.
4. See Warren H. Donnelly, "An Assessment of the Proliferation Threat of Today and Tomorrow and Replies to Questions Asked by Senator William Proxmire," (Washington, D.C.: Congressional Research Service, The Library of Congress, September 24, 1984). See also "Nuclear Proliferation: Nuclear export policies of major nations," *International Currency Review* (London) Vol. 13, No. 1 (1981), pp. 66-70.
5. According to a late November 1984 report from the Pentagon's Defense Nuclear Agency, cited in a *Los Angeles Times* Editorial, December 4, 1984.
6. *New York Times*, April 29, 1977.
7. For Indian intelligence reports claiming that Pakistan exploded a nuclear device in China during 1983, see *Boston Globe*, March 27, 1984; *The Times* (London), March 29, 1984. See also Steve Weissman and Herbert Krosney, *The Islamic Bomb* (New York: Times Books, 1981). Leonard S. Spector, *Nuclear Proliferation Today* (New York: Viking, 1984), pp. 19-20 and 70-109, denies that Pakistan exploded a nuclear device.
8. For a summary of phosphate rock deposits in the Middle East, North Africa and Pakistan see "International Trade in Phosphate Rock: Present and Projected to 1985," Florida State University prepared for the Bureau of Mines (December 1975), pp. 113-117. For the scientific bases and risks of this process see W. Davis, et al, "Potential Radiological Impacts of Recovery of Uranium from Wet-Process Phosphoric Acid," (Oak Ridge, Tennessee: Oak Ridge National Laboratory, January 1979); Richard C. Ross, "Uranium recovery from phosphoric acid nears reality as a commercial uranium source," *Engineering and Mining Journal*, Vol. 176 (December 1975) pp. 80-85; Fred J. Hurst, Wesley D. Arnold and Allen D. Royen, "Recovering uranium from wet-process sulfuric acid," *Chemical Engineering* (January 3, 1977) pp. 56-57; H.C. McIntyre, "New uranium source: wet process acid," *Canadian Chemical Processing*, Vol.

166   THE DEADLY CONNECTION

62, No. 1 (January 1978) pp. 12-13; Edward J. Bouwer, John W. McKlveen, and W.J. McDowell, "A Solvent Extraction-Liquid Scintillation Method for Assay of Uranium and Thorium in Phosphate-Containing Material," *Nuclear Technology*, Vol. 42 (January 1979) pp. 102-111; Michael Spriggs, "The potential of unconventional sources of uranium," *Nuclear Engineering International* (April 1980) p. 47. For its application in Israel see Leonard S. Spector, *Nuclear Proliferation Today*, p. 125; in Morocco see *The Middle East* (April 1978) and Zakya Daouad, "Uranium: la carte de l'avenir," *La Malif* (Casablanca), No. 112 (January 1980) pp. 8-10; in Tunisia see *Middle East Economic Digest* (26 June 1981) p. 35 and for the decision to postpone the Tunisian project to extract uranium from phosphoric acid because of low world uranium prices, see *Middle East Economic Digest* (10 August 1984) p. 48.

9. For a succinct discussion of the effects of disorganic development on the Third World see A. Sivanandan, "Imperialism and disorganic development in the silicon age," *Race & Class* (London), Vol. XXI, No. 2 (Autumn 1979) pp. 111-126.

10. See Michael Klare, "Intervention and the Nuclear Firebreak in the Middle East," in *MERIP Reports*, No. 128 (November-December 1984) pp. 3-6.

Text of a speech delivered at the October 13, 1984 Midwest Freeze Rally, Chicago. Notes have been added for publication. The author wishes to thank Ms. Leila Blacquebelaire for her research assistance.

Joseph Gerson
Roger Hurwitz
Dan Petegorsky

The United States
in the Middle East

Since 1945, when a State Department described Middle East oil
as "a stupendous source of strategic power, and one of the greatest
material prizes in world history,"[1] successive U.S. administrations
have claimed the nations and resources of the Middle East as part
of the American sphere of influence. Our government has
dominated the diplomacy of the region; bought and toppled
governments; dispatched thousands of Marines; and threatened
to use nuclear weapons to establish and maintain U.S. primacy
in this oil-rich strategic region stretching from the north coast of
Africa to the Persian Gulf.

Three fundamental interests underlie U.S. policy in the Middle
East. The first is the desire to control production and distribution
of the region's oil and to assure continued access to its strategic
waterways. The second is the desire to confront perceived Soviet
threats in the area and to contain the spread of Soviet influence.
The third is a commitment to the survival and security of the state
of Israel. The pursuit of these various goals has at times been
complementary, but at times also contradictory.

In the Beginning

At the conclusion of World War II the United States was the
preeminent economic, military and political power in the world.
War-ravaged Europe was just beginning to rebuild. The former
Mideast colonial powers, Great Britain and France, no longer had
the strength to compete with the U.S. in the Middle East. U.S.
policymakers moved quickly and aggressively to consolidate the
United States' privileged position in the region. This position
allowed control over nearly half of the world's proven oil reserves,

"the jugular vein of Western capitalism,"[2] as described by former Chairman of the Joint Chiefs of Staff, Maxwell Taylor.

U.S. military involvement in the Middle East in the post-war period began when the Truman Administration intervened in the Greek Civil War. The Administration provided both military and political support for the conservative government to defeat progressive and nationalist forces. President Truman was motivated in large measure by the fear that a victory on the part of the insurgents would threaten the U.S. position in the Mediterranean and in the Middle East as a whole. Intelligence analysts argued in 1948 that such a victory would jeopardize U.S. control over Mideast oil.[3]

The readiness of the United States to intervene on behalf of interests in the Middle East was formalized in the Truman Doctrine, a masterpiece of cold war rhetoric which committed the

U.S. "to support free people who are resisting attempted subjugation by armed minorities or by outside pressures."

President Truman's interventions in the Middle East were not limited to Greece or to the kind of counter-insurgency that the U.S. supported there. In repeated statements Truman claimed that he had threatened to drop the "superbomb" on the Soviet Union to force its withdrawal from Kurdistan and Azerbaijan, two northern provinces of Iran which the Soviets had occupied with American and British approval during World War II. The Soviets did, in fact, eventually leave Iran. There is, however, no certainty that this resulted from President Truman's alleged nuclear intimidation (as Senator Jackson of Washington and others claimed). It may also have resulted from more conventional diplomatic pressures. President Truman's claim to have forced Soviet evacuation of Iran within 24 hours of his delivering the nuclear threat served later as a paradigm for U.S. nuclear war strategy.[4]

Following President Truman's efforts to consolidate control of the region for Western interests and to contain the spread of "communist influence," President Eisenhower extended the pattern of U.S. intervention into the heart of the Middle East. His actions ranged from the use of the CIA to overthrow a nationalist government in Iran (1953) to threatening the use of nuclear weapons to prevent the spread of the Iraqi anti-monarchist revolution to neighboring Kuwait in 1958.

The Eisenhower Years

Eisenhower's own "doctrine" recast the Truman Doctrine in more explicit anti-communist terms, calling for "the employment of the armed forces of the United States to secure and protect the territorial integrity and political independence of nations requesting such aid against ... aggression from any nation controlled by international communism." However, the doctrine was most frequently employed to rationalize U.S. intervention against internal threats to client states and proxies in the region. Whatever "external aggression" there was came from the American side.

In 1951 the Iranian Parliament unanimously voted to nationalize the Anglo-Iranian Oil Corporation. Afraid that this precedent would be followed by other petroleum rich countries in the Middle East, American and British oil companies, with the support of their governments, organized a boycott of Iranian oil. The boycott weakened the nationalist government in Iran but was unable to reverse this popular Iranian initiative. To bring the "crisis" to a close the Eisenhower Administration instructed the CIA to topple the Iranian government of Dr. Mohammad Mossadegh and reimpose the unpopular Shah, who had fled abroad. The Shah went on to "do our bidding" for the next 25 years, serving as a pillar of U.S. power in the Middle East.[5]

The 1953 coup d'etat in Iran was followed the next year with the creation of the Central Treaty Organization, otherwise known as the Bhagdad Pact. Ostensibly aimed at containing the Soviet Union on its southern flank, this treaty was a means for the U.S. to provide economic and military aid to Turkey, Iraq, Iran and Pakistan and thus preserve the status quo in the "northern tier" of the Middle East. With the increase in aid came a tightening of internal security measures in the member countries.

These attempts at regional organization were opposed by Egypt's President Nasser. Having come to power through the 1952 officers' revolution, Nasser rapidly became a symbol of nationalist pride and aspirations in the Arab world. His increasing stature in the region posed a threat to the economic and political interests of the United States, the former colonial powers (France and Britain), and frightened Israel as well. The CIA first attempted to buy Nasser's loyalty with cash. But after the U.S. and its Western allies refused to provide him military aid or to assist in the construction of the Aswan High Dam, he began to look to the Soviet Union for assistance. This developing relationship with Moscow won him the enmity of Secretary of State Dulles.

In what became known as the Suez Crisis of 1956, however, events took an unexpected turn: the Eisenhower Administration found itself intervening on behalf of President Nasser against an invasion of Egypt by the combined forces of Great Britain, France and Israel in an attempt to regain control of the Suez Canal. The United States joined with the Soviet Union in insisting that the invading forces be withdrawn immediately. This cooperation between the superpowers, however, did not come before a period of great tension that included a Soviet nuclear threat and an American alert of strategic nuclear forces to counter any Soviet moves.[6]

Eisenhower's forceful action was not intended as a defense of Nasser or a condemnation of resurgent European colonialism; it was a signal to Britain, France and Israel that the United States saw the region as part of its sphere of influence, and would not tolerate intervention by other powers. Once this message was conveyed, Eisenhower could return to the more traditional U.S. role of opposing nationalist forces in the region. In 1958 he sent

14,000 Marines to Lebanon to thwart what he claimed was the spread of Nasserite-inspired revolution.

Wilbur Crane Eveland, the United States' principal CIA operative in Lebanon in the 1950's, has described how the challenge of Lebanon's disenfranchised people to the power of the Maronite establishment led the CIA to purchase the 1957 parliamentary elections for the favorites of Lebanese President Camille Chamoun.[7] The rebellion that followed resulted directly from this gross U.S. intervention into Lebanon's domestic political process and was quelled when Eisenhower dispatched the Marines to Beirut.

The invasion of Lebanon was also designed to send a message to Iraq. Shortly before the Lebanese crisis, revolutionaries sympathetic to President Nasser had toppled Iraq's conservative, pro-Western monarchy. Fearful that the revolution might spread to neighboring oil-rich Kuwait, Eisenhower ordered the Joint Chiefs of Staff to prepare to use nuclear weapons if necessary in defense of the Kuwaiti monarchy. The President was well aware of the risks that his actions entailed.[8]

President Eisenhower's heavy-handed intervention in Lebanon under the pretext of preventing the spread of communist revolution was a portent of things to come under the Johnson Administration. From the Dominican Republic to Vietnam, the image of U.S. troops arriving in Third World countries to defend U.S. interests from local threats was common in the 1960's.

U.S. Strategy and the Six Day War

During the Johnson Administration one of the cornerstones of subsequent U.S. policy in the Middle East was established: the "special relationship" between the U.S. and Israel. U.S. policy had been supportive of the Israeli state since its creation in 1948, despite such episodes as Eisenhower's insistence on an Israeli withdrawal from Egypt during the Suez Crisis. But prior to 1967 there was considerable debate within policy circles about the wisdom of identifying the United States exclusively with Israel against the Arab countries. According to Stephen Green, President Kennedy most clearly articulated this position in a conversation with Israeli Prime Minister Golda Meir:

> The United States, the President said, has a special relationship with Israel in the Middle East really comparable only to that which it has with Britain over a wide range of world affairs. But for us to play properly the role we are

called upon to play, we cannot afford the luxury of identifying Israel—or Pakistan, or certain other countries—as our exclusive friends...[9]

Two events changed this situation dramatically. The first was the deepening American involvement in Indochina. As U.S. troops became increasingly bogged down in Vietnam, President Johnson faced mounting public opposition to the presence of U.S. forces abroad. This opposition made it difficult for the Administration to consider direct large-scale military intervention in other areas of the world. In what later became known as the Nixon Doctrine, the U.S. began to rely on regional surrogates to act on behalf of American interests. Massive quantities of the most modern U.S. weaponry were sold or given to Middle East countries, especially Israel and Iran, which were then expected to police the area on behalf of their U.S. ally.

Under the Shah, Iran received both military hardware for its army and training for its internal security forces, SAVAK. SAVAK was then used to suppress internal dissent, maintaining the stability necessary for the Shah to play the role assigned to him by Washington.

The 1967 Arab-Israeli war (the "Six Day War") was the second event that, under the Johnson Administration, changed the shape of U.S. Mideast policy. Israel's stunning defeat of Egypt, Jordan and Syria in the war established it as the preeminent military power in the region.

For U.S. policymakers, Israel's victory was also a victory for the United States over the Soviet Union, which, since the 1950's, had supplied Nasser's army. The war demonstrated to President Johnson Israel's value as a strategic ally in the Middle East. By relying on Israeli power together with the Shah's Iran as primary surrogates, the U.S. could maintain its predominance over any indigenous threats in the region and curb the spread of Soviet influence without having to use U.S. troops in combat.

This view was attractive to many in Washington, and it led to a great increase in U.S. aid to Israel. It had, however, several flaws. First, while reliance on regional allies might free American Administrations from actions such as Eisenhower's 1958 invasion of Lebanon, the U.S. was nonetheless forced at times to use drastic measures to protect its regional surrogates. These measures included nuclear threats against the Soviet Union. Second, while the U.S. assumed that strong support for Israel and for the Shah would secure its position in the Middle East, this support was also a major cause of anti-American feeling in the region.

Following the humiliating defeat of the Arab states in the 1967 war a new force emerged in the region which would prove to be as potent a challenge to U.S. policymakers as Nasser had been: an independent Palestine Liberation Organization. Prior to the Six Day War the Arab states had assumed primary responsibility for the Palestinian question and the confrontation with Israel over the occupation of Arab lands. With the defeat of Nasser and the pan-Arab nationalism that he represented, the PLO emerged as an independent force for Palestinian nationalism. The activities of the PLO began to pose increasingly serious problems not only for Israel, but for conservative and autocratic Arab states and for the U.S. as well. In Jordan, as later became the case in southern Lebanon, the size of the Palestinian refugee community and the organization of the PLO created economic, social and political structures that competed with the State itself.

When Palestinian guerillas began to launch armed attacks against Israel from neighboring Arab states, those states faced mounting retaliatory attacks from Israel. Jordan came under particular threat from the Israelis. It demanded that King Hussein cease providing the PLO with a base of operations. Hussein's attempt to comply with Israel's demand and to assert Hashemite sovereignty throughout Jordan encountered serious resistance. Palestinians comprised half of Jordan's population and sympathy for the PLO cause was strong. Civil war resulted, with the PLO seeking to topple Hussein's regime. When the Syrians moved to support the PLO in the war, the U.S. and Israel intervened to protect King Hussein.

As in the Lebanese crisis of 1958, American behavior during the Jordanian civil war was based on a perception that the Soviet Union was behind all the trouble. In the years since the 1967 war, the Soviet presence in the region had become stronger. Nixon and Kissinger were especially troubled by Soviet arms shipments to Syria and Egypt. "One thing was clear," wrote Nixon in his memoirs, "we could not allow Hussein to be overthrown by a Soviet-inspired insurrection." Nixon saw dire consequences if the U.S. failed to act decisively: "It was like a ghastly game of dominoes, with a nuclear war waiting at the end."[10]

Although the Administration worked out a joint plan of action with the Israelis, Nixon's worst fears were that direct Israeli military action against the Syrians in support of Hussein would precipitate a Soviet intervention. His strategy was to scare off the Russians (and through them the Syrians) leaving Hussein to deal with the PLO. He orchestrated a major show of force that included the dispatch of two nuclear capable aircraft carrier task forces to the Mediterranean, eighteen F-4 fighter planes to Turkey, and orders to place three Army battalions in Europe and the 82nd Airborne Division at Fort Bragg on full alert.[11]

In the end, Syrian intervention in Jordan proved to be minimal and ineffective. Hussein's forces dealt a crushing blow to the PLO, and the King ejected the PLO from Jordan in what has become known as Black September. While Nixon and Kissinger celebrated having faced down the Russians (as they saw it), the tensions that surrounded the Jordanian crisis contributed to the outbreak of the next Arab-Israeli war in 1973.

Kissinger at Work

Before the 1973 war the Nixon Administration had little incentive to pursue a comprehensive settlement of the Arab-Israeli conflict that would challenge the Israeli government's increasingly harsh occupation of the West Bank and Gaza and provide a solution to the Palestinian question. Following the 1967 War the U.S. supported U.N. Resolution 242, which called on Israel to withdraw from the territories it had occupied in exchange for peace; but it had put little effort into seeing the resolution implemented.

President Nixon and Henry Kissinger feared that plans for a comprehensive settlement (such as Secretary of State Rogers' proposals of 1969-71) would expand the role of the Soviet Union in the region. Nixon and Kissinger were far less concerned with establishing a just peace in the region than with preserving and expanding U.S. power and influence.

Anwar Sadat, who became Egypt's President following Nasser's death in 1970, was determined to force Washington to pay greater attention to Egyptian and Arab grievances. First, he launched a diplomatic initiative that hinted at Egyptian readiness to make peace with Israel in return for an Israeli withdrawal from the conquered territories (1971). The Nixon Administration, however, was reluctant to put any pressure on its ally Israel to come to terms with Egypt so long as Egypt was still seen as a Soviet client. Israel's military power was perceived to be unmatched. Sadat's next move in 1972 was to oust Soviet military advisers from Egypt. But the event that finally wrested Washington's attention was the 1973 war that Sadat and the Syrians launched with the backing of Saudi Arabia.

Although the 1973 war ended with the military defeat of the Arab forces, the war itself had a profound effect on the perceptions of people in the Middle East and in Washington. The surprising success of the Egyptian army in the first stages of the war damaged the image of Israeli invincibility that had arisen from the Six Day War. In addition the war showed planners in the Nixon Administration that their hopes of maintaining the status quo in the region were unrealistic, and that more serious effort would be necessary to deal with Arab concerns. This last point was driven home by another of the war's effects—the emergence of OPEC and the "oil weapon" as a force to be reckoned with. The United States' unquestioning support for Israel had placed U.S. access to the region's vital oil reserves in jeopardy.

Finally, the war again brought the U.S. and the Soviet Union into direct nuclear confrontation. In a study of the use of force in U.S. foreign policy, Barry Blechman and Stephen Kaplan list 18 occasions in which nuclear threats had been directed at the Soviet Union through the actions of American armed forces. Of the four most overt and explicit of these threats, three occurred during Middle East crises: the Suez crisis of 1956; the Lebanese crisis of 1958; and the 1973 Arab-Israeli war. (The fourth was the Cuban Missile Crisis). At the end of the war President Nixon ordered a nuclear alert of American forces as the Soviet Union threatened to intervene to protect the encircled Egyptian army which was being denied food and water by the Israelis.[12]

The 1973 war presented U.S. policymakers with a serious dilemma: How could they continue to support Israel as they had in the past, while at the same time consolidate the role of the moderate and conservative Arab states in the U.S. sphere? If one goal of U.S. policy was to ensure continued privileged access to the region's resources and waterways, how could this be reconciled with a policy that set the United States at odds with the increasingly powerful Arab oil states over the question of unqualified support for Israel?

One answer to this dilemma was the strategy worked out by Henry Kissinger in the series of ceasefire and disengagement agreements that he negotiated between Israel and Egypt in the Sinai and between Israel and Syria in the Golan Heights (1974). These agreements were to form the model for the "step-by-step" process that culminated in the Camp David Accords. Unlike the comprehensive approach, which called for a broad resolution of Middle East conflicts in the context of a multi-lateral international conference, the step-by-step approach was to be implemented through limited bilateral agreements negotiated between Israel and individual Arab states under U.S. auspices. These limited agreements might hint at a comprehensive settlement for the sake of satisfying pan-Arab and pro-Palestinian sentiment in Arab countries, but they were not aimed at producing such a settlement. Instead, Kissinger's hope was to minimize any role for the Soviet Union or the PLO, which by 1974 had been recognized by the Arab states as the sole legitimate representative of the Palestinian people.

By September of 1975 Kissinger's step-by-step approach had come to fruition. The second Sinai accord confirmed Egypt's determination to seek its own interests in negotiations with Israel, and to do so in such a way that the broader issues of the Arab-Israeli-Palestinian conflict were evaded. In brokering the agreement the United States gave the Israelis a series of far-reaching assurances that amounted to a long-term military, security and political alliance. In addition, the Administration secretly promised never to negotiate with the PLO until that group first accepted UN Resolution 242 and recognized Israel.

Carter and the Middle East:
Diplomacy and Militarism

At the outset of his Administration, President Carter affirmed the American commitment to the "security and survival of Israel." In his first meeting with Egyptian President Sadat and Foreign Minister Fahmy, Carter expressed his reluctance to put major pressure on Israel to reach a comprehensive peace agreement out of fear that "it would be personal political suicide for me."[13]

Carter did, however, unnerve many of Israel's U.S. supporters in the spring of 1977 by stating that the Palestinians were entitled to a "homeland." Later that year Carter again signalled his willingness to tackle the Palestinian question. The signal came in the joint U.S.-Soviet Declaration of October, 1977, which spoke in part of "the legitimate rights of the Palestinian people" and committed itself to a settlement that would insure those rights. The fact that a joint statement with the Soviets was issued at all appeared to mark a shift away from Kissinger's step-by-step process and back to a comprehensive approach to the Mideast problem. The declaration even called for Palestinian representation at a Geneva Conference.

Within days of the declaration, however, intense pressure from the Israeli government and from the pro-Israel lobby in the United States led President Carter to back down. The Geneva Conference was never convened. President Sadat's historic visit to Jerusalem in November of that year further blocked efforts to negotiate a comprehensive Middle East peace settlement. Instead, Sadat's visit prompted the Carter Administration to support bi-lateral Egyptian-Israeli negotiations under U.S. sponsorship. This process culminated in the 1978 summit involving the U.S., Israel and Egypt that produced the Camp David Accords.

The Camp David Accords also concluded the process begun by Henry Kissinger of bringing Egypt firmly into the U.S. camp. With the signing of the accords Egypt became a full U.S. client. The peace agreement was underwritten with the commitment of a staggering $4.5 billion in military aid and sales to Egypt and Israel, and an understanding that the level of U.S. aid to Egypt would henceforth be comparable to Israel's aid package.

While the Camp David Accords did bring thirty years of war and belligerency between Israel and Egypt to an end, and should be appreciated for that, they did not deliver all that was promised. Functionally, the Camp David Accords gave the Begin government in Israel diplomatic space and time to confiscate and integrate significant portions of the West Bank and Gaza into Greater Israel and to annex the Golan Heights (1981). In addition to providing for the return of the Sinai to Egypt in exchange for the normalization of Israeli-Egyptian relations, the accords set up talks to negotiate "autonomy" for the Palestinians under Israeli occupation. This section of the accords, however, was interpreted in completely different ways by the Israelis and the Egyptians. While the Egyptians and the United States saw the talks as a step towards returning the occupied territories to Arab control, Prime Minister Begin announced that Israel would continue to claim sovereignty over the lands. The talks eventually broke down and were suspended.

The Carter Administration, however, was soon to suffer a far more serious blow to its Middle East policy. The overthrow of the Shah of Iran in the beginning of 1979 and the subsequent "hostage crisis" destroyed what remained of the Nixon Doctrine, shook the basis of U.S. power in the Middle East, and led the United States to accelerate its efforts to achieve a first-strike nuclear capability. Billions of dollars worth of the world's most sophisticated weaponry, the counsel of the CIA, and repeated statements of presidential support were not enough to protect the hated Shah from his people. A generation of repression, torture and economic mismanagement finally took its toll. Decades of repression of political thought and action had created an environment in which the home grown, but repressive, Islamic government of Ayatollah Khomeini came to power.

Afraid that the Soviet Union might invade Iran to fill the power vacuum left on its southern border after the Shah's collapse, the

Administration sent 25 U.S. warships (including 3 aircraft carriers), 150 Phantom jets, 1,800 Marines and a classified number of tactical nuclear weapons to the Persian Gulf. The President justified this military posturing with the Carter Doctrine, which announced that "any attempt by an outside force to gain control of the Persian Gulf region will be regarded as an assault on the interests of the United States and will be repelled by the use of any means necessary, including military force."[14]

The Administration moved to buttress the U.S. military posit ion in the Middle East further with the creation of a new Rapid Deployment Force that would allow the United States to introduce combat forces swiftly into Middle East conflicts and establish an American military presence. Agreements to provide military bases and staging areas for the RDF were negotiated with Oman, Kenya, and Somalia, and joint military exercises were initiated with Egypt. More ominously, President Carter took steps to make the nuclear threat implied in the phrase "any means necessary" more credible by committing the United States to a first-strike nuclear policy.

Although President Carter's drastic measures were triggered by the events in Iran, they were also in response to a more fundamental change in the United States' global strategic position vis-a-vis the Soviet Union. By this time the Soviets had achieved nuclear parity with the United States. While this fact did not threaten the capacity of the U.S. to deter a nuclear attack by the Soviet Union, it did limit the capacity of the U.S. to intervene freely in the Third World under the shield of nuclear superiority. Parity also gave the Soviet Union greater options in the region. The possibility that the Soviets might take a significantly more active role in a region just several hundred miles from their borders was underscored later in 1979, when, just weeks after the beginning of the Iranian hostage crisis, the Soviet Union invaded Afghanistan.

There were at least two problems with the Carter Doctrine. First, there were serious doubts that the U.S. could actually achieve an effective first-strike capability. Second, events in Afghanistan notwithstanding, the major threat to U.S. power in the Middle East did not come from the Soviet Union but from the struggles of people in the Arab countries and in Iran to overthrow the ruling autocracies and monarchies. In the wake of the Iranian Revolution, these struggles threatened to take on a strongly fundamentalist and anti-Western character. In Saudi Arabia, for example, tensions exacerbated by rapid modernization led to the takeover of the Grand Mosque at Mecca by religious extremists in November, 1979.

U.S. policymakers seeking to ensure the stability of their allies in such circumstances faced serious problems. While trends within the region itself compelled countries such as Saudi Arabia to identify more strongly with Arab and Islamic interests, the inherent instability of the situation compelled Saudi Arabia and other conservative countries to rely even more on the United States for military assistance. In 1978, the Carter Administration had pushed through the Congress a sale of 60 F-16 fighter planes to Saudi Arabia. Following the outbreak of the Iran-Iraq war in September, 1980, the U.S. flew 4 AWACS surveillance planes to Saudi Arabia in a show of support. Although such gestures underscored the importance placed by Washington on maintaining the stability of the Saudi monarchy and its friendliness to American interests, they also angered the Israelis and gave the fundamentalists more reasons to condemn the pro-Western leanings of the regimes.

Reagan: Incompetence and Intervention

The Reagan Administration brought to its handling of Middle East affairs an even more obsessive vision of an evil Soviet empire responsible for every challenge to U.S. power in the region (and elsewhere). This vision has obscured its view of developments in the Middle East, causing it to lurch from mistake to mistake. While the Reagan Administration has thus far managed to avoid a deep involvement in the Iran-Iraq war, its overall record justifies a senior Egyptian diplomat's observation in March, 1984 of "a U.S. inability to expand or even understand the essentials needed to conduct the peace process."[15]

The Reagan Administration wasted little time in reaffirming the American commitment to use any means necessary—including the threat of nuclear war—to guarantee U.S. control over the strategic resources of the Middle East. Its thinking was reflected in Defense Secretary Caspar Weinberger's "Defense Guidance" statement and was summarized in an article by Robert Tucker in *Foreign Affairs*.[16] Tucker proclaimed that while Central America is only symbolically important to the United States, the Persian Gulf is central to U.S. power in the world. He wrote, "We must either rely on the threat of responding with nuclear weapons or concede that as matters now stand there is no effective response we can make."

President Reagan proceeded to deploy ground-launched cruise missiles aimed at the Middle East and northern Africa in Comiso, Italy. This was in addition to the new Pershing 2 and cruise missiles that were being deployed in Western Europe as part of the first strike arsenal. The Rapid Deployment Force, now renamed the Central Command, was more than doubled in size, and was integrated with conventional and nuclear U.S. forces based in Japan, the Philippines and elsewhere in the Pacific. The Reagan Administration also rushed to bolster the military capability of its regional allies. In October, 1981 the Administration obtained Senate approval for an $8.5 billion arms sale to Saudi Arabia, the largest single arms deal in U.S. history. The Administration further attempted to involve Israel, Saudi Arabia, and other Arab clients in a tacit alliance, the "strategic consensus," aimed at confronting the Soviets and lending mutual support against internal threats. These efforts, however, came unravelled in Lebanon.

Early in the Lebanese civil war, the Ford Administration had supported Syria when it intervened militarily in Lebanon in 1976 to prevent a victory by leftist forces and their PLO allies. The Carter Administration had similarly been willing to consider Lebanon as part of Syria's sphere of influence. The Reagan Administration, however, saw Syria as a Soviet proxy. In 1982, then Secretary of State Alexander Haig gave the green light to Israel's disastrous invasion of Lebanon. Haig hoped that an Israeli blow would destabilize the Assad government in Syria, as well as destroy the PLO, which it regarded as the vehicle of Soviet-sponsored terrorism throughout the world.

During subsequent mediation efforts aimed at the evacuation of the PLO from Lebanon, the Reagan Administration repeatedly rejected the suggestion that neutral United Nations forces be used to guarantee the safety of Palestinian and Lebanese Moslem civilians from the threat of Israeli and Lebanese Phalangist attacks. Instead, to increase its regional presence in the short term, the Administration demanded the creation of a multi-national force of U.S. and Western European troops under U.S. leadership. However, the premature withdrawal of these forces at the request of President-elect Bashir Gemayel enabled the subsequent massacre of hundreds of defenseless Palestinian and Lebanese civilians in the Sabra and Shatilla refugee camps (September, 1982). The multi-national force was belatedly returned to Beirut.

In the spring of 1983, Secretary of State Shultz undertook a round of shuttle diplomacy ostensibly aimed at negotiating mutual Israeli and Syrian withdrawals from Lebanon. The Syrians, however, were excluded from the negotiating process, which culminated in the "May 17th Agreement." Syrian resistance to this agreement, which they perceived as rewarding Israel for its invasion, led to its eventual abrogation by the Lebanese government and further humiliation for the United States throughout the region.

Later that fall, following Shultz's shuttle diplomacy, President Reagan abruptly altered the mission of U.S. forces in Lebanon, providing support for the isolated Gemayel government against its Druse and later its Shiite opponents. Shortly thereafter, the Beirut Marines barracks were destroyed, with an enormous loss of lives. President Reagan and his advisers rejected the counsel of the Pentagon and dispatched part of the Rapid Deployment Force to the Lebanese coast. This new fighting force, the largest assembled since the Vietnam War, consisted of 30 warships (including 3 aircraft carriers and the Battleship New Jersey), 300 warplanes, 4,000 Marines, and an unknown number of nuclear weapons. Yet the flotilla's bombardment of Druse and Shiite positions during the next four months failed to secure the stability of the Gemayel government or to prevent its falling further under Syrian influence. Instead it further alienated the United States from its friends and allies in the Arab world.

Having failed to remove Syria from Lebanon through diplomatic or military means, the Reagan Administration turned once again to Israel's military potential as a basis for assuring U.S. domination of the region. In late 1983 it revived the "strategic cooperation accord" with Israel (part of its original strategic consensus plan), which the U.S. had suspended in 1981 to punish Israel for annexing the Golan Heights. The Administration stated publicly that the new accord would be an anti-Soviet, anti-Syrian pact. Undersecretary of State Lawrence Eagleburger, however, let slip that its scope was considerably larger, "in and beyond the Middle East."

In its diplomacy regarding the Israeli-Palestinian conflict the Reagan Administration was neither more subtle nor more successful than it was in Lebanon. Realizing that its support for the Israeli invasion had alienated Saudi Arabia, Egypt, Jordan, and other Arab clients and allies from the United States, the Administration launched a "peace initiative" in September, 1982 to regain support in the Arab world. The Reagan initiative opposed Israeli annexation of the West Bank and the Gaza Strip. At the same time, it excluded the PLO from a role in the settlement and ruled out an independent Palestinian state. Instead, it envisioned a confederation between the West Bank and Jordan.

As it turned out, the initiative pleased no one. The Begin government in Israel immediately rejected it. The PLO hesitated, supporting instead the Fez Plan, which called for an independent Palestinian state, as well as an implicit recognition of Israel. Jordan's King Hussein, disgruntled by the Administration's inability to dislodge Israel from Lebanon or to take the diplomatic initiatives needed to win PLO acceptance for an enhanced Jordanian role in negotiations, denounced the United States, saying that it had "disqualified itself" as the sole force capable of mediating the Arab-Israeli conflict. The King saw no reason to risk his life and his throne for the sole benefit of the Reagan Administration.

For the Future

As the first four years of the Reagan Administration drew to a close, several clear patterns had emerged and a series of decisions faced the President, Congress and the American people. Reliance on Israel as our principal strategic asset had become the favored U.S. approach to the Middle East. Congress, under pressure from the Israel lobby, had converted the entire $2.6 billion annual Israeli aid package from loans to grants, had voted to give Israel duty free access to U.S. markets, and supported significant increases in aid for the Fiscal Year 1986. In the past such aid has not only subsidized the Israeli economy, but has also supported the invasion and occupation of Lebanon, the occupation of the West Bank and Gaza Strip, and the construction of a nuclear-capable military force.

In the past decade the United States has tightened the nuclear trigger and instilled fear, anger and despair as a result of its approach to the Middle East. Resistance to the United States has grown, and our government has been sharply denounced by traditional friends throughout the region. Americans have become the targets of terrorist violence throughout the Middle East.

Alternative policies are possible. In recent years an international consensus, embraced by nearly all the world's countries—with the principal exception of the United States, Israel and Libya—has developed regarding the Israeli-Palestinian conflict. This consensus recognizes the right of the Israelis and the Palestinians to national self-determination and security and calls for Israel to return to its pre-1967 boundaries. It calls for the creation of an independent Palestinian state in the West Bank and Gaza Strip that would coexist peacefully with a secure Israel. The United States should support this consensus.

The United States should also renounce its commitment to fight a war for oil. Money now being spent for first-strike nuclear weapons and for the Rapid Deployment Force could be better spent by making Western industrial nations more energy efficient and by developing non-nuclear energy alternatives.

The United States has enormous power to help determine who lives, who dies, and how—in the Middle East and globally. The question remains whether we in the United States will exercise our power for our collective survival and freedom.

Notes

1. Joe Stork, *Middle East Oil and the Energy Crisis* (New York: Monthly Review Press, 1975).
2. *Christian Science Monitor*, June 16, 1978.
3. See Lawrence S. Wittner, *American Intervention in Greece, 1943-1949* (New York: Columbia University Press, 1982).
4. See "Call to Mutiny" by Daniel Ellsberg in this book and first published in *Protest and Survive* by E.P. Thompson and Dan Smith (New York: Monthly Review Press, 1981).
5. The quotation is from Ronald Reagan in his second debate with Walter Mondale during the 1984 Presidential election. Two excellent histories of Iran are: Ervand Abrahamian, *Iran: Between Two Revolutions* (Princeton, N.J.: Princeton University Press, 1982); Richard W. Cottam, *Nationalism in Iran* (Pittsburgh: University of Pittsburgh Press, 1979).
6. Donald Neff, *Warriors at Suez* (New York: Simon and Schuster, 1981).
7. Wilbur Crane Eveland, *Ropes of Sand: America's Failure in the Middle East* (New York: W.W. Norton & Co., 1980).
8. For an analysis of U.S. decision making in the Lebanese crisis see William B. Quandt, "Lebanon, 1958, and Jordan, 1970," in Barry M. Blechman and Stephen S. Kaplan, *Force Without War: U.S. Armed Forces as a Political Instrument* (Washington, D.C.: The Brookings Institution, 1978), pp. 222-257.
9. Stephen Green, *Taking Sides* (New York: William Morrow and Company, Inc., 1984), p. 181.
10. On the Jordanian crisis as it was viewed in the White House see Seymour M. Hersh, *The Price of Power: Kissinger in the Nixon White House* (New York: Summit Books, 1983), pp.234-249, and Quandt, "Lebanon and Jordan," pp. 257-288.
11. Blechman and Kaplan, *Force Without War*, pp. 47-49.
12. Blechman and Kaplan, *Force Without War*, p. 48.
13. Ismail Fahmy, *Negotiating for Peace in the Middle East* (Baltimore: The Johns Hopkins University Press, 1983), p. 196.
14. President Carter's "State of the Union" address, January 23, 1980.
15. The diplomat spoke to two of the authors of this article in a not for attribution conversation.
16. Robert W. Tucker, "The Purposes of American Power," *Foreign Affairs*, Winter 1980-81.

Carol Bragg

Central America and the Deadly Connection

To understand U.S. nuclear policy in Central America and the danger that U.S. military intervention in the region might escalate to the point of nuclear war, it is helpful to look at the historic relationship of the U.S. to Central America.

President Reagan's view of Central America as unquestionably and irrevocably within the U.S. sphere of influence (i.e., our "turf") is a logical extension of President James Monroe's 1823 warning to the nations of Europe not to interfere in the affairs of the American countries or to try to add to their possessions on the American continents. In addition, the current massive U.S. military buildup in Central America and the Caribbean is a modern-day incarnation of President Theodore Roosevelt's "Big Stick" policy. As Roosevelt put it: "There is a homely adage which runs, 'Speak softly and carry a big stick; you will go far.' If the American nation will speak softly and yet build and keep at a pitch of the highest training a thoroughly efficient navy, the Monroe Doctrine will go far." The Reagan Administration may not speak so softly, but it obviously wields a big stick.

Throughout the 20th century and much of the 19th, the U.S. has regarded Central America as critical to U.S. economic and military interests. In addition, because of its geographical proximity to the U.S. (our "backyard"), Central America holds a unique strategic significance for the U.S.

U.S. involvement in Central America since the late 1800s has consisted, by and large, of economic exploitation and military intervention. The U.S. has intervened militarily in Central America and the Caribbean more often than in any other region of the world—some 39 times since 1833.[1] U.S. troops have been sent to maintain order, to "protect" the local populations from domestic insurgents and foreign agitators, to defend U.S. national security, and to guarantee the interests of American business. The U.S. has always assumed that it has the right to intervene militarily in Central America and to control the outcome of internal struggles within the Central American countries. Successive U.S. presidents have justified U.S. invasions by invoking the Monroe Doctrine, the "Big Stick" policy, or Containment, but the result has always been the same: bloodshed, mass poverty, and the perpetuation of repressive rule by military dictatorships.[2]

U.S. companies, (the former United Fruit Company, the leading force in pushing for the 1954 coup in Guatemala, being among the most notorious) have reaped enormous profits from the cash crops —coffee, bananas, sugar, cotton and beef—of the region. In the past two decades, U.S. financial institutions and other corporate interests have deepened and diversified their investments in the area. Construction and subsequent control of the Panama Canal and use of sea lanes in the Caribbean have been important to U.S. commerce. And the Canal, as a passage between the Atlantic and Pacific Oceans, is strategically important to the U.S. Navy.

As early as 1927, Congress was informed by the President (then Calvin Coolidge) that the U.S. was fighting "Bolshevism" in Nicaragua.[3] General Wallace Nutting, former head of the U.S. Southern Command, has said that the loss of Guatemala to Marxism would be considerably more serious than the loss of El Salvador.[4] If one subscribes to the view of General William Westmoreland, commander of U.S. troops in Vietnam, that "the domino theory has validity in Central America,"[5] and also accepts the notion of the "Evil Empire," the stakes in the region must appear extraordinarily high. One need only look at a map to realize that the "dominoes" are falling our way: Nicaragua, El Salvador, Guatemala. Given the devastation and suffering the U.S. caused in Southeast Asia, one is sobered at the thought of the death and destruction the U.S. military might wreak on the land and peoples of Central America in a last-ditch effort to preserve "freedom" and "democracy" on our doorstep.

The U.S. Military Buildup in Central America

Since 1979, when the Sandinistas overthrew the dictatorship of Anastasio Somoza in Nicaragua, the United States has spent hundreds of millions of dollars on weapons, training, military advisers, airfields, and other military facilities in Central America and the Caribbean. Additional millions have been spent on improving U.S. military capabilities in the region and on training and equipping rapid deployment troops which could be dispatched quickly during a crisis. In addition, the CIA has engaged in extensive "covert" military operations aimed at political destabilization.

Current U.S. military intervention in Central America is the most massive ever in the region. It is aimed at subverting (or overthrowing) the Nicaraguan revolution, defeating the insurgents in El Salvador, suppressing opposition movements in other parts of the region, and installing governments supportive of U.S. goals and U.S. perceived needs in the region.

In *El Salvador*, the U.S. is financing and directing the war against the guerrillas (primarily the Farabundo Marti National Liberation Front). Through a combination of military and economic aid, the U.S. is underwriting between 30 and 40% of the budget of the Salvadoran government.[6] The U.S. has supplied an enormous arsenal of weapons including at this writing 35 Huey UH-1H transport helicopters (armed and used as attack helicopters), six A-37 counter-insurgency fighter bombers, two C-47 gunships outfitted with machine guns and night-vision equipment, reconnaissance planes, howitzers, rifles, and grenade launchers.

U.S. reconnaissance flights originating in Honduras and Panama provide information and direct Salvadoran ground combat and bombing missions. The Salvadoran military has recently stepped up its aerial bombing as part of its "area denial" program. Aerial attacks are aimed at forcing civilians out of guerrilla-held and contested territory, thereby cutting off the popular base of support for the guerrillas. Aerial sorties have increased in number from 10 to 30 daily.[7] The fighting in general and this policy in particular have generated an estimated 500,000 Salvadoran refugees.

U.S. advisers have assisted in the restructuring of the Salvadoran military and have provided training to Salvadoran troops. Increasingly, U.S. personnel are involved in military strategy and in planning day-to-day operations. Meanwhile, the size of the Salvadoran government forces has increased from 22,000 in early 1983 to nearly 50,000.[8] Although talks with the guerrillas are stalled and the future of President Duarte's reformist efforts are uncertain, U.S. officials predict that the war will be over within two years and the guerrilla threat reduced to a mere "nuisance."[9]

In *Honduras*, the U.S. has established a permanent forward base which, according to a Senate staff expert quoted in the

Philadelphia Inquirer, would "enable the 82nd Airborne Division to be deployed for combat in Central America in less that 24 hours."[10] Under the guise of extended military exercises (notably Big Pine I, II and III) carried out since 1983, the U.S. has constructed or improved seven airstrips, two of which are capable of accommodating U.S. fighter aircraft. All seven are capable of handling C-130 transport aircraft, which would be the primary means of moving troops and military supplies into the region were the U.S. to commit combat troops.

Two radar sites manned by U.S. personnel monitor air and sea traffic in the region and provide intelligence to the Honduran and Salvadoran militaries. Roads have been built, housing units and medical facilities erected, wells dug, and fuel storage and ammunition depots set up. U.S. plans include the construction of a $150 million permanent naval base in Honduras.[11] U.S. personnel in Honduras now number between 1800 and 2000.

Joint military exercises in Honduras have been used to train Honduran and Salvadoran troops as well as to lend combat support to the Honduran and Salvadoran militaries.[12]

In addition, the U.S. provides extensive covert support to the *contras* based in Honduras, the 8-11,000 member Nicaraguan Democratic Force led by former members of Somoza's National Guard.[13]

In *Guatemala*, the CIA directed the 1954 military coup which overthrew the left-leaning, democratically-elected Arbenz government. The U.S. has provided substantial assistance to the military ever since, although direct military aid to Guatemala was "banned" by Congress between 1977 and 1985 due to the Guatemalan government's refusal to comply with U.S. human rights stipulations. Nevertheless, Guatemala was able to purchase military equipment, weapons, and training from the Defense Department, the Department of Commerce, and private American companies. The U.S. State Department licensed the sale of 20 Bell "civilian" helicopters to Guatemala, many of which have been fitted with machine guns or used to transport troops. In 1984, Congress authorized $300,000 for military training for Guatemala, opening the way for renewed U.S. military assistance.

The Guatemalan government is involved in a bloody war against its Mayan Indian population and leftist guerrillas. It has carried out a "scorched-earth" policy of crop burning, confiscation of crops, and slaughter of livestock, combined with bombing, shelling, selective killings and massacres in areas where the guerrillas have had widespread support. Recently, the government has adopted a "Development Center" counter-insurgency strategy, forcing civilians to live in "model villages" in military-controlled areas.[14]

In *Nicaragua*, the CIA supervised the 1984 mining of Nicaraguan harbors and developed the "Psych-Operation Manual on Guerrilla Warfare," instructing *contras* in sabotage and assassination techniques. It has provided money, arms, and training to the 12-18,000 *contras* based in Honduras and Costa Rica, helped plan and organize terrorist attacks in Nicaragua, and coordinated the activities of the different *contra* groups in order to increase pressure on the Nicaraguan government.

The U.S. has attempted to undermine the Nicaraguan revolution by discrediting the 1984 elections (reports indicate that the U.S. Embassy in Managua actually paid leading non-Sandinista candidates not to run[15]). The United States is squeezing the Nicaraguan economy through *contra* attacks, repeated threats of military escalation, and a variety of economic measures including an embargo on trade and pressure on multilateral lending institutions. The November 1984 crisis over the alleged delivery of Soviet MiG fighter aircraft to Nicaragua, which put Nicaragua on full alert against a U.S. invasion, was conveniently timed to coincide with the coffee harvest.

In *Costa Rica*, the CIA is providing support to 3-5,500 *contras* in the Democratic Revolutionary Alliance, led by former Sandinista commander Eden Pastora. Costa Rica formally abolished its armed forces in 1949 and in 1983 renewed its commitment to neutrality, but it has been drawn increasingly into neighboring Central American conflicts. Costa Rica maintains a lightly-armed Civil Guard and a Rural Guard to maintain internal order within the country and to defend against external aggression. U.S. military assistance to Costa Rica increased 4-fold between 1983 and 1984 to $9 million,[16] creating deep discord in a country struggling to uphold its non-military tradition.

In *Panama*, the U.S. maintains a series of military bases and training facilities, including the headquarters of the U.S. Southern Command, the nerve center of increased U.S. military activity in Central America. "Southcom," as it is called, analyzes data from U.S. radar sites in Honduras and intelligence ships off the coast of Nicaragua; provides many of the advisers the U.S. sends to Honduras and El Salvador and the personnel that participate in military exercises like Big Pine I, Big Pine II, and Big Pine III; oversees the military exercises carried out in the region; and monitors U.S. military aid funds for the region.

Panama is the site of Howard Air Force Base, the only official U.S. air base in Central America. Until recently, the U.S. Army

School of the Americas was also located in Panama. The Army School trained more than 42,000 Latin American officers and soldiers from 22 nations since it began operations in 1946.[17] Nearly half the students there in early 1984 were from El Salvador. Under the terms of the Panama Canal Treaty signed in 1977, authority to continue the School expired October 1, 1984. The U.S. and Panama were unable to reach an agreement regarding its continued operation, and the School was relocated to Florida. The U.S. is the chief supplier of weapons and training for the Panama Defense Forces, the Panamanian military. U.S. and Panamanian forces hold annual joint military exercises to practice defense of the Canal. Panama has participated in the Contadora process (together with Mexico, Venezuela, and Colombia), which has produced a draft treaty seeking an end to the military conflicts in Central America. Meanwhile, however, the U.S. has attempted to involve the Panamanian Defense Forces in regional military actions by expanding the Canal Treaty's definition of joint defense of the Canal to include Central America and the Caribbean.[18]

Nuclear Weapons in Central America and the Caribbean

The Treaty of Tlatelolco, signed by the U.S. in 1967, prohibits the testing, production, storage, installation, deployment, use, control, and any form of possession of any nuclear weapons in Latin America and the Caribbean. The U.S. government, however, maintains that the Treaty does not prohibit the transit or transport of nuclear weapons.[19]

There are currently no nuclear weapons on the ground in Central America. But nuclear weapons play a major role in U.S. military planning and preparations at Key West (Florida), Guantanamo Bay (Cuba), and in Puerto Rico. In addition, U.S. naval exercises in the Caribbean and maneuvers off the coast of Central America involve ships armed with nuclear weapons.

U.S. naval facilities at Key West, Florida, virtually abandoned since a major Navy pullout in 1973, are now being renovated in response to increased tensions in Central America and the Caribbean. Key West, the southernmost city in the continental U.S., is strategically located at the junction of the Gulf of Mexico and the Atlantic Ocean and is only 90 miles from Cuba. The U.S. is establishing a forward base there, capable of handling nuclear-armed destroyers and warships. In addition, Key West is now the home of U.S. Forces Caribbean, which coordinates U.S. naval activities in the Caribbean, the Gulf of Mexico, and those parts of the Pacific that border Central America. The 1983 invasion of Grenada was coordinated by this command.[20] There are also plans to activate a base at Key West for nuclear anti-submarine warfare.[21]

The U.S. is expanding and upgrading its military facilities at the U.S. Navy Base at Guantanamo Bay, Cuba. This base serves as a training ground for all U.S. warships that practice in the Atlantic.

Puerto Rico, historically a staging ground for U.S. intervention in Latin America, is undergoing rapid military buildup. Roosevelt Roads, a U.S. Navy base in eastern Puerto Rico, and its accompanying naval air station, service nuclear-capable ships, submarines, and aircraft. Preparations are underway for coordinating command and control of nuclear-missile-carrying submarines from Roosevelt Roads, and there are plans to activate a base there for nuclear anti-submarine warfare.[22] In western Puerto Rico, facing Central America, Ramey Air Force Base, closed in 1964, has been reopened and is being used by the U.S. Air Force for training missions. Ramey at one time housed more than 30 B-52 bombers[23] and can potentially be reactivated as a dispersal point for U.S. nuclear-armed bombers. Although it does not appear that the U.S. stores nuclear weapons in Puerto Rico, there is clear evidence that the U.S. intends to take nuclear weapons into Puerto Rico in a crisis or during wartime.[24]

At any one time, at least 20 U.S. ships in the Caribbean are practicing naval and air maneuvers for possible intervention. Approximately 80% of the combat ships in the U.S. Navy (aircraft carriers, battleships, cruisers, destroyers, frigates, attack submarines) are nuclear capable. In addition, many support ships also carry nuclear weapons. Seven aircraft carriers regularly enter the Caribbean. All carry at least 90 aircraft, including A-6 and A-7 aircraft capable of carrying three and four nuclear weapons, respectively.[25]

Since 1981, the U.S. has conducted three major naval exercises in the Caribbean. Ocean Venture '81 involved 120,000 troops, 240 ships, and 1000 aircraft from NATO countries, Argentina, Venezuela, Uruguay, and Colombia and included a mock invasion of the island of Vieques.[26] This exercise is considered to have been a practice invasion of Grenada.

Ocean Venture '82 involved 45,000 soldiers and sailors, 350 aircraft, and 60 ships, including the aircraft carriers *Independence* and *Forrestal*. This exercise included a mock invasion of "Brown" (presumably Cuba), following that country's attacks on U.S. ships and stepped-up support for leftist guerrillas in a Central American country (presumably El Salvador). Ground troops included members of the Army's 101st Airborne Division, part of the Rapid Deployment Force. In an article about Ocean Venture '82 in *The Nation*, Michael Klare reports that when he asked several senior officers whether the Rapid Deployment Force was available for use in the Caribbean, they informed him that they were not permitted to answer that question.[27] The Rapid Deployment Force is "dual-capable," trained and equipped to use both tactical nuclear and conventional weapons.

In April and early May of 1984, Ocean Venture '84 took place, involving over 30,000 troops, sailors, and pilots, the aircraft carrier *America*, and more than 250 aircraft.

In addition to these large-scale naval exercises, there have been a number of other naval maneuvers off the Atlantic and Pacific coasts of Central America. In 1983, the battleship *New Jersey* spent time off the Pacific coast of Nicaragua on its way to the Middle East to shell Druze military positions in Lebanon. In August 1983, the aircraft carrier *Ranger* conducted maneuvers off the Pacific coast. In March, 1984, an aircraft carrier battle group headed by the *America* was dispatched to the Caribbean coast of Central America. Later the same month it was replaced by a guided-missile cruiser, a guided-missile destroyer, and other warships. The battleship *Iowa* was one of 25 warships on maneuvers in the Caribbean on Election Day, 1984. In early 1985, the *Iowa* operated in the Gulf of Fonseca, off the Pacific coasts of El Salvador, Honduras, and Nicaragua.

The battleships *New Jersey* (stationed in Long Beach, California), *Iowa* (to be based on Staten Island), *Wisconsin* (to operate out of the Gulf of Mexico), and *Missouri* (to be homeported in San Francisco or Honolulu) are each being recommissioned and outfitted with Tomahawk sea-launched cruise missiles. The Navy plans to deploy 4000 Tomahawks on 14 aircraft carriers and 140 surface ships and submarines, 758 of them a nuclear-armed land-attack version with a 1500-mile range. The remainder of the Tomahawks will be conventional-armed land-attack missiles with a 700-mile range and ship-to-ship missiles with a 300-mile range. The conventional land-attack Tomahawk, according to retired Navy Captain James Bush, is applicable only to Third World intervention and could have been well used during the Vietnam War. In June 1984, the Navy confirmed that it had started deploying the nuclear-armed Tomahawks. According to a report of the Congressional Research Service, 108 of the nuclear-armed Tomahawks have already been delivered to the Navy.[28] At least some of the Tomahawks aboard each battleship and its accompanying fleet will be nuclear-armed. In a crisis, any one of the four battleship fleets could be moved to within striking range of Central America.

The Deadly Connection in Central America

There are three distinct functions that nuclear weapons serve in U.S. policy in Central America.

First, the entire U.S. strategic nuclear arsenal (particularly first-strike weapons) and to a lesser extent the tactical nuclear weapons deployed on ships and aircraft in the Caribbean and off the Pacific coast of Central America help to restrict the extent to which the Soviet Union and Cuba can provide military support to the Sandinistas in Nicaragua or the guerrillas in El Salvador without fear of retaliation. Central America has become the Reagan Administration's testing ground for fighting "Soviet-Cuban adventurism" in the Third World. Nuclear weapons are the ultimate "Big Stick" for enforcing the Monroe Doctrine of non-interference in "our" hemisphere. Naval exercises like Ocean Venture '82, involving the mock invasion of "Brown" with elements of the Rapid Deployment Force and B-52 bombers,[29] are intended to serve as a warning to Cuba and the Soviet Union that the U.S. will not tolerate arms shipments to leftists in Central America or challenges to U.S. war efforts in the region.

Second, nuclear weapons are a motive for continued U.S. conventional intervention in Central America, insofar as that intervention (whether in the form of military aid to the Panamanian government or in the form of efforts to overthrow the Sandinistas in Nicaragua) helps to secure use of the Panama Canal for the U.S. Navy. Interestingly, the Canal today is probably of greater military significance to the U.S. than it was 10 years ago. Pentagon officials acknowledged during the Canal Treaty negotiations in 1976 and 1977 that the Canal was less crucial to the U.S. than it once had been; there are now two navies (Atlantic and Pacific fleets) and the Canal cannot accommodate our largest aircraft carriers. The Canal *can* accommodate the battleships which are part of our "power projection" forces. This is evident from the fact that the *New Jersey* passed through the Canal on its way to shell Lebanon, and the *Iowa*, assigned to the Atlantic fleet, went through the Canal to engage in maneuvers in the Gulf of Fonseca, off Nicaragua's Pacific coast. One of the functions of the new battleship fleets armed with Tomahawk cruise missiles is to replace aircraft carrier battle groups when the carriers are needed elsewhere in times of crisis. Continued U.S.

access to the Panama Canal will be critical to the speed with which those battleships can be moved between the Atlantic and Pacific Oceans.

Third, nuclear weapons have been and continue to be used as a threat in Central America. Since the end of World War II, the United States has threatened to use nuclear weapons at least 22 times.[30] One of the earliest of these involved Central America. In 1954, U.S. Strategic Air Command (SAC) B-52 bombers armed with nuclear weapons were dispatched to Somoza's Nicaragua to back up the CIA-sponsored coup in neighboring Guatemala.

There are three general reasons for, or circumstances in which, the United States has threatened to use nuclear weapons. The first is to obtain concessions from adversaries of the United States— for example, trying to force the Soviets to withdraw their missiles from Cuba as in 1962 and trying (unsuccessfully) to intimidate the Vietnamese into revising the terms of the peace treaty in 1972. Second, the U.S. has given serious consideration to the use of nuclear weapons in a number of "last-resort" situations in which U.S. or allied troops were surrounded, cut off, or in danger of defeat—the Chosin Reservoir in Korea in 1950, Dienbienphu in Vietnam in 1954, the Berlin crisis in 1961, and the battle of Khe Sanh in Vietnam in 1968. Similar situations will become increasingly dangerous as the distinction between nuclear and conventional weapons narrows and as jurisdiction over tactical nuclear weapons falls to officers *lower and lower* on the echelon of military command.

Finally, threats to use nuclear weapons have also been made for the purpose of minimizing public opposition to or gaining support for the seemingly more acceptable (but perhaps equally destructive) use of conventional force. The tactic is to generate support for the "lesser of two evils" by falsely creating an either/or situation. During the Vietnam War, there was "much public discussion, in newspapers and in the Senate, of reports that the White House had been advised of the possible necessity of nuclear weapons to defend marines surrounded at Khe Sanh."[31] In fact, General Westmoreland had secretly instructed his aides to do research on the feasibility of using nuclear weapons. According to Ngo Vinh Long, the Johnson Administration used these threats to persuade the American public and the Congress to support sending additional hundreds of thousands of troops to Vietnam, realizing that the use of tactical nuclear weapons would be so shocking to the public that mere conventional escalation would seem acceptable by comparison.[32]

In a similar manner, in February 1985, Secretary of State George Schultz hinted at the possible need to use American GI's to overthrow the Nicaraguan government if Congress did not approve military aid to the *contras*. Were the U.S. to decide to send actual U.S. combat troops into Central America, one could imagine the Administration publicly discussing the option of using *nuclear* weapons as a subterfuge for mustering public and Congressional support for the otherwise unpopular option of committing U.S. combat forces.

The danger of nuclear weapons being used in Central America will increase precipitously with any major escalation of U.S. military intervention there, particularly a naval blockade of Nicaragua, an invasion of Nicaragua, or the commitment of combat troops to El Salvador. Were U.S. ground troops to become bogged down in protracted combat in El Salvador or Nicaragua, some might be tempted to try to break the stalemate or stave off defeat by resorting to the threat to use or the actual use of tactical nuclear weapons. Were a Cuban or Soviet ship to attempt to run a U.S. blockade of Nicaragua, and should an exchange of fire ensue resulting in damage to or destruction of a U.S. ship, there would be considerable potential for quick escalation to nuclear war.

One of the factors that makes nuclear weapons so dangerous in Central America is that, unlike in Europe or the Middle East, it is possible that the U.S. could use nuclear weapons in the region without fear of provoking a Soviet military response. The Soviets have essentially said that they would not consider their national security jeopardized by U.S. actions in Central America unless Cuba were directly threatened. The potential that very limited use of nuclear weapons would escalate into global nuclear war may, therefore, be significantly less in Central America than in other parts of the world. In this situation, the greatest and only restraining force may be that of American and international public opinion.

The U.S. perception that the Soviets would not risk escalation to global nuclear war over U.S. military actions in Central America is a real problem in the context of the history of U.S. threats to use nuclear weapons. Not all U.S. threats to use nuclear weapons were successful in achieving their goals. Although various threats against the Soviet Union and China—aimed at restricting their activities in other countries—may have achieved the desired results, the numerous threats made both publicly and secretly against the Vietnamese during the Vietnam War were not effective. The difference may be that in the Third World national liberation struggle, where the "enemy" believes it has everything to gain and has nothing to lose, and is fighting on its own territory, intimidation doesn't work. Repeated threats which are not followed by action eventually lose their effect.

The United States has repeatedly threatened to use nuclear weapons but has never acted on its threats, even in cases where the threats did not work. In the past, this was because of the destructive power of nuclear weapons. Henry Kissinger addressed the problem of nuclear impotency ("the more powerful the weapons, the greater becomes the reluctance to use them") in a book entitled *Nuclear Weapons and Foreign Policy*, published in 1957. The solution, said Kissinger, is to adopt a "strategy which makes room for the possibility of fighting limited (nuclear) wars..." This philosophy is behind the development of smaller, more accurate, first-strike and battlefield nuclear weapons, including the newly-deployed Tomahawk sea-launched cruise missiles. These weapons are designed to be used and to convey the threat that they can and will be used.

In my view, one of the dangers in Central America is that the U.S. may use nuclear weapons in part as a demonstration of will in order to restore credibility to its threats to use nuclear weapons elsewhere in the world.

Notes

1. Figures on the number of times the U.S. has intervened in Central America and the Caribbean range as high as 45. The figure used here is cited in the American Friends Service Committee's "A War By Any Other Name: A Statement on the United States and Central America" (September, 1984), p. 4.
2. The ideas in this paragraph are drawn from Tom Nusbaumer's Introduction to "Central America in Perspective," *Intervention*, Spring, 1984, p. 8.
3. Cited in Marcus Raskin, "Foreign Policy in the Backyard," *Intervention*, Spring, 1984, p. 18.
4. Phil Berryman, "The Central America War," *The Deadly Connection: Nuclear War and U.S. Intervention* (AFSC: 1983), p. 82.
5. Quoted in *Intervention*, Spring, 1984, p. 9.
6. From Phillip Berryman's "The Kissinger Commission Report: A Critique" (AFSC: January, 1984), cited in the Newsletter of the Inter-Church Committee on Human Rights in Latin America, Spring, 1984, p. 7.
7. AFSC, "The Best Kept Secret of 1984—The U.S. Invasion of Latin America," January, 1985, p. 2.
8. Ibid.
9. Janet Shenk, "Proxy President," *The Nation*, March 2, 1985, p. 229.

10. Cited in Duane Shank's article "Central America" in *Freeze Focus*, June, 1984, p. 9.
11. Center for Defense Information, *The Defense Monitor*, Vol. XIII, No. 3, 1984, p. 7.
12. Ibid., pp. 7 and 9.
13. Ibid., p. 13.
14. Inter-Religious Task Force on Central America, *Update Central America*, February, 1985, p. 4.
15. Cited in "Nicaragua-Baiting," *The Nation*, November 24, 1984, p. 540.
16. AFSC, "The Best Kept Secret," p. 2.
17. Mary Day Kent and Eva Gold, "The U.S. Army School of the Americas" (NARMIC/AFSC: May, 1984), p. 1.
18. Eva Gold and Mary Day Kent, "A View of the U.S. Role in the Militarization of Central America" (NARMIC/AFSC: January, 1984), p. 4.
19. William M. Arkin, "The Treaty of Tlatelolco, Nuclear Weapons and Puerto Rico," August 13, 1984, p. 2.
20. Chris Vaughan, "Key West Riding High Again on Wave of Navy Prosperity," Providence *Sunday Journal*, February 24, 1985.
21. Arkin, "Treaty of Tlatelolco," p. 3.
22. Ibid., p. 2.
23. Mobilization for Survival, "Nuclear Weapons and Intervention in Central America and the Caribbean," April, 1984.
24. Arkin, "Treaty of Tlatelolco," p. 3.
25. Mobilization for Survival, "Nuclear Weapons and Intervention," p. 3.
26. NARMIC, "The Central American War: A Guide to the U.S. Military Buildup" revised April, 1983, p. 7.
27. Michael T. Klare, "Testing Out Haig's New War Policy," *The Nation*, June 19, 1982, pp. 750-751.
28. Pacific Campaign Against Sea-Launched Cruise Missiles, "Status Report 1," November 1, 1984, p. 3.
29. Use of B-52s is cited in Michael T. Klare, "Testing Out Haig's Policy," p. 750.
30. Barry M. Blechman and Stephen S. Kaplan, *Force Without War: U.S. Armed Forces as a Political Instrument* (Washington, D.C.: The Brookings Institution, 1978), memoirs of past presidents and their cabinet officials, *Time* magazine, and the daily press.
31. Cited in Daniel Ellsberg, "Call to Mutiny," *The Deadly Connection: Nuclear War and U.S. Intervention* (AFSC: 1983), p. 21.
32. Ngo Vinh Long, "Vietnam: Conventional War and the Use of Nuclear Threats," *The Deadly Connection: Nuclear War and U.S. Intervention* (AFSC: 1983), p. 53.

Charito Planas

The Deadly Connection:
A View from
the Philippines

Many Americans do not know that the Philippines are the most important former colony of the United States. They are not aware that, as Boone Schirmer has observed, the Philippine-American War robbed Filipino revolutionaries of victory against Spanish colonialism. That first U.S. military intervention in the Philippines was in many ways a model for the many U.S. interventions that followed, including those that are being planned and acted out today in El Salvador. Many Americans do not realize that, as Dr. Stephen Shalom has said, the Philippines was a testing ground for the economic, political, and military policies of U.S. imperialism in the Third World.[1]

Let me briefly refer to our history. It is a history of occupation, colonization, and domination by foreign powers. We were under Spain for more than 300 years, colonized by the United States of America for 48 years, and occupied by the Japanese for three and one half years.

The Spaniards claimed that when they came to our country they discovered us. But before they came we had our own culture; we were trading with our neighboring countries. We even had our own laws. When the Americans came, it was in the name of God, to civilize us, to Christianize us, and to educate us. But the real reason was given by your own Massachusetts Senator, Henry Cabot Lodge, when he urged President McKinley to retain us as a colony of the United States because we were a good source of cheap labor. William Howard Taft, first U.S. governor of the Philippines, asked Washington to hold the Philippines as a colony in order to guarantee a stable climate for U.S. investment in our country.

The Spanish said they liberated us from the influence of the devil, and when the Americans came, they said they liberated us from Spanish oppression. When the Japanese invaded us, they said we were liberated from U.S. imperialism. When the U.S. came back to the Philippines, they said we were liberated from Japanese fascism.

During World War II, we fought side by side with the Americans. (Actually, we fought in front of the Americans, as has always been the case.) Then we were granted our independence. Do you know on what date we were granted our independence? It was July 4, 1946.

But before we were granted independence, we had to meet two conditions. We had to extend equal rights to the Americans in the exploitation of our natural resources. We also had to allow the presence of U.S. military bases in the Philippines for 99 years from 1946. Upon acceptance of these conditions, we became subservient to U.S. influence.

Later on, a group of Filipino nationalists, organized in a movement called the Hukbalahap, led a second war of resistance (the first was the Philippine-American War). This second war took place in the mid '50's, and this time the nationalists were again defeated. They were defeated not by U.S. troops, but by Philippine government troops aided and armed by the U.S. government, organized and led by U.S. advisors of the Joint U.S. Military Advisory Group or JUSMAG.

This was the United States' first indirect military intervention in the Philippines. It was at this time also that the C.I.A. succeeded in securing the election of Ramon Magsaysay as president of the Philippines. Magsaysay openly made the CIA chief, Colonel Edward Lansdale, his advisor after the election. Following his success in the Philippines, Colonel Lansdale was sent to Vietnam, where of course he failed.

The second indirect military intervention in the Philippines by the United States took place in 1972, when Marcos declared martial law and established one-man rule. The United States used to take pride in the Philippines as a showcase of democracy. But when our freedom was denied by the declaration of martial law, there was no protest by the U.S. government, nor did it impose sanctions as it did in Poland. What took place instead was a vast increase in U.S. military aid to the Marcos government.

What are the signs today of large-scale U.S. intervention in the Philippines? For one thing: increased military aid. I would like to point especially to the international military education training (IMEP) which was increased from $700,000 to 1.3 million dollars

in the Philippines. Training under this program has included
techniques of torture uniformly used by Third World military
personnel. Another sign is the emergence of standard counter-
insurgency tactics used by the U.S. in Vietnam like "strategic
hamlets" and "free fire zones." As in El Salvador and other U.S.-
backed regimes in Latin America, we now have paramilitary terror
groups, massacres, summary executions and disappearances.
Another sign is the participation of U.S. marines in military
repression outside U.S. bases in the Philippines. On September
29, 1981, the U.S. marines appeared in support of Philippine
marines who were terrorizing people protesting against a nuclear
power plant being built by Westinghouse in Bataan. Still another
example: U.S. war exercises. The world is aware of the Rapid
Deployment Forces' exercises that took place in Egypt. But do
you know that there have been annual joint military exercises in
the Philippines from 1980 to the present, where thousands of U.S.
marines have participated with Philippine marines in a mock war?
We have seen the string of visits by U.S. dignitaries with their
foreboding statements. There was for instance Vice President
Bush, who went to the Philippines to visit Marcos not only to
pat him on the back but to embrace him and say, "We admire
you for your adherence to democratic principles and democratic
processes." Bush was followed first by a visit from then Secretary
of State Haig, and second, by Defense Secretary Weinberger, who
assured Marcos that the U.S. would remain unswerving in its
promise to help the Philippines militarily, economically, and in
every other way.

In a policy statement made public in spring 1985 the U.S. State
Department said, "The U.S. does not want to remove Marcos
from power to destabilize the government of the Philippines."
The Pentagon says that we have no external enemies, yet our
armed forces have been increased from 60,000 to 300,000, all
armed by the U.S. government. Against whom? Against Filipinos
whose only sin is to love their country. All this can be better
understood if we remember that when Deputy Secretary of
Defense Carlucci came to the Philippines he agreed with Marcos'
chief of staff, General Ver, that internal control of subversives
and regional global defense capabilities were related.

President Reagan has asked Congress to increase U.S. military
aid to Marcos in 1986 by 150%, "to assist in defeating the ongoing
insurgency." Why is there this "ongoing insurgency"? Because
of the unending stream of injustices that have taken place for
centuries. As Bishop Lebayen of Quezon Province writes, "To
understand revolution is to examine why the poor, most cautious,

law-abiding peasants turn to violence. Imagine the injustice it takes to convert these people into guerrillas willing to take on a professional army in a struggle that must risk the little that they have and their families, with all its consequences!" Cardinal Sin, the leader of the Philippine Catholic church which claims the adherence of 85% of the people, explains the fundamental mistake of U.S. policy toward the Philippines in this way. "We believe that your government's present policies are leading to a misdefinition of our real problems. It is shifting the focus away from the economic and political injustices that are the real cause of our problems and injecting the international dimensions of the U.S.-Soviet conflict into our domestic situation."

The policymakers of the United States have never learned from past mistakes. In China they supported Chiang Kai Shek with all the arms and money that he needed, and he lost. In the Vietnam War, the U.S. experimented with its latest weaponry and spent billions of dollars; it cost tens of thousands of American lives. They had to give up. In Iran, the United States provided the Shah with the most sophisticated weaponry, and he didn't even have the chance to use it. What is the lesson to be learned that the U.S. government refuses to learn? That people's power is stronger than military hardware. Because it refuses to accept the lesson of people's power, it depends on military might and on bases outside the United States. It engages in the madness of the nuclear arms race, so that a major part of its wealth is being used to discover the latest weaponry, to kill as many people in the shortest time possible. This is happening at a time when so many people are hungry. As Sister Christine Tan of the Philippines has said, the wealth of the earth is being utilized not that mankind may be more humane but that mankind may be annihilated.

U.S. military bases in the Philippines today are instruments of U.S. interventionist policy, and as such bring the Filipino people under the shadow of nuclear holocaust. Maud Easter mentioned the fear of the Koreans that nuclear war will take place, and that it will start on the Korean peninsula because of the many nuclear weapons that the U.S. has deployed in South Korea. We, too, have U.S. nuclear weapons deployed on Philippine bases. We have strong reasons for our fears.

The Pentagon has projected the possibility of limited nuclear war for three areas in the world: Europe, the Korean peninsula, and the Mideast. The U.S. bases in the Philippines provide a means to project limited nuclear war to the Mideast and the Korean peninsula, two of these three areas. There is a great probability that such limited nuclear war would escalate to full-fledged nuclear war between the United States and Soviet Russia. In this case the peoples of both the Philippines and the United States would be the objects of nuclear retaliation. The policy of limited nuclear war in the Mideast or Korea undermines the security of both our countries. If one believes this and is opposed to such policies, then one must oppose the concrete means by which such policies are made possible. U.S. bases and nuclear installations in the Philippines help make a policy of limited war in the Mideast and Korea possible. Therefore, they must be opposed.

The Arkin report of February 1985 that the U.S. government plans to deploy nuclear bombs to the Philippines without consulting the Philippine government has caused a storm of public protest in my country, with cries for an investigation going up even in the Marcos-controlled legislative assembly. In the wake of the Arkin exposure, former Vice President Emmanuel Pelaez, who was a member of the Philippine panel that negotiated the bases agreement in 1979, has publicly declared that the agreement that expires in 1991 "should not be renewed." I urge you to include in your efforts not only the freezing of the production, testing and deployment of nuclear arms, but also opposition to the maintenance of U.S. military bases outside this country. As a Filipino, as an Asian, as a member of a Pacific nation, I appeal to you. I urge you to give serious consideration to the demand of removing U.S. nuclear weapons and installations from the Philippines, and finally to dismantle U.S. bases in the Philippines.

The continuity of purpose between a U.S. colonial government in the Philippines yesterday and the U.S.-backed Marcos dictatorship today is confronted by the struggle of the Filipino people to win national freedom and democracy. The people of the Philippines are aware that their own determined struggle for national liberation coupled with the militant solidarity and support of all progressive people and countries in the world can oppose, frustrate, and defeat U.S. intervention and nuclear war.

Notes

1. *The United States and the Philippines: A Study of Neo-Colonialism*, Institute for Study of Human Issues, Philadelphia, PA, 1981.

Talk given at the Deadly Connection conference, 4 December 1982. It has been updated by the author.

Maude Easter

Korea: Still a Nuclear Trigger

Where do we picture a nuclear war beginning? In Europe? In the Middle East? Well, Koreans would say: "Look at our part of the world: a tense, divided and overarmed peninsula, with more than 150 American nuclear weapons already based on our soil."

The Koreans would be correct. There is a serious threat of radiation devastating their homes. By accident of geography, the Korean peninsula has been caught between its immediate and powerful neighbors—the Soviet Union, China and Japan—for centuries, and for the past 100 years has had to deal with American intervention as well. In addition to the constant danger that an accident or a small dispute between North and South Korea could escalate into a conflict involving on-the-site American nuclear weapons, Koreans also fear they may be used by the big powers as guinea pigs to try out tactical nuclear warfare.

The Korean peninsula was divided by American and Soviet military occupation at the end of World War II. Despite a prior history of over 1200 years as one country, the tensions of the continuing Cold War have kept North and South Korea from any progress toward much longed for reunification. The U.S. has been deeply involved in South Korea and has supported a series of unpopular, military-based governments. The U.S. does not recognize North Korea and refuses direct dialogue to reduce tensions. When we speak of U.S. intervention in Korea, therefore, we mean intervention in the South, but all Koreans, North and South, have suffered the effects of the prolonged hostilities.

The division of the peninsula, about the size of the states of Pennsylvania and Indiana, has been a major factor in the militarization of both North and South Korean societies. The sixth and seventh largest armies in the world face each other along a narrow strip of land. There are over 600,000 persons under arms on each side. Because the forces of North and South are basically balanced, not counting the presence of foreign American troops in the South, the likelihood of planned invasion by either side is not great. However, any of the constant border incidents could mushroom into a major confrontation, rapidly involving other countries.

Koreans have good reason to fear that nuclear weapons might be tried out on their territory. As far back as 1953, American military leaders and even some members of Congress publicly urged that limited or tactical nuclear weapons be used in the Korean War. During the Korean War General MacArthur requested authorization to use the bomb and Eisenhower called for its use a few days after the war began.[1] In the summer of 1975, during the frightening roar of bomb-shaking with which the Pentagon tried to cover its defeat in Indochina, the Secretary of Defense again threatened tactical nuclear warfare in Korea.[2]

The U.S. has based approximately 150 nuclear arms in South Korea, some very close to the volatile demilitarized zone which separates the North and South. Submarines carrying Polaris missiles regularly dock at the South Korean port of Chinhae, and cruise missiles are scheduled to be deployed with the Seventh Fleet. Lance surface-to-surface missiles, specially designed to carry nuclear warheads, are stationed with U.S. troops. The Pentagon has announced plans to deploy the neutron bomb in Northeast Asia for use against tanks, with the only possible target North Korean forces.

Koreans fear that racist attitudes in the U.S. might lower the barrier to nuclear use in Korea. One woman commented to me, "Hiroshima has made us wonder whether the U.S. values Asian lives as much as those of Westerners."

Koreans in the South also must fear their own government will follow the example set by the United States. The U.S. Congressional Fraser Commission revealed that, despite having signed the Nuclear Non-Proliferation Treaty, South Korea in the early 1970's decided to build its own nuclear weapons. So far the Seoul (South Korean) government has been frustrated in obtaining a reprocessing plant, but continues negotiating with France for one. A study by the Ford Foundation revealed that South Korea could already be producing over 35 crude bombs a year from existing nuclear power waste. Even the U.S. CIA has cited South Korea as a county "most likely and able to proliferate."

In the fall of 1981 the South Korean government increased fears that South Korea already has the bomb by repeatedly threatening to reduce North Korea "to ashes."

South Korea, with great encouragement from the American nuclear industry and from the U.S. government, has embarked on the most ambitious nuclear power program in the world. Seoul plans to build 15 plants by the year 2000. Three plants are already functioning and six others are under construction. Six nuclear reactors have been sold by Westinghouse, with 85% funding provided by the U.S. tax-supported Export-Import Bank. Westinghouse is delighted for this assistance in remaining in the nuclear business. For Koreans, however, nuclear wastes have clearly become a focus of concern. With no long range disposal site planned, some have already been reported leaking into the ocean, and the question of their diversion for weapons development remains the most threatening of all.

On the Korean peninsula nuclear activity appears to be entirely on the southern side of the border. Even the most hostile observers of North Korea, including the CIA's of both the South and the U.S., do not allege nuclear weapons development in the North. The North has no nuclear power program and only one small research reactor. There are neither foreign troops nor foreign nuclear arms in the North. North Korea has called repeatedly for the establishment of a nuclear free zone in Northeast Asia. The Korean peninsula is one case where U.S. nuclear weapons are deployed against a clearly non-nuclear enemy.

Koreans know the destruction of nuclear war. Over 100,000 Koreans were in Hiroshima and Nagasaki when the atomic bomb fell, mainly working as forced labor in the Japanese munitions factories. Fifty thousand Koreans died from the blast or its immediate aftereffects. Twenty thousand survivors have returned to South Korea, most in poor health, impoverished and ostracized. The Association of Atomic Bomb Sufferers in South Korea has taken the great risk of calling publicly for the total abolition of all nuclear weapons. They say, "Never again."

So, we as Americans must face the possibility of the U.S.'s using Koreans again as nuclear guinea pigs, for the cruise missile or the neutron bomb, to try out tactical nuclear warfare, or as hostages to their own government's ill-advised nuclear plans. In addition, however, we must also face what rattling nuclear swords over the heads of Koreans has already meant for their lives.

Nuclear weapons are not simply a superpower game to frighten us into unlimited military spending; they have also been used by the U.S. to excuse and protect American intervention in many Third World countries.

What is the nature of this American intervention in Korea? As mentioned above, it is in South Korea that the U.S. has found a military and economic haven. North Korea has no foreign troops on its soil and has little foreign corporate investment. North Korea and South Korea are on opposite ends of the development spectrum. The South, advised by the U.S. and multilateral institutions such as the IMF and the World Bank, has developed an export-led economy, highly dependent on the U.S. and Japan. The North has trade with about eighty countries, but its goal has been economic self-sufficiency, and it has structured its economy to take advantage of its own raw materials. According to a study done by the U.S. CIA in 1978, the two economies are equivalently industrialized. However, the distribution of benefits is more level in the North than in the South. Soviet involvement in the North was extensive in the 1940's and the first half of the 1950's. It was greatly reduced as the Sino-Soviet split emerged, though North Korea continues to receive aid from the Soviet Union. North Korea is now closer diplomatically to China than to the Soviet Union. It criticized the Vietnamese invasion of Kampuchea and refused to support the Soviet invasion of Afghanistan. The North has received only a third as much military hardware from the Soviet Union and China combined as the U.S. has supplied to South Korea.

So, now let us examine the area where the U.S. is involved—specifically the dynamics of U.S. military intervention in South Korea. American military commanders told the Armed Services Committee that they like Korea because "no one is trying to raise the rent" and because they believe "Korea represents the best possible training ground in the world for U.S. ground combat troops with...a real live adversary north of the DMZ." The largest American military exercises in the world are held each spring in South Korea. In a holdover from the Korean War, the U.S. Commanding General is also in charge of almost all South Korean troops, which is seen as an affront by many sensitive Koreans.

The U.S. has provided over $10 billion in military aid to South Korea, more than to any other country except Vietnam. South Korea has been a magnificent market for arms manufacturers, including General Dynamics, Northrup, Litton, McDonald Douglas and Hughes Aircraft. As with many Third World countries, U.S. military aid at first provided free arms until dependency was established on American technology, and then shifted to subsidized sales, for which the Korean people will be paying for generations.

Among U.S. provisions have been equipment for domestic repression. Koreans have not forgotten that during the latest military coup, in 1980, the tanks, tear gas, and helicopters used

to control resistance all said "made in the USA." While I was
in Asia, the U.S. approved sales of interrogation equipment to
the Korean government, then as now under international criticism
for torture of political prisoners. Only public outcry recently
stopped the Reagan Administration from shipping 500 electric
shock batons usable for crowd control or torture. The result of
this lavish American arming and training of the South Korean
military has been predictable. No other institution in the society
has received so much nurturance from the outside. No other
institution can wield so much power. Many in the democratic
movement in South Korea have been imprisoned, forced
underground, and not surprisingly, are becoming increasingly
angry at the U.S.

American intervention has been economic as well.
Approximately 130 U.S.-owned multinational corporations have
direct investment in South Korea. General Motors, Motorola,
Radio Shack, and Cargill are among those which have set up
factories. The South Korean government allows them to pay wages
roughly one-tenth what they would pay American workers for the
same job.

Over 2000 U.S.-owned corporations do business in South
Korea. For example, Sperry Rand computers process the pass
cards which all must carry. Bechtel is constructing most of the
nuclear power plants; Jantzen contracts for clothes from
sweatshop garment factories; Nike and Adidas buy millions of
running shoes from the Kukje Corporation, notorious for its 1982
campaign of intimidation and violence against South Korean's
last remaining democratically elected trade union.

Foreign corporations in South Korea are looking for what they
call "a good business climate." As on the Mexican border, as
in the Philippines and in Thailand, they benefit from a harshly
controlled labor movement. In South Korea strikes are banned.
In industrial zones set up specially for foreign investors, even
government-controlled unions are forbidden. All foreign investors
enjoy a five year tax holiday. Pollution rules are notable for their
non-enforcement.

As is often the case, there is a differential impact of this
economic intervention on men and women. Obviously, all have
suffered from a lack of political and economic control over their
future, but women have been especially harshly affected. In light
industries like textiles and electronics, which have dominated
South Korean exports, women make up 80-90% of the workforce.
They are young, averaging 19 years old, and are horribly
underpaid. Lint in the air, chemical fumes and dangerous

machinery create lifelong medical problems for the textile workers. Seventy percent of those employed at an American-owned electronics factory in Seoul had suffered vision damage at the end of one year, from the intense, tiny microscopic work involved in supplying America's "computer revolution." A woman at the Radio Shack factory commented to me, "Why should I ruin my eyes to make this car radio, when my family can't afford a car, let alone a car radio?" A good question. These women are the human side of what the U.S. government touts as South Korea's "economic miracle."

Women also bear the burden of raising children even more exclusively than in this country. They know the pain of too expensive medical care, of exorbitant school fees, and of virtually non-existent childcare. In fact, South Korea has one of the lowest social service budgets in the world. If we want to see what the U.S. might be like—if Reagan fulfilled his dream of unleashing the corporations, shifting even more massive resources to the military, and making invisible the safety net of social services— then let us look at South Korea.

Women in Korea have also been the most vulnerable to American cultural intervention. Coke, General Foods and Nestle target them as consumers with pressure to be "modern and western." The U.S. military plays a special role, licensing over 10,000 prostitutes a year around American military bases. The tourist industry, including hotels operated by Hyatt, Hilton and Regency, also encourages the sale of women's bodies by the swimming pools and in the hotel lobbies. Prostitution is a great disgrace in Korean culture and undertaken only by a woman in financial desperation. Government reports indicate that 75% of workers in South Korea earn less than the subsistence salary needed to support an average family. Money for food and shelter is hard to find.

Is there a possibility of ending U.S. intervention in South Korea, of giving Koreans a chance to shape their own economic and political future? Could Northeast Asia become a nuclear free zone?

Koreans are struggling under extremely repressive conditions to get back control of their own country. However, U.S. nuclear policy and U.S. intervention is something over which we have more control than they. Our voices need to be stronger than those of the arms contractors, the nuclear power merchants, and the computer chip makers. Those of us who know the dreadful details of U.S. intervention must work together with those who understand the horrors of the U.S. nuclear arsenal. And we all need to work closely with people from Korea and other Third World countries, because they know from direct experience that nuclear weapons, an unleashed Pentagon, and runaway corporations are all part of the same problem.

Notes

1. Bruce Cumings, *Nation*, April 7, 1984.
2. *New York Times*, June 21, 1975.

Talk given at the Deadly Connection Conference, 4 December 1982.

Ngo Vinh Long

Vietnam: Conventional War and the Use of Nuclear Threats

Since we do not have too much time, I will neither deal with Southeast Asia in general nor Indochina in particular, although developments there since 1975 have been very disturbing. The military, economic and diplomatic pressures exerted by the United States and China on the Indochinese states, for example, are threatening to engulf the region in another war. Neither do I have time to explain to you what American military aid to the ASEAN countries, which has almost quadrupled since the end of the Vietnam War, is doing to those countries individually and to the region as a whole.

I would like very much, however, to relate the nuclear issue with American intervention in the Third World. Basically, I have three very brief statements to make. First of all, the United States government has considered the use of nuclear weapons or has threatened to use nuclear weapons against Third World countries only in the "worst-case" situation, i.e., after America has failed to establish its domination over a certain Third World country by other means. Second, the threat of using nuclear weapons against Third World countries even in this "worst-case" situation has been made largely for domestic American consumption; that is, to justify lesser means of destruction and intervention. And third, although nuclear weapons are not designed to be used against Third World countries, American policymakers may be forced to use nuclear weapons to drive home the point that the U.S. would not tolerate revolutionary take-over. This is because in the post-Vietnam era, introducing American ground forces into foreign lands to keep the dominoes from falling has become much more difficult.

Let me elaborate on my first two points by taking them together since they are closely connected. You may remember that the first, vague threat of using nuclear weapons in Asia was during the Korean War. At that time, someone, possibly General MacArthur, talked of considering using 40 or so "stink" bombs (nuclear bombs) to seal the border of China and North Korea should the Chinese dare to cross the Yalu River. I don't think these threats were ever conveyed directly or indirectly to the Chinese. Rather, as I said, they were made for domestic American consumption so as to get the American public and American politicians to support conventional military intervention.

The next time the United States considered nuclear weapons in East Asia was during the battle of Dienbienphu in 1954 when the French forces were about to be overrun. Having raised the specter of nuclear disaster over Indochina, however, the United States then used other means to subvert the Indochinese societies and revolutions. Another time, threats of using tactical nuclear weapons in Vietnam were made during the battle of Khe-sanh in 1965. But the Johnson Administration used these threats to get the American people and the Congress to support the introduction of several hundred thousand additional American troops and several thousand airplanes to Vietnam instead. The American policymakers realized that they could inflict much more destruction on Vietnam by "conventional" means such as the B-52s and the ground troops than a few tactical nuclear bombs which, while not as damaging physically, might be so shocking to the American and world public opinion that it would be counter-productive.

The third time the Vietnamese were threatened with nuclear weapons was in 1972, after Nixon and Kissinger decided to renege on the draft peace agreement which Kissinger had initialed in September of that year. The threats were supposedly conveyed to Vietnam privately through Pakistan and China. But they were already leaked to the press before that. Again, Washington never made good on that threat. Instead, the American policymakers tried to show that they were restrained by ordering the Christmas bombing of North Vietnam with B-52s and other bombers. Now, B-52s typically flew in formations of 4, 8 or 16 airplanes per mission. Each B-52 carried enough bombs to destroy an area ½ mile in width and a mile and a half in length. Since there was very little overlapping, the B-52s could destroy much more than the nuclear bomb used over Hiroshima with much less political fall-out.

In fact, the destructiveness of conventional means cannot be overemphasized. During 1979 and 1980 when I travelled around Vietnam, I was really flabbergasted by the destruction inflicted on that society. The physical destruction is what comes to your mind first because, after all, the United States had expended an amount of high explosives that was equal to five times the total tonnage of bombs dropped on all fronts during the Second World War on that tiny country the size of Massachusetts, Connecticut and Rhode Island put together. But to many foreign visitors to Vietnam, even the physical destruction is not readily noticeable because vegetation comes back to a certain extent as a result of the favorable tropical climate. You have to know what used to be there before to see the difference. From 1959 to late 1962 I was a military mapmaker for the American Military Attache in Vietnam and as a result, I travelled throughout the southern part of Vietnam and parts of Laos and Cambodia. In 1979 and 1980 when I travelled around Vietnam, I was shocked because in places where there used to be rain forest down to almost the borders of the villages, now you can see for miles and miles in front of you. In fact, in some provinces in the central region of Vietnam, there is more scrap metal on the ground than there is vegetation. In the district of Ben Hai, which is the district that straddled the former DMZ, in some villages there are about 400 pounds of scrap metal per square yard. It is literally metal ground. But what is much more heart-rending is to see the tens of thousands of people who are crippled, who have but one leg, one arm, one eye, for example, and who are carrying with them until their dying days the wounds of the Vietnam War. When you have met these people and talked with them, you realize that those who died, like the victims of Hiroshima, for example, might have been luckier than they.

Even much less noticeable to the untrained eyes are the psychological wounds and cultural destruction caused by the war and the American economic and cultural penetration. To cite but only one superficial example: During the war years the United States poured so many American cigarettes into Vietnam that they became a symbol of class and progress. And so, even now as you travel around in the urban areas of the southern part of Vietnam, where over 60 percent of the peasant population became "urbanized" during the war years, you would see many people who are just sitting pretty, chain-smoking American cigarettes. Each pack of American cigarettes cost about 25 dong, or about 50 kilograms of subsidized rice, or the monthly salary of a worker.

Yet you have thousands of people in Vietnam right now, some of them cadres even, who are literally blowing the economy of Vietnam up in smoke. And if you cannot support this expensive habit, then your pipe-dream is to leave Vietnam and make it to America, the land of milk and honey and cigarettes and Coke. I don't mean to be flippant. Rather, I want to suggest that the threats of American economic and cultural penetration are very real to Third World people.

This brings me to my third and final statement. At the present time, the threats of American intervention by conventional means (military aid to American client regimes, police training, pacification efforts, etc.) and economic and cultural penetration are very real to many Third World people—much more real than the threats of nuclear weapons. Moreover, Third World people have learned from the examples of the Korean and Vietnam Wars that the threats of nuclear weapons did not work, basically because the Chinese and Vietnamese called America's bluff every time, and because the United States meant those threats for domestic American consumption.

But what if the present American intervention provoked Third World peoples to organize and fight back as they already have in Nicaragua and El Salvador and suddenly confront the United States with 6 or 7 Vietnams at the same time? Will the United States then be able to contain the revolutionary forces by the "conventional" means or will the United States be able to introduce American troops to maintain its client regime? In other words, what will the United States do when it is faced by half a dozen "worst-case" situations at the same time? I think that in the post-Vietnam era, when the introduction of American ground forces into foreign lands to protect American interests and to teach the natives a lesson has proved to be counter-productive, if not to say disastrous, the use of nuclear weapons to make an example out of a certain Third World country may become a reality. So the irony here is that while nuclear weapons are made to be used primarily in the First World, the possibility of having them used against Third World countries becomes ever greater with continued American intervention and penetration into Third World countries. Therefore, if we get side-tracked by the technological or numerical details of nuclear weapons and focus all our attention on how many nuclear weapons the superpowers can lob at each other and forget the other threats to Third World countries, we may help bring about what we fear most.

Question and Answer Session

Both Randall Forsberg and Daniel Ellsberg have stated and you have reiterated that nuclear weapons are essentially for use in the Third World, at least that is a lot of it, and that they're for use in situations where the countries cannot retaliate with nuclear weapons. Why didn't the U.S. use nuclear weapons in Vietnam when it became clear they could not win it by conventional means?

First of all, I think you have seen a slight and subtle difference in my analysis from that of Ellsberg and Forsberg. Ellsberg, for example, maintains that nuclear weapons have been used against Third World countries in much the same way a cocked gun is placed at someone's head. And that is enough. I am saying that so far threats of nuclear use have been made basically for domestic American consumption to rationalize American intervention by conventional means, if not to say to get public support for the use of conventional means. But I think in the case of Vietnam, at least, that cocking of the gun never worked in the sense Ellsberg talks about. It did not work at Dienbienphu in 1954; it did not work at Khe-sanh in 1965; and it did not work in 1972 when the United States tried to intimidate the Vietnamese into revising the peace agreement. The Vietnamese called the American bluff every time because, in their analysis, the use of tactical nuclear weapons might have speeded the end of the war and might not have caused that much destruction in Vietnam in the long run.

Regarding the second part of your question, let me remind you that during the last days of the Vietnam War President Gerald Ford went to Congress and feverishly demanded that the U.S. be allowed to bring in airplanes to evacuate Americans and Vietnamese. He also pushed for $300 million in supplemental aid. Now, according to press reports at the time, on the very day that Vietnam was liberated, the B-52s were rolled out into the flight lanes in Guam and elsewhere. And even a whole week after Vietnam was already liberated, Gerald Ford continued to go to Congress to ask for the authorization to use the planes as well as the supplemental military aid.

The question is why? The answer is that if they got the authorization they would have come in and bombed the hell out of Vietnam just like President Johnson had wanted to "come out of the saloon shooting." Well, many people in the peace movement fought until the very last day, in fact we fought until a couple of weeks after the war ended, to make sure that the Ford Administration would not give the authorization. But since they did not have an excuse to bomb Vietnam, they used the very same planes to bomb Cambodia after the so-called Mayaguez incident.

I am saying all this because I want to show to you that although the United States wanted to blast Vietnam as it was leaving, it did not want to consider the use of nuclear weapons. That would have been counterproductive. You must give the American policy-makers and Pentagon analysts some credit for their intelligence. And you have a saying in this country: "You don't use an elephant gun to kill a mouse." In their analysis, they had destroyed Vietnam so much over the years in every way and had proven that they had been able to reap a lot of success by conventional means that dropping nuclear weapons in Vietnam would, in a way, rob them of the successes that they had reaped.

After all, the purpose of the Vietnam War was to teach people elsewhere the lesson that the United States had many weapons in its arsenal to destroy revolutionary movements and that revolutions don't pay. You just don't want people to draw the wrong lesson by using nuclear weapons. At least not yet. You want people elsewhere to learn how well-nigh impossible it is for the Vietnamese to rebuild their country after the United States was through with them. And the difficulties faced by the new socialist government could then be used as propaganda against revolutions and socialism. Hence the continued political, economic and military pressures mounted by the United States and its allies against Vietnam since after the fall of Saigon.

Talk given at the Deadly Connection Conference, 4 December 1982.

Kassahun Checole

South Africa
and the Threat
of Second Tier Nations

I have been asked to speak on disarmament and the southern African situation, and I will do so. However, I feel it is impossible to address this topic without at the same time dealing with the problems of security faced by smaller and newly independent nations, and the interventionist role of the superpowers. I will have, therefore, to expand this topic.

First, the disarmament movement cannot be seen in a narrow, regional perspective, nor can the southern African situation be viewed in the same light. There is a need to take a global, or if you like, a world systems perspective in an attempt to understand the tasks and problems and prospects for change and reconstruction in southern Africa.

The interconnection between disarmament, national security, and intervention is real and immediate. There is in the meantime a fourth factor that is as vital and urgent: this is the problem of development and reconstruction. The relationship between economic and social development in the Third World, on the one hand, and global disarmament, on the other hand, is an organic one. Peace and disarmament activists who cannot see this interconnection need to reconsider their single-issue perspective.

I will not argue that all single-issue struggles are wrong, or imply that single-issue struggles as a tactic, or even a strategy, for peace and change is wrong. What I would argue for is that single-issue struggles be informed and tempered by a recognition and an understanding of the crucial interlink between the fragmented single-issue struggles and the global framework.

With the above points in mind, we can now move to a discussion of the disarmament problem as it relates to the Third World and southern Africa in particular. The Third World, unfortunately, is a vague and all-encompassing term, yet it is useful in describing a single, historically constituted continuum between the industrialized West and the non-industrialized nations. But it is not a definitive term, and as such, the Third World constitutes qualitative varieties in degrees of development. One, therefore, cannot talk in the same terms of Brazil and Nicaragua, or South Africa and Mozambique. There is here a real distinction, a real difference not only in mere economic terms, but also in political and social orientation, as well as in the degree and quality of relations with the superpowers.

In talking about the Third World, there is a real need to understand the second tier of nations. Second tier nations are important in the context of the struggle for global disarmament, for the security of nations and peoples, and for the interventionist role of the superpowers. The second tier nations, such as South Africa or Israel, are not only direct and indirect agents of Western economic and strategic considerations, but they also, and more importantly, have a greater relative degree and chance for independent action. It seems to me that these characteristics of the second tier nations are dynamic and an area of meaningful growth.

In this context it is very important that disarmament and peace forces not narrowly focus on the superpowers. Disarming the superpowers will be a beginning, but the more crucial question will be how to temper the aggressively expansionist and expressly oppressive character of the second tier nations. After all, the transfer of arms and armaments technology, such as nuclear arms and nuclear power, to the Third World is not of the same degree and quality in all cases. The Soviet Union, for example, an industrial and military complex in its own right, is deeply involved in arms peddling and in transferring arms to Cuba, but it is not to the same extent nor of the same quality as that transferred by the United States to South Africa.

In any event, I wanted to bring out this explicit danger that we face today, and point out, if I may, that the disarmament movement in the West may begin to view itself in a similar light as the national liberation forces in the Third World. Now some may argue that the struggle for disarmament is long and protracted, that it is strategic, but most important of all, it is global. That is also how the national liberation forces view themselves.

There is one more item that needs to be said in the above vein. Just as aggressively expansionist second tier nations are assured of the vital linkage in trade, in investment, and in the transfer of arms and technology from the superpowers, they are also most assuredly dictatorial and internally repressive. Thus, they not only cause a threat to their neighbors, but also actively violate the human rights of their citizens. It seems in fact that there is a mathematical relation between the transfer of arms and technology to the second tier nations and the degree of violation of human rights. The apartheid policy of South Africa is perhaps the most vivid example of this fact.

It is not invalid to argue, then, that the superpowers, in transferring oppressive arms and technologies to the Third World nations, always quote as their defense the argument of national security. But there is security, and there is security. In the last few years, since the independence of the Portuguese colonies in Angola and Mozambique, the South African state, which clearly represents Western interests, and openly espouses itself as Western/Christian/civilization ideology, has repeatedly attacked and conspired against its neighboring nations. South Africa claims as its defense the threat caused by communist expansion in the regions of its national interests. Although a grossly overextended and grossly false argument, it is nonetheless the argument that has an unqualified support of the major Western powers. In reality, it is the state of South Africa that directly threatens the security of its neighbors. South Africa had actively worked to prevent the forces of decolonization from taking place in southern Africa. It had viewed the former Portuguese colonies and the minority ruled state of Rhodesia as its buffer zone against the alleged threat from the north. Its role in Angola, in Mozambique, and in Zimbabwe, is quite widely known and does not require repetition here. What is important is that today, even after the reality of independence, South Africa refuses to live in peace with its neighbors, and is engaged in various acts of sabotage, conspiracies, and direct intervention.

The reasoning behind South Africa's continuous acts of aggression is not hard to locate. The apartheid state has two, what are called preventive, goals in acting as it does. In the first instance, its goal is to prevent the influencing potential, which the freed development of the majority-ruled peoples in southern Africa could have over its own subjects. The second is to ensure that the region as a whole remains dependent upon and controlled by its economic dominance. These are the two essential objectives mitigating South African aggressiveness towards its neighbors.

There is no way that South Africa can ensure these two preventive goals without heightened repression against its citizens internally, and continued aggression against its neighbors. The maintenance of South Africa's apartheid power, anchored as it is in acts of repression and aggression, can only be ensured by the support—which is economic, military, and political—that it has been able to garner from the NATO alliance and Japan.

Today, intervention is a global policy of the superpowers. In the case of the United States, intervention is often directed through its second tier allies, such as South Africa and Israel. When the American state acts to intervene directly on its own as it did in Vietnam, and today in Central America, it faces the power of the peace movement internally, and has the costly burden of pacifying both internal dissent and the presumed foreign threat. It is very, very vital to understand this. Second tier intervention, however, is a more useful instrument of American foreign policy. It is less costly in the material and political sense and is mainly good for home consumption. Measure, if you will, the degree of opposition and dissent against the American role in the Middle East and southern Africa with that of the role of America in Central America. Apparently, the opposition to American involvement in Central America is more visible, more sustained, and in many ways, reminiscent of the Vietnam war days. Intervention is a ghastly but real and vital policy of the superpowers. But the peace movement cannot simply focus on direct intervention alone, nor can by extension the disarmament movement's focus be placed only on the first tier nations (these are the United States and the Soviet Union). If such are the tactics of struggle for disarmament, we will be erring tremendously. Instead, we have to understand the interconnection between disarmament, security, and intervention. Again, South Africa is a clear example in which the reality of continued support from the West has granted that it now become an important security threat to its neighbors.

Apartheid South Africa is a nuclear power. It is not a small second tier nation. This development of its existence as a nuclear power is tied to the vital support of the West, in particular, and the active collaboration of its equally interventionist and second tier friends, Israel and many South American nations. I could mention Brazil, Argentina, and Chile in particular. The nuclear might of South Africa and its interventionist capacity means that its neighboring countries have to devote more resources to the defense of their peoples. It means that they have to scrap or delay their development or reconstruction plans. And it means they have to have a costly independent alliance with one or the other superpower.

The business of intervention is a good business for arms peddlers. Several nations are now being forced to spend much more money for arms than they would have done for development and reconstruction. But their security needs are real, although not equally real in all cases. The decision of American support in El Salvador and Soviet support in Ethiopia, for example, which forces these nations to spend over forty percent of their national income toward pacification is certainly not a real security need, but it is still good business for the arms peddlers. It is vital, therefore, that the disarmament movement focus on the inter-link between the call for disarmament and the need for development and social justice. A vital factor here is the real security needs for smaller nations, and the interventionist role of the superpowers, direct or indirect. Again, there is no better example of this reality than the present situation in southern Africa of which I will be able to elaborate in our discussion today.

Finally, let me say that the peace and disarmament movement ought to see itself in the same light as national liberation movements. The two movements share the same vision—a better tomorrow and a humane and peaceful environment.

The liberation movements view the struggle as being one of strategic nature, that it is long and protracted and that it is part of the global struggle for social change, peace and development.

There is here an essential link of vision and perspectives, and it ought to be translated into a real and concrete one.

Question and Answer Session

I attended a rally on October 24, 1982 and Johnny Makatini mentioned the Lebanonization of southern Africa and compared the situation in southern Africa with the strategy that South Africa has taken towards that entire area to the strategy that Israel has taken in the Middle East.

Well, it is very hard to speak for Johnny Makatini who is a very good spokesman for the African National Congress, but I can say a few things about what South Africa is doing. Perhaps the term "Lebanonization" might be a very difficult one to utilize here but South Africa's policy in southern Africa is similar to that of Israel in the Middle East.

I will give you one example. In the last few years, South Africa has adopted what is called a "nation building" policy in a country where only 4 million whites rule over 25 million non-white people, of which 18 or 19 million are Black African. What this minority has decided as a policy over the last five years is to form nations within a nation, states within a state. The South African state argues that all tribal entities in South Africa should retain their identity and become tribal states. They have divided the people into a variety of small nations, which are recognized by no one in the world except South Africa—though perhaps Israel will in the future. If you belong to one of these artificially created small states, you have no right to security protection as a citizen of the South African state itself. So what in fact they have done is to have removed people from their own country and given them a false identity, which limits their right to move, their right to participate in the economy of the nation and their rights to education, medical care, etc. I would imagine that this is as close as they come to the policy pursued by Israel in Lebanon.

What I was referring to was forms of intervention in other countries such as Mozambique and Zimbabwe.

In that case I would have a different view. South Africa's intervention in southern Africa as a whole is not a new one. The intervention in Angola, in particular, is important. When the Portuguese were forced to leave Africa, and Angola was about to become independent, South Africa and the United States intervened to create artificially two movements they supported, one is called UNITA and the other is FNLA. One is based in Zaire and the other in South Africa. The creation of these forces led to civil war. What South Africa has done, and very cleverly so, is to maintain that civil war from 1974 till the present. As a result, Angola has not had peace since 1975. It has been fighting a war against underdevelopment, and also a war of defense against aggression.

Similar examples can be found in Mozambique and in Zimbabwe. In Mozambique, South Africa has created what is called the Mozambique National Resistance, which are indigenous people who have been supported and armed by the South African government to destroy and subvert the economic development of Mozambique. In Mozambique, the Resistance does two things: it attacks the railroads which are vital for the country, and it attacks places where research and development are going on. As a result, it stalls the development process. Eventually, it will lead to some form of destabilization of the state, which is in fact the aim of South Africa. South Africa pursues this goal throughout the entire region: active intervention, active processes of destabilization.

Could you tell us more about our country's political and economic interests in South Africa, which lead to the various forms of destabilization. General public feeling here may abhor what is occurring in South Africa and yet feel that we cannot really oppose it since it is they over there who are really doing it. Does one oppose it openly or does one also try to withdraw companies from there as some major church denominations have tried to do? Could you say more about our real interests in South Africa as a second tier nation, as really an extension of us?

There is a very good article in the March 1982 issue of *Multinational Monitor*, and I strongly recommend you look at it. American investment in Africa as a whole is limited to three main countries: South Africa, Libya, and Nigeria. American investment in Africa is mainly concentrated in South Africa. However, the rate of income from investment is not as high as it is in Libya. That is why American investment is still in Libya. But there is one catch. In Libya, the government guarantees the income of the workers; the average annual income of Libyan workers is $16,000, which is about the average rate for American workers. But the average income of a black worker in South Africa is merely $5,470. So the choice of South Africa is not a rate of return choice, but it is actually the labor cost factor which is decisive. American corporations have chosen South Africa over Libya precisely because the labor costs are much cheaper there than they are in Libya.

So if we consider that, we can understand the political issue. The United States is committed to maintaining the power of the South African government. This is a political commitment. In contrast to the Carter Administration, that tried to pressure the South African government, the Reagan Administration is committed to improve relations with South Africa. At this time, South Africa has asked IMF, for the first time, to provide 2.5 billion dollars in aid. The United States government, which controls IMF, decided that South Africa should have this money. This was done in spite of the opposition of many countries.

The Reagan Administration has also liberalized the transfer of technology that can be used for repressive means in South Africa. South African police can now import cattle shockers, which was illegal under the Carter Administration. South Africa can now import the big IBM computer. Furthermore, there is today a stronger relationship between the South African armed forces and the American military. There are more representatives from South Africa coming to the U.S. to visit military installations and to exchange intelligence information. These are real and concrete ways of supporting South Africa.

If the issue were investment, then American capital would go to Libya, because the rate of return is higher there. But the issue is lower labor costs, political expediency and security.

Do you have an operational definition of second tier nation?

Which are precisely the second tier nations?

Second tier nations are in a transition situation. In fact, they are capitalist and in a development process advancing towards industrialization, but still have not fully reached it. They have internal capital accumulation that has taken place somewhat but not fully because it is in collaboration with foreign capital. Most of these states are trying to break away. The greatest growth rate in capitalist investment today happens to be in Brazil.

There is the role that American investors play in South Africa in supporting South African industry, allowing South Africa to devote resources toward building up their own indigenous military forces.

Let me return to the issue of South African nuclear capacity. It is very interesting. South Africa's nuclear development initially started with France and West Germany, with only a little help from the United States. Today, it is almost independent from France and West Germany. France, for all practical purposes, has terminated its relationship with South Africa because there is now a social democrat government that is more socially conscious than were previous governments there. In any case, South Africa's nuclear development was perfected by the help of a three-tier relationship with Israel, Brazil, and Argentina. Jointly, they created a defense commission; they created a treaty in which they resolved to come to the defense of each other if ever attacked. If you remember the Falklands crisis, the greatest support for Argentina came from Israel and South Africa. So the nuclear industry in South Africa is very much linked to that in South America and Israel. Now the United States is no longer in a position to control completely the military behavior of these countries because of their growing degree of autonomy. The second tier countries are all working toward independence from the superpowers. Not all are advancing, however, at the same speed. The Philippines, for example, has actually regressed.

Talk given at the Deadly Connection Conference, 4 December 1982.

The Washington Office on Africa

U.S.-South Africa Nuclear Alliance

We can ascribe our degree of advancement today in large measure to the training and assistance so willingly provided by the United States...

A. I. Roux, President of
the South African Energy Board, 1976

On the night of September 22, 1979, a U.S. Vela satellite detected an intense flash of light in the South Atlantic off the coast of South Africa. Many scientists and intelligence officials suspected a nuclear explosion. The CIA told select members of Congress they strongly suspected that South Africa and Israel were responsible and that a task force of South African warships had conducted secret exercises in the same area as the double flash. Yet, the Carter Administration refused to state that it suspected South Africa of exploding a nuclear bomb.

Two years earlier, the Carter administration had evidence that South Africa was preparing a nuclear test. On August 6, 1977, the Soviet government told the White House that Pretoria was preparing to explode a nuclear device in the Kalahari Desert. U.S., British, French, and West German intelligence confirmed this finding. Pretoria was told not to explode the bomb. On August 23, however, President Carter told the press that he had "assurances" from Pretoria that the structures in the Kalahari were not intended for a nuclear test.

Carter equivocated because these events spotlighted something highly embarrassing to U.S. and European governments: the apartheid bomb had become a reality. Three decades of Western assistance in building South Africa's nuclear program had mushroomed.

South Africa's acquisition of nuclear weapons capability is part of a larger picture of Western political, economic, technological, and military support for white minority rule. This support has strengthened the Pretoria regime as it has instituted increasingly sophisticated forms of repression and control over the Black majority population struggling for its liberation. The Apartheid Bomb marks a new era in Pretoria's military and political dominance in Africa.

History of Collaboration

Western nuclear collaboration with South Africa began in 1945 when Britain and the U.S. were searching for a reliable supplier of raw uranium for their nuclear weapons program. Pretoria was the ideal partner with its vast uranium reserves in South Africa and occupied Namibia, and a cheap labor force of miners under tight, state control. The U.S. and Britain bought up all of South Africa's uranium and totally financed the development of its uranium mining and processing industries. Pretoria benefitted immensely from huge revenues and increased Western reliance on its natural resources, and used these advantages to further its own nuclear program.

Washington was happy to oblige Pretoria's desire for its own nuclear industry. In 1957, as part of Eisenhower's "Atoms for Peace" program, the U.S. and South Africa signed an agreement whereby the U.S. provided South Africa with technical nuclear training, its first research reactor, SAFARI I, and the highly enriched, weapons-grade uranium to fuel it. (SAFARI I was completed in 1965 and the U.S. supplied South Africa weapons-grade uranium for the reactor until 1976.) With this assistance, South Africa was able to build its own research reactor, SAFARI II, by 1967. The two reactors are located at the Pelindaba facility north of Johannesburg. ("Pelindaba" is a Zulu expression meaning "We don't talk about this any more.")

Pretoria continued to expand its nuclear program—including its ability to make nuclear weapons—by building the Valindaba pilot uranium enrichment plant with U.S. and West German assistance in 1975. ("Valindaba" means "We don't talk about this *at all*.") Later that year, Pretoria announced its intention to build a large commercial enrichment facility with the hope of becoming a major enriched uranium exporter in the 1980's.

In 1976, work began near Cape Town on building South Africa's first commercial nuclear power reactor, Koeberg. Built by the French consortium Framatome, Koeberg was due to start up in 1983.

South Africa's Nuclear Weapons Capacity

The Western countries' attempt to justify their collaboration as assistance to South Africa's nuclear energy program. South Africa designed that program to make it energy self-sufficient and able to resist an international oil boycott or other economic sanctions. Yet, "peaceful" nuclear power and nuclear weapons are just two sides of the same coin.

Nuclear reactor technology was originally designed to produce plutonium for nuclear weapons. As nuclear critic Amory Lovins has noted: "(N)uclear reactors are essentially bomb factories that produce electricity as a byproduct." When the Koeberg power reactor is running at full capacity, it will produce enough plutonium to produce an atom bomb every two weeks. Furthermore, the SAFARI I research reactor already runs on weapons grade uranium. While these two reactors are under International Atomic Energy (IAEA) safeguards, many experts have noted the laxness of IAEA oversight, making diversion of materials for nuclear weapons possible if a government so chooses. Furthermore, South Africa has refused to sign the Nuclear Non-Proliferation Treaty or to submit its enrichment plant to any safeguards. Pretoria has already indicated Valindaba can enrich uranium to weapons-grade. In this context, there can be no *peaceful* nuclear collaboration with South Africa.

Why the Bomb?

South Africa hopes to gain great political and military benefits by simply possessing nuclear weapons and developing an extensive nuclear industry. Pretoria realized early on that its survival could be prolonged if it could create a greater Western dependence on its raw uranium supply and other natural resources. In addition, by *threatening* use of the bomb, Pretoria could effectively block international efforts to impose sanctions on it for its racist policies. Its politics of intimidation could also stonewall African support for the liberation struggle to eliminate apartheid.

South Africa has always seen itself on the frontline defending the West against communism, a view that most U.S. administrations have shared. If Western assistance continues, South Africa could develop and *use* tactical nuclear weapons as part of its "total strategy" to retain power. Pretoria might use such weapons on a neighboring country hoping to destabilize it or weaken the liberation movements struggling for freedom. Or Pretoria might use the bomb on South African territory if it felt its hold on power was on the verge of collapse. As one Johannesburg lawyer told the *New York Times* in 1977: "As far as the Afrikaners are concerned, a South Africa that is not governed by them is not worth preserving."

Reagan and the Apartheid Bomb

Despite this overwhelming threat to the survival of the world, the Reagan Administration has *increased* nuclear assistance to South Africa by allowing exports of computers and other high technology goods to Pretoria's nuclear program. It has also negotiated with South Africa for the resumption of enriched uranium supplies, cut off when Congress passed the Nuclear Non-Proliferation Act in 1978, and allowed Pretoria to acquire needed enriched uranium from Europe through two U.S. brokering companies for its Koeberg reactor. This assistance is part of Reagan's "constructive engagement" policy designed to befriend Pretoria and provide it with increased economic, political, and military aid. Reagan has increased this nuclear assistance at the expense of deteriorating relations with Black Africa, which has repeatedly condemned the cozy relationship between Washington and Pretoria. The administration is not naive about Pretoria's nuclear weapons capability and how these exports strengthen it: in October 1982, a State Department spokesman concurred that South Africa has, or is "very close" to having the bomb, and that Pretoria wants U.S. technology to assist it further. Just as the Reagan Administration spent billions of dollars increasing its nuclear arsenal at the expense of domestic social programs, so it openly supports the apartheid regime building its own nuclear arsenal at the expense of its Black majority, the African continent, and, perhaps, the whole world.

Published with the permission of the Washington Office on Africa

THE DEADLY CONNECTION

Part VI
Toward Strategies
for Survival

Melinda Fine
Jennifer Leaning
Everett Mendelsohn
Pam Solo

The Future in our Hands: A Call to Common Security

The major assault by the Reagan Administration calling for massive increases in nuclear weapons, legitimization of military intervention, extending the arms race into space, further distorting our domestic economy, and adding increased pressure on the economies of the Third World demands an urgent response. Recognizing the interdependence of the world community, we call for a redefinition of security in the belief that no nation can achieve security in isolation. Now is the time to freeze and reverse the arms race. Now is the time to encourage nations of the world to find their own means of settling disputes, without superpower intervention. Now is the time to reverse disfigured economic priorities. It is time for a new vision of common security among all nations.

We live in an increasingly dangerous world, where we have allowed the threats of war to become our only response to conflict and where the weapons we threaten to use will annihilate us all. The costs of pursuing this habit of war have now become too great to ignore. To refuse to explore alternatives further erodes the moral, psychological and political vitality of our nation. Yet trapped by our technologies as much as by our psychological dependency, we are reluctant to face perilous consequences. We must challenge ourselves to new and creative thinking in our common search for survival.

The U.S. and the U.S.S.R., societies locked in an arms race, have come to equate security with weapons. In the decades since the second World War, both countries have actively promoted that equation among nations worldwide, in an effort to entice or engage them in economic and political alliances simply based on these arms sales. This increasing reliance on the sale of arms has distorted the spending priorities of the industrial world. Human, material, and financial resources are increasingly dedicated to the military, while the quality of life is in a continual state of decline. Development efforts in the Third World are steadily losing ground. At home, the poor and middle class Americans feel the impact of the distorted spending priorities first and most severely.

New military technologies have made us less secure, not more so, and have rendered boundaries between nations almost meaningless. The destructive capability, increased accuracy, and short delivery time of today's nuclear weapons have drastically escalated our peril, while developments in conventional weapons have blurred the line between nuclear and non-nuclear war. Under the most moderate of scenarios, scientists estimate that current strategic stockpiles are three to four times larger than what is required to shroud the entire planet in a nuclear winter.

Technological and economic developments have created an interdependence among the world's nations which poses opportunities as well as dangers. Our actions have consequences beyond our borders. Whether or not we acknowledge this reality, as the arms race makes us less secure it also endangers the world; as we drive our own resources into a war economy, we constrict the futures of people everywhere. There is no more urgent political or human imperative than defining a vision of common security. Such a code of common security offers realistic alternatives to the nuclear arms race, the development of conventional weapons, the stationing of troops and bases around the world, and massive sales of arms. Common security envisages other ways to resolve conflict, form alliances, and secure stability for the world community.

Toward a New Definition of National Security

The devastating capacity of nuclear weapons has forced us to unmask the notion that security can be gained through arms. Security is understood as the ability to preserve territorial boundaries; to maintain economic relations with the rest of the world on reasonable terms; and to protect national institutions and culture from outside disruption.

Security for those of us in the United States has acquired further meaning. We see the need for security in order to protect some deeply held values: the "right to life, liberty and the pursuit of happiness." In our institutional experience, these rights have been translated into cherished expectations of democracy: the right to free speech, right to free association, the right to participate in decisions that affect our lives, to choose leaders accountable to the people, the right to equal opportunity for all.

It is this heritage we invoke when we speak of national security and participate in debates on foreign and military policy. Yet this heritage also defines a vision this nation aspires towards—a society that defends diversity and strives for social justice.

Our definition of national security must change and evolve to be consistent with our own image of ourselves, with the fundamental values we seek to protect and with the new realities of a thoroughly interdependent world. Our economic relationships and our foreign and military policies must be measured against our own principles and values as a nation. To redefine national security in light of our recognition of interdependence, we must do the following.

Identify our vital national interests. Mutual dependence on the import and export of raw materials means that the United States cannot insulate itself from reliance on others, nor can smaller nations remain completely independent of the superpowers. Attempts to gain privileged access to Third World resources through military means embroils us in local conflicts, undermines rather than strengthens our local economy, and thwarts economic growth of developing nations.

Assess the Soviets' international role realistically. Until our response to the Soviet Union refects a realistic assessment of its global role, we will continue to exaggerate its significance in other parts of the world and will waste precious national resources in an arms race no one can win. We will continue to divert the scientific talent of the country away from solving our own social and economic problems. Working from distorted images, we will continue to miscalculate the U.S.S.R.'s capacities and intentions and respond in heavy-handed patterns that continue to lose us friends and allies around the world. Misreading local conflicts and transforming them into superpower confrontations is one of the major ways we can anticipate escalation to global war.

Acknowledge the right of Third World nations to choose their own political and economic course, and refrain from using indigenous conflict as an opening for either Soviet or U.S. intervention. We must recognize that local conflicts have local solutions and restrain our tendency to turn these conflicts into opportunities for expanding our influence. Attempting to interpret these conflicts as opportunities for superpower intervention or expanding influence only ends up undermining relations with the people of the region and becomes exceedingly costly to people in these regions in lives and resources needed for economic and social development.

Local conflicts are fueled and sometimes generated by superpower rivalries in areas such as the Middle East, Europe and Latin America. Both the Soviet Union and the United States compete for political influence, exploiting local conflicts for their own purposes, using their own security interests as justification. Local conflicts are thus transformed into U.S.-U.S.S.R. confrontations through the imposition of Cold War politics, arms sales, the infusion of military advisors and aid. Local problems, whose roots lie in poverty, maldistribution of land, religious, political or cultural differences become the "theater" for superpower competition. The local conflicts deepen because their roots are ignored or forced into a "resolution" that reinforces a polarization into East-West affiliations. The origin or the conflicts continue to fester. Fundamental to the recognition that local conflicts can be better solved by local solutions is a respect for the cultural, historical and political diversity of the world community. The political and economic futures of those who participate in this community must be of their own choosing.

Accept the full autonomy of our allies and enable them to participate in determining their own security needs. Our allies should be responsible for defining their own security needs and appropriate vital interests. In addition, they should shoulder the burden of costs for achieving those security needs. In so doing, our allies should be entitled to hold views which differ from those of the United States and to pursue these views without fear of economic, military, or political ramifications. Such reciprocity and joint sharing of responsibility would strengthen rather than undermine alliance relationships.

Affirm that true security is reached not by amassing weapons but by restoring the internal integrity of our nation, and devote economic resources to the attainment of that integrity. To pit increased military spending against the social and economic progress of our nation erodes the real basis for the security we seek. Massive arms allocations drain fundamental social investment, thus threatening the health of our people and undermining those democratic freedoms we seek to protect.

Common Security: A Global Imperative

Each nation will find security only as it works to ensure the security of all other nations; no country can ensure its survival in isolation. The yardstick for true security must not only be defense of national borders and institutions but also the promotion of the economic, intellectual, and moral quality of life among and within nations. Recognizing the interdependence of all the world's nations, we call for an international common security code which affirms the following.

Nations have a right to security. A secure existence is one of the most elementary desires of humanity. This shared aspiration, expressed in our world by the creation of nation states, must be respected by all, regardless of differing political convictions.

Military force is not a legitimate instrument for resolving disputes between nations. The justification of self defense, a frequent resort of those who use force to challenge the integrity of other nation states, must be examined most critically. Prevailing definitions of self defense must be kept restrictive and remain in accordance with international procedures as specified in the Charter of the United Nations. These procedures state that nations must retain their right to use force only in their own defense or in collective defense of victims of aggression. Restraint should characterize the underlying tenor of all international relations, not only in acknowledgement that others have the right to live in a secure world, but also in the straightforward recognition that only through common action can security be attained.

Military superiority cannot guarantee security. The drive to win advantage over another to gain security at the other's expense rests on the false premise that security can be attained unilaterally, even in the nuclear age. Policies which seek advantage—either through the accumulation of arms, the distortion of negotiations for unilateral gain, or, most dangerously, the exercise of military power—should be renounced. This renunciation must be accompanied with the establishment of parity.

The current nuclear arms race must be frozen and the level of arms greatly reduced. With parity and the elimination of threat postures established as guiding principles for military relationships, it is essential that nations of the world act in concert to reduce nuclear and conventional armaments substantially. In making such reductions, particular attention should be paid to those types of weapons which raise the greatest concern on either side, as these carry the greatest danger of provoking war. Reducing armaments would allow nations to redirect resources toward economic and social development, and would contribute to creating a political atmosphere where, with a lesser risk of war, peaceful relations among nations might flourish.

Initiatives Toward Common Security

The superpowers should assume the major responsibility for initiating efforts to reduce reliance on arms and build toward common security, but all nations should share in significant progress toward this end. We advocate a series of independent, bilateral and multilateral steps which could occur simultaneously and on different levels.

The U.S. and U.S.S.R. should initiate a complete halt to the testing, production, and deployment of all nuclear weapons and their delivery systems. Such a halt could begin with an immediate and verifiable cessation of testing and deployment, to be followed by a halt to production within a one year time period. Following the superpower lead, other nuclear nations should initiate similar halts to testing, production, and deployment of their own nuclear systems.

Funding for Star Wars—the "Strategic Defense Initiative"— should be suspended. Rather than wasting billions of dollars desperately needed for economic and social revitalization, the U.S. administration should acknowledge that military security in a nuclear age is anachronistic, and security achievable only by ridding the world of nuclear weapons, themselves.

The U.S. and U.S.S.R. should begin to implement Article Six of the Nuclear Non-Proliferation Treaty by signing and ratifying the Comprehensive Test Ban. Nuclear nations should stop the flow of nuclear technology to non-nuclear nations, and thus create an environment in which developing nations abide by non-proliferation policies.

Nuclear free zones should be created, beginning in non-nuclear regions. The U.S. and U.S.S.R. should respond to calls for nuclear-free zones by the Pacific Rim nations, New Zealand, the Baltic States, and others by halting the testing and deployment of nuclear weapons in these regions. High priority should be placed on creating nuclear free zones in regions of conflict, such as the Middle East, the Pacific, South Africa, and Central America.

The U.S. and U.S.S.R. should adopt a strict bilateral agreement of non-intervention and non-interference in the Third World, beginning with an immediate halt to the presence of military troops in a region and followed by a halt to military aid, advisors, and economic destabilization. Allies of the superpowers should abide by the principles of this policy and not serve as conduits for interventionary activities.

Technological developments which narrow the firebreak between nuclear and conventional systems and facilitate military intervention should be halted. Conventional forces should be frozen and then reduced to a fifty percent level. This fifty percent reduced should be mothballed and provide a steady source of parts and replacement weapons, creating the conditions for economic conversion and reducing the defense dependency in the public sector.

Military research and strategic analysis should take place within the context of re-orienting weapons toward non-provocative defense. Gains made in halting nuclear weapons should not be traded for militarization of space or increased reliance on conventional arms. Instead, a thorough redefinition of national and global security must seek to confine military force only to what is needed for defensive purposes.

Accomplishing any one of these steps would significantly·contribute to achieving a common security among nations. In order to begin the process by which such steps could be taken, we call upon the superpowers to develop a set of independent initiatives, leading the way toward a series of reciprocal actions. We challenge the superpowers to begin a process of disengagement from local conflicts in Central America, Afghanistan, and the Middle East; to suspend underground warhead tests for a definite period of time; to withhold arms sales and technology transfers to nations in the Middle East, South Africa, and the Pacific.

We call upon all the world's nations to exert pressure on the superpowers to take these steps. New Zealand, in declaring its ports nuclear free, the Baltic States, in working constructively for a nuclear-free zone, leaders of the Five Continent Peace Initiative, in advocating a nuclear weapons freeze, and the Contadora nations, in calling for a locally guided process to resolve the security needs of nations in their own region, all signify the political strength of the world community that acts from a recognition of interdependence. Only by working together can we achieve a common and stable security for us all.

Some of the material in this chapter is drawn from the Palme Commission Report on Common Security.

Jack O'Dell

Disarmament and Intervention: What Is to Be Done?

Fundamentally, our concern is that the dichotomy between foreign policy and domestic policy be ended. We live in a culture that tends to specialize, and even overspecialize. The history of our movements essentially is one of people concentrating on one issue. There were moments when we focussed on one problem, especially in periods of war, like Vietnam. Ordinarily people concentrate on what is called domestic issues, and other folks concentrate on what is called foreign policy. Ending that dichotomy is extremely important. A holistic view will make it possible for us to work more effectively, whatever our individual or organizational specialization may be.

The greatest mass movement of this millenium, measured by the numbers of people involved, was the anti-colonial national liberation movements which swept away the political foundations of the colonial system from 1945 to 1975. Now this movement has entered its second phase, one of economic reconstruction designed to complete the emancipation process by reorganizing their economic and social relations with those industrial nations of the West that developed at their expense.

This transition to a new international economic order, as the fulfillment of true independence in the Third World, is closely connected with the struggle to end the arms race and defeat the policy of military intervention aimed at arresting this process of economic independence. It is the connection that confirms that peace and justice are inseparable. The arms race is targetted against the people of the Third World, directly and indirectly. It is also targetted against the poorest strata of the working population within the United States and Western Europe, because it represents a decision taken to sacrifice their living standards and their aspiration for justice in favor of an escalating militarism.

What then is our challenge and the response that reflects our self-interest? It is to be fully conscious participants in helping to shape contemporary world developments in the interest of human progress. The solidarity movements which oppose military intervention have to concern themselves with actively supporting the stated objectives of the peace movement, because the deployment of nuclear weapons is itself a form of intervention and military intimidation—part of the general strategy of destabilizing whole regions of the world as the basis for escalating the arms race and maintaining the status quo. The Trident submarine in Washington State, for example, is in direct conflict with the mass peace movement in Asia that desires to establish the Indian Ocean as a "zone of peace." The deployment of the Cruise or Pershing II in Comiso, Sicily is a decision directed against the whole of North Africa, in addition to being a violation of the national rights of the people of Sicily.

Conversely, the network of organizations that have now become a movement determined to prevent nuclear war and halt the arms race will be consistent to the extent that we respond to the problem of military intervention, because there are examples and forms of intervention that carry the possibility of escalating into a nuclear weapons showdown. There was Israel's invasion of Lebanon. The South African regime's invasion of Angola in 1982 should also be remembered. Both attacks are examples of military interventions which appear to have been approved by the American government in the spirit of Cold War confrontation. Both had the potential of escalating to a scale in which nuclear weapons could have been introduced, and in each case the aggressors, Israel and South Africa, had nuclear weapons capability as a result of their relations with the U.S. and other members of the NATO alliance.

This is a development of such seriousness that it should not be ignored or passed over by the disarmament movement or the various groups in our country dealing with apartheid and the Middle East. The production and deployment of nuclear weapons and military intervention with conventional weapons are twin tactics used against people's efforts to establish peace and justice.

Our respective peace organizations that have now become a movement to prevent nuclear war, *to be consistent*, must be actively opposed to military intervention. Clarifying these links and building active cooperation between these constituencies is part of a strategy for keeping our movement moving.

A second component is the unity between disarmament and non-intervention wings of the peace movement and the coalition that is focusing on anti-racism and human needs. Today we are faced with a period of relative and absolute impoverishment of large numbers of working people. The decline in the industrial base in steel, in autos, electronics, industrial design, massive farm bankruptcies that are the highest anytime since the Depression, small business bankruptcies—all of this represents a new situation, a new relationship of our economy to the world economy. We now have an administration prepared to dismantle much of the public sector of the economy in order to adjust to this new situation. Significant achievements of the last forty years of social legislation are either being compromised or thrown out in the search for more tax dollars to pour into this nuclear arms madness. Hot lunches for children, medical assistance for the elderly, the CETA job training program for our youth who are chronically unemployed, legal services for the poor, financial aid programs for college students—these and many others—took years of struggle to put into place and are now being callously scuttled to finance a new generation of weapons.

A century and a half ago, the people of this country built a movement for the abolition of slavery which was ultimately victorious because slavery, and the economic class it directly benefited, had become destructive of the Union. In more recent times, we abolished segregation because that system of racist insult and deprivation violated the humanity of our citizens and became destructive to the U.S. credibility in a changing world that rejected such institutionalized racism. Now we are challenged as a society to build a movement for the abolition of nuclear weapons because their continued existence threatens the survival of life on this planet.

If the traditional peace organizations actively embrace the human needs dimensions of the struggle for peace, they have the opportunity to become the conscience of the nation—a center of moral authority and political power capable of reshaping in a progressive pattern the social outlook of the majority of our population. An America committed to change through reduction and abolition of nuclear weapons will be a better America simply because it will be less dangerous to itself and the world. An America committed beyond just this objective, to reconstruct its economic and political life for full employment, available health care, and quality education, will not only be better because it is less dangerous, it will be more civilized, more humane and more in step with world development. That is the preferred option.

From embracing the goal of an end to the destructive arms race to establishing as a new national purpose the effective use of the national resources that are freed up through relief from the burden of the arms race—that is the transitional process we must seek.

So the third element of the strategy would be the unity of the disarmament and peace movements with the human needs movement, and the unity of these forces with movements in Europe and Japan. I have recently had the privilege of being on two delegations that went to Western Europe. Two things stand out from these visits: first, it is important for us to appreciate the depth of the feeling among the peoples of Europe with respect to avoiding nuclear war. Europe knew the destruction of World War II and these memories are still very much with them. I was also struck on these tours in the Federal Republic of Germany, Holland, and Belgium that in each instance our hosts arranged meetings for us with people who have been in the anti-fascist resistance movement. They talked about the conditions that existed during the Nazi occupation. I remember one of the brothers who was with us during our visit in Germany. At the closing session, he said, "We are not going to allow these missiles to be put into our country. And it may mean civil war, but so be it. Because we know what an occupation army is. The first time one of our peace demonstrators gets killed by an American soldier as we demonstrate against these missiles, the first time that happens we will know the American army is an occupation army, and we will treat it accordingly."

That is something for us to think about seriously. We have a government that is putting us to a test of wills. There is a whole philosophy in this administration that if you just press on everything will be all right. They are testing us to see if we have the stamina, the continuity, and the ability to maintain and withstand the pressure. A classic case in point was a demonstration of one hundred thousand people in Comiso, Sicily against the preparation and building of the missile silos. The day after the demonstration, they proceeded to begin to build the silos. That is an example of United States military arrogance that we must confront.

I remember one woman on my last visit to Europe who was part of the general audience. She raised a question as they reviewed the situation in West Germany. "What is our source of hope?" Others responded that our source of hope is in the people. I think that is what we need to underscore. What is the source of our hope? Our hope is in the mass movement; it is in the power of organized public opinion as a force for social change. The movements for disarmament and peace, and against military intervention, are now international in scope. These movements will definitely leave their imprint on the decade of the eighties.

The scores of organizations that came together in coalition for peace on June 12 in New York, and the success of the Freeze Campaign in the post-June 12 period, confirms that the activists have created a watershed period in our national history. They have given us a green light to build the biggest movement for disarmament and against military intervention in the contemporary world.

This will be the contribution of the people of the U.S. to the international community. Of all the urgent issues facing different areas of the world, *peace* is the *one* issue on which the mass of the population of our country has joined the world community. On this issue alone, the people of the U.S. have managed to break out of the isolation, misinformation, lies and the cultural diet of national chauvinism, to join the stream of human history. If our movement fulfills its responsibility, it will open up an enormously significant period in our political education that will ultimately and profoundly affect people's thinking on international issues.

There is an enormous amount of outreach to be done. What do we do with all this information presented as the "Deadly Connection"? The answer is "spread it." Knowledge is power. Let it reproduce itself. People don't expect us to know everything. Give them the information we do have. Follow that old saying that "what you are speaks louder that what you are saying." People are more concerned with our intent than with our content. You can respond to a question by saying, "Well, I don't know all about that," and people will understand. But share what we are learning through the churches, the PTA's, the block clubs, the beauty parlors, the barber shops, the talk shows, and letters to the editors. Get the message out, then listen to the response, because listening will help us understand the language that will enable us to communicate all the better.

Finally, we have heard from the President that peace is not a policy, it is a goal. We want peace as a policy. I believe that our movement must be guided by the vision of bringing to power here in the U.S. during this decade a national government committed to the objectives of the abolition of nuclear weapons, the building of our cities, the restoration of human needs programs that have been sacrificed to the military budget, and a government that accepts political negotiations rather than military intervention as a cornerstone of foreign policy. We should utilize national elections and all local elections to bring such a government into existence, to make this program irreversible as an objective of public policy.

Talk given at the Deadly Connection Conference, 4 December 1982.

Joseph Gerson

The Deadly Connection: Resisting the Nuclear Navy

After a brief but intense struggle in the spring and summer of 1983, the people of New England insured that we will not soon play host to the battleship *Iowa* or the destroyers, cruisers, tactical and strategic nuclear weapons—including sea-launched cruise missiles—which accompany it. Homeporting struggles in New York, Texas, California, Washington, and Hawaii have indicated important directions for the peace movement in the United States and have begun to forge links with people of the Pacific and North Atlantic.

The *Iowa* Task Force is organized around the battleship *Iowa*, now refurbished after lying for years to rot in the Philadelphia Navy yard. The *Iowa* will initially be armed with 32 Tomahawk sea-launched cruise missiles (SLCMs) and is capable of carrying as many as 360. Each missile is designed to carry nuclear warheads of the two-to-three hundred kiloton range. The *Iowa* also boasts guns with a sixteen inch diameter for which they have been so well known. In addition to the *Iowa* and its cruise missiles, the fleet will include two guided missile destroyers, a cruiser, a destroyer, and at least two frigates. The additional ships are capable of carrying another 160 sea-launch cruise missiles, and they will certainly carry dozens of tactical nuclear weapons mounted on missiles, torpedoes, and depth charges. The fleet is the embodiment of the "deadly connection," the integration of nuclear warfighting policy and military intervention in the Third World.

In New England, when we began to learn about the battleship *Iowa* Task Force and started organizing to prevent its deployment and homeporting, we found that it raised a number of critical issues, some of which the disarmament and freeze movements in the United States had not fully considered. The deployment of sea-launched cruise missiles threatens the possibility of negotiating a nuclear weapons freeze or any other serious arms control measures. The presence of tactical and strategic nuclear weapons poses an immediate danger to people in communities near the homeport site. Economic risks, as well as safety risks, sail with the fleet. And the task force's nuclear weapons can be used for Third World intervention as well as against the Soviet Union.

The *Iowa* Task Force has at least three missions. First, with its cruise missiles, the fleet is part of President Reagan's plan to fight and "win" a prolonged nuclear war with the Soviet Union. It can also be used as part of a preemptive first strike against the Soviet Union. Thus, it plays a role in providing a nuclear shield for U.S. intervention in the Middle East and other regions of the Third World. The task force's second mission is reminiscent of the navy's primary role during the First and Second World Wars and is the function that backers of the task force prefer to emphasize. This is to keep Soviet ships out of the Atlantic and to defend U.S.-European sea lanes in time of war. The task force's third likely mission is as part of the Rapid Deployment Force, now called the Central Command, or for gunboat diplomacy elsewhere in the Third World. Since being recommissioned, the *Iowa* has spent considerable time off the Nicaraguan and Salvadoran coasts, seeking to intimidate those who challenge the Monroe Doctrine and U.S. hegemony in the region. Like the battleship *New Jersey*, which participated in wargames off the Indochinese and Central American coasts and bombarded Lebanese villages in 1983, the *Iowa* can be quickly moved in times of crisis to the Mediterranean or to Central America with its nuclear and conventional weapons turned against the people, governments, and resources of North Africa, the Middle East, Nicaragua, or Cuba.

More than a decade after the navy moved its ships and sailors out of the Northeast to insulate them from the anti-war protest that attended the Indochina War, the Reagan administration developed a sophisticated strategy to win the hearts and minds of people in Massachusetts, Rhode Island and New York. Rather than select its preferred site for the *Iowa* task force and then begin negotiations with the local powers that be, the Navy arranged a contest between the three possible homeport sites. The community which could demonstrate that it had the best facilities, the lowest cost, and the most popular support for the fleet would be rewarded with the fleet, the jobs, and the profit which came with it. None of this was done under the watchful eye of an informed or involved public.

Quietly, in each of the potential homeports, impressive coalitions were assembled to win the *Iowa* task force for their community. In March 1983, when Massachusetts Governor Dukakis first announced that the state and the City of Boston had jointly submitted a proposal to base the fleet in Boston, he announced that it would bring three thousand civilian jobs and a $143 million annual payroll to revitalize the depressed harbor economy. In Rhode Island the same payroll figure was used, but only thirteen hundred jobs were promised. The *New York Times*, which publishes "all the news that's fit to print," headlined that the fleet would bring nine thousand jobs and a $500 million payroll.

Though a few people in powerful positions knew these figures were grossly inflated, the task force's spending power and its multiplier effect brought together many corporate and labor leaders to back their respective community's homeporting proposal. In Massachusetts the breadth of the coalition for the homeporting proposal was such that in January 1983— before the public had been told of the possibility of bringing the task force to Boston—the entire Massachusetts congressional delegation signed a letter to Secretary of the Navy Lehman calling for the fleet to be based in Boston. Senator Kennedy, one of the primary advocates of the nuclear weapons freeze in the Senate, was one of the moving forces behind the effort to bring the *Iowa* task force to Boston. Congressman Edweard Markey, who at the time harbored ambitions of serving in the Senate and was the leader of the freeze efforts in the House of Representatives, also loyally signed on to the homeporting proposal and the letter to Secretary Lehman.

Digression on Strategy

Little of substance has been written about why World War II vintage battleships are being taken out of mothballs and refurbished to play a major role in the most powerful navy of the twentieth century. Still less has been written about the capabilities of, and reasons for, deploying sea-launched cruise missiles. As a result, our effort to block the *Iowa* task force led me to articles from military and policy journals with such exciting titles as "John Lehman: No Second Echelon Role for His Naval Forces," "John Lehman: The Hard Liner Behind Reagan's

Military Buildup," and "Maritime Strategy vs. Coalition Defense"—tedious material unless one is trying to understand what lies behind official pronouncements about a battleship task force and what cruise missiles are designed to do. As a result of this reading and dozens of telephone conversations with researchers and journalists, I learned more about naval strategy than I ever thought I wanted to know.

In the course of my inquiry I was reminded that strategic thinkers, people who ponder power relations in the game of nations, view our country like nineteenth century Britain. They see the United States as an "island power" distant from the geopolitically crucial Eurasian continental heartland (to which the economically and strategically important Middle East is now added), and dependent on naval domination of the seven seas to retain its role as *the* leading military power. The killing power of sixteen inch diameter, sixty-eight foot long guns that protrude from the silhouettes of battleships, and which can hurl twenty-seven-hundred pound shells a distance of twenty three miles, were brought to life—so to speak—as essential to gunboat diplomacy. These shells can penetrate twenty feet of reinforced concrete from a distance of four miles and can be shot at a rate of sixteen tons per minute.

I learned about what were, for me, obscure parts of the planet, places like the G.I.U.K. Gap, the strategically important funnel in the North Atlantic between Greenland, Iceland, Ireland, and the United Kingdom. It is through this water that the Soviet Northern Fleet must pass to gain entry into the Atlantic from the Norwegian Sea.

Charles Myers, Jr., a former fighter pilot who worked as a consultant for a number of major weapons manufacturers, is generally credited as the man primarily responsible for bringing back the battleship. As a fighter pilot who flew ground support missions during the Vietnam War, he knew that bad weather often prevented aircraft from providing the firepower needed to protect the landing operations of marines and soldiers. In Myers's view, "At a time when we have to worry most about conflicts in the Third World, the most important non-nuclear function of the Department of the Navy...is forcible entry...We want the battleship because it can do the job without risking anybody's life. Do you realize that 80% of our targets were within main battery range of the New Jersey? The same would be true in the Middle East."[1]

In a remarkable *New York Times Magazine* cover story which heralded the "Return of the Battleship," author William H.

Honan described how Myers' advocacy of the battleship complemented the thinking of John Lehman, President Reagan's navy secretary. "Myers' battleship plan contained an element that Lehman found particularly compelling—the addition of Tomahawk cruise missiles to the ship's armament. This missile, with a range of up to 1,500 miles, could make the battleship one of the most potent of all capital ships."²

Lehman understood that with sea-launched cruise missiles, the battleship could become a platform for long-range strategic attack against the Soviet Union. On the seas it could be used to destroy Soviet ships from a distance of three hundred miles, and it could serve as an off-shore fortress for Third World intervention. To critics who argued that World War II and the sinking of the British destroyer *Sheffield* by a single, aging Argentine Exocet missile proved that battleships are vulnerable relics, Lehman countered that the surface-to-air missiles, nuclear-armed anti-ship missiles, and nuclear-tipped torpedoes and depth charges carried aboard the ships accompanying the *Iowa* and other battleships would provide adequate protection.

In a world in which "naval strength is measured in terms of the number of available offensive platforms—ships that mount weapons capable of taking the war to the enemy,"³ the battleship task force provides the Reagan administration with new weapons systems that can place both the Soviet Union and Third World nations on the defensive. The commitment to place four such battleship task forces in Lehman's six-hundred ship Navy was quickly integrated into the military budgets sent to, and passed by, Congress.

The Fleet Threatens a Freeze

The deployment of the *Iowa* battleship task force makes a bilateral U.S.-Soviet nuclear weapons freeze much more difficult to negotiate. A central element of the freeze concept is the ability of each side to identify or verify the presence of the nuclear weapons possessed by the other superpower. The cruise missile is too small to be easily detected. To make matters worse, the Lehman Plan is a floating version of the MX shell game. Four thousand sea-launched cruise missiles are scheduled to be deployed aboard battleships, destroyers, cruisers, and submarines, but only 758 have been designated to carry strategic nuclear warheads. Thus, once sea-launched cruise missiles are deployed, a nuclear freeze can be verified only if we invite the KGB and other Soviet agents to inspect every port visited by the U.S. Navy—a dismal prospect at best. Republican Senator Mathias described the problem this way: "If you start this particular kind of arms race, it will be absolutely impossible to get reductions. In five years, the Russians will catch up, we will put ourselves in a position in which all the principles of arms control will be destroyed."

Michael Klare, a then fellow at the Institute for Policy Studies and defense correspondent for *The Nation*, pointed out that the *Iowa* task force made a mockery of the U.S.-Soviet negotiations then in progress in Geneva. The negotiations, demanded by our European allies, were designed to limit the number of intermediate range nuclear weapons in Europe. The *Iowa* task force, when fully armed, would have allowed the Reagan administration to circumvent any agreements negotiated at Geneva. Based in the GIUK Gap, its sea-launched cruise missiles and their strategic nuclear warheads will be stationed just off the European coast. In the words of Christopher Paine of Physicians for Social Responsiblity, "The nuclear SLCM represents a monstrous and wholly gratuitous complication for arms control—which is perhaps why the Reagan Administration is so enthusiastic about it."[4]

There is some debate about the Tomahawk missile's strategic role. The navy concedes it is part of its "seamless web," and that it has a second strike capacity which could be used to coerce Soviet survivors of a U.S.-Soviet nuclear exchange. (In strategic game-playing, the power that can coerce the other side after the first massive nuclear exchange is thought to have won the war!) While navy spokesmen deny that the sea-launched cruise missile has any first strike capabilities, researchers from the Center for Defense Information, the Institute for Policy Studies, and the Institute for Defense and Disarmament Studies explain that when used in conjunction with Pershing II missiles, the slow but "smart" cruise missiles can be most effective in a first strike attack against the Soviet Union's harbors and missile silos.

Even in its more publicized mission of "defending the sea lanes" in the Atlantic, the *Iowa* task force has a controversial and potentially dangerous role to play. In Navy Secretary Lehman's words, the Carter administration's naval strategy "was not to go into high-threat areas, to stay south of the GIUK gap....Our naval strategy is to size the Navy to be able to go into the highest-threat areas of our vital interest...Why should we stay in a pulled-back defensive maritime strategy, when the payoff of going north of the GIUK gap and going after (the Soviets) and their interdiction capabilities is so high."[5]

In addition to this more aggressive approach to the Soviets, one Boston-based naval expert pointed out that every ship assigned to protect the *Iowa* is armed with tactical nuclear weapons. If these one-kiloton nuclear weapons are used in a local sea conflict with the Soviet Union, the confrontation could easily escalate into a global nuclear exchange. Very few mock war games are able to contain a "limited nuclear exchange."

A Weapon for Middle East Intervention

Like the land based cruise missiles deployed at Comiso, Italy, the weapons of the battleship *Iowa* task force can be used for both strategic attacks against the Soviet Union and for intervention in North Africa and the Middle East. Reminding us of recent policy statements by the Navy, Michael Klare pointed out there "is a 100% possibility" that in times of crisis the *Iowa* task force can be integrated into the Rapid Deployment Force and dispatched to the Middle East. There the *Iowa*'s cruise missiles and 16-inch guns could play significant roles in a war for oil, a deepening conflict in Lebanon or between Israel and its Arab neighbors, to maintain King Hassan in Morocco or to depose Colonel Qadaffi in Libya. In a private meeting during our campaign to block the homeporting of the *Iowa*, Massachusetts' Lieutenant Governor, now Senator, John Kerry—himself a backer of Boston's homeporting proposal—warned us not to underestimate the possibility that the *Iowa* could be dispatched from the North Atlantic to Central America. His insights on this aspect of the *Iowa*'s mission proved more informed than his understanding of the strategic, tactical, and safety implications of the deployment and homeporting of the *Iowa*.

The 1982 *New York Times Magazine* celebration of the battleship's return also suggested an interesting scenario in which the *Iowa* would be used to reinforce intervention by the Rapid Deployment Force in the Persian Gulf. To prevent the Soviet Northern Fleet from moving into the Mediterranean and thus countering U.S. moves, the *Iowa* task force could remain on station in the North Atlantic, confining the Soviet Navy to the Norwegian Sea. Daniel Ellsberg, in his essay "Call to Mutiny," explains that the new generation of first strike weapons are designed to bluff the Soviets and to serve as a shield for U.S. intervention in the Third World. He explains: "The whole panoply of new arms and deployments, from the usable neutron warhead and the Rapid Deployment Force to the Pershings and the MX serve to implement presidential claims to have wired up the Middle East to a Doomsday Machine."[6]

Safety and Jobs

When we began our organizing in New England, we underestimated the safety issues related to the *Iowa* task force. The incredible dangers that we found accompanying the fleet came to worry mayoral candidates, environmentalists, elected officials, and the press. We posed safety questions that have rarely been raised in the United States, which the navy was not anxious to hear, and which homeport backers could not answer. While we were initially able to raise concern and to mobilize people's energy over the threat the fleet posed to the nuclear weapons freeze, the safety issues we raised probably had the most telling impact.[7]

The proposal to base the *Iowa* task force in one of the most densely populated harbors of the northeastern United States marked a turning point in U.S. military policy. It demonstrated, among other things, just how little concern our government and military leadership have for the people they are ostensibly protecting. Although the navy and homeport backers argued that the people of Boston, Rhode Island, and New York had nothing to fear, we found a court case in Hawaii in which the Navy had conceded a record of 379 nuclear weapons accidents between 1965 and 1977. Captain James Bush, a retired Polaris submarine commander, brought a Government Accounting Office study to our attention. It stated that one consequence of a nuclear weapons accident could be the release of plutonium downwind in a "radiological cigar-shaped cloud extending from the accident scene for about twenty-eight miles, with a maximum width of about 2.5 miles."[8] Millions of people live within a 28 mile radius of the Boston and New York naval yards. In Boston it seemed that our effort to stop the homeporting proposal turned a critical corner when Captain Bush read this quotation to the assembled City Council.

We also learned that no environmental impact study was to be made before the navy awarded its homeporting contract. Even if such a study were made, navy policy precludes consideration of the possibility of a nuclear weapons accident in its environmental impact studies. Our loose coalition was the first community voice to ask if dangerous liquified-natural-gas (LNG) tankers and the *Iowa* task force would be in Boston harbor at the same time, and what the impact of a LNG explosion would be on the *Iowa*'s nuclear weapons.

The pain of increasing unemployment and the desperate effort of many people to find work meant that we also had to challenge the outrageous promises of jobs and profits made by homeport supporters. Every city, state, and federal official we interviewed indicated their primary reason for backing the deployment of the *Iowa* lay in the jobs and prosperity they thought it would bring. Like the *Boston Globe*, which argued that cruise missiles were "not an appropriate consideration in the negotiations over basing the North Atlantic surface action group in Boston,"[9] many members of Congress attempted to avoid the contradictions inherent in backing both the nuclear weapons freeze and the *Iowa* Task Force. For them, money and jobs were the name of the game.

We found that the *Iowa* task force was not the answer to Boston's economic problems. A study prepared by the Reagan administration reported that "The near-term economic benefits of a major new military base may not be sufficient to offset the cost of required additional community facilities and services." After extensive public debate and many inquiries by the press, we learned that the task force would provide only 1,300 short term construction jobs and a mere 325 permanent jobs—not the 3,000 or 9,000 promised by homeport supporters. The prospect of a $143 million or $500 million payroll began to fade when more accurate figures were used.

In addition to shattering the economic promises of the navy and homeport backers, we thought it necessary to suggest alternative possibilities for the development of Boston's harbor area to demonstrate our concern for the economic life of Boston and to demonstrate that non-military development would be more profitable to the city. The working group of business consultants, real-estate developers and architects that we assembled found the area under consideration was ideal for housing, high-technology training centers and light industrial development. After our victory in Boston the City and State developed a three billion dollar development plan for the harbor area with no role for the navy.

In Conclusion

In August 1983, much to the chagrin of the corporate and established political leadership of Massachusetts and Rhode Island, the navy announced that Staten Island, New York was its preferred homeport for the *Iowa* task force. Many reasons were given for the decision, but the most telling seemed to be "the quality of life" in Boston and Rhode Island. The vacated and deteriorating commercial district of Stapleton, New York was more appealing to the Navy than the beautiful harbors and culture of New England. Behind the label "quality of life" lay noisy public debates, teach-ins, demonstrations against the *Iowa* task force and its missions, and countless press inquiries which we had generated. New York City, the home of many American disarmament and peace organizations, had remained largely silent through the critical summer of 1983. As a result, the *Iowa* task force and its nuclear weapons were assigned to the shadows of the Staten Island Ferry, the Statue of Liberty and the World Trade Center. Since the navy opted for New York harbor, activists and organizers have mobilized considerable opposition to the homeporting proposal. Using information gleaned in the New England homeporting struggle, community activists have shattered the promises of jobs and profits sailing with the *Iowa* task force. They have won the support of a majority of New York's City Council for a "nuclear free harbor," and many members of New York City's congressional delegation have withdrawn their unquestioning support for the homeporting proposal.

The homeporting struggles in New England and now New York demonstrate the wisdom of the hackneyed slogan "think globally, act locally." These campaigns have made our communities just a little bit safer. They have served as models for similar struggles in Texas, California and Hawaii, and they have helped to build cooperation between American activists and people in the Pacific and North Atlantic who are similarly threatened by these weapons systems. The framework of the deadly connection provided us with a means to understand the capabilities and dangers posed by the *Iowa* task force and helped us to build coalitions needed to resist it.

Notes

1. *New York Times Magazine*, 4 April 1982. Note also, the battleship *New Jersey* was briefly brought back into active service during the Vietnam War.
2. Ibid. Technological changes in the Tomahawk now give it a range of between 1,800 and 2,300 miles.
3. Ibid.
4. *The Nation*, 9 April 1983.
5. *Defense Week*, 8 June 1981.
6. Daniel Ellsberg, "Call to Mutiny," in *Protest and Survive*, ed. E.P. Thompson and Dan Smith, (New York: Monthly Review Press, 1981).
7. Since the 1983 campaign in New England, Simeon Sahaydachny has

compiled a more telling indictment of the nuclear safety hazards that accompany homeporting proposals. It is published by the Riverside Church Disarmament Program and the Lawyers' Committee on Nuclear Policy.

8. "Areas Around Nuclear Facilities Should Be Better Prepared for Radiological Emergencies" *EMD* 78:110 (30 March 1984).

9. *The Boston Globe,* 9 April 1983.

About the Authors

MICHAEL BEDFORD is director of *Third World Reports*, and lived and worked in Asia and the Pacific. He has written widely on U.S. military and foreign policy and is a member of the International Advisory Committee of the Council for a Nuclear Weapons Freeze.

CAROL BRAGG is the Peace Education Field Secretary for the American Friends Service Committee in Rhode Island.

KASSAHUN CHECOLE teaches at Rutgers University and is a visiting Professor at El Colegio de Mexico. He is an Eritrean activist and publisher of Africa World Press and the Red Sea Press.

NOAM CHOMSKY is Institute Professor at M.I.T., eminent scholar in the field of linguistics, involved in radical social change movements, and critic of American political life. Author of *Towards a New Cold War* (1982), *Fateful Triangle: The U.S., Israel and Palestinians* (1984), and other books.

MAUDE EASTER is co-director of the Committee for a New Korea Policy, an educational and resource center. She worked for the American Friends Service Committee in Asia and as a lobbyist for the National Organization for Women (NOW).

DANIEL ELLSBERG served as a strategic analyst at Rand Corporation (1954-64), consultant to the Department of Defense, joined the Defense Department in 1965. He returned to Rand in 1967 where he worked on Secretary of Defense McNamara's study of U.S. decision-making in Vietnam, more popularly known as *The Pentagon Papers*. Since his trial for sharing *The Pentagon Papers* with the American people, he has been a leading peace activist.

MELINDA FINE is the International Coordinator of the Nuclear Weapons Freeze Campaign. She works with peace organizations in Europe and the Pacific and provides education and analysis on foreign policy issues to the Freeze.

RANDALL FORSBERG is the founder and director of the Institute for Defense and Disarmament Studies, chair of the National Advisory Board of the Nuclear Weapons Freeze

Campaign, author of "Call to Halt the Nuclear Arms Race" (1980), member of the Boston Study Group, and co-author of *The Price of Defense.*

JOSEPH GERSON is Peace Secretary of the American Friends Service Committee's New England Regional Office. He has served on the staff of Clergy and Laity Concerned, the War Resisters' International and as director of Arizonans for Peace.

ROGER HURWITZ is a doctoral candidate at the Massachusetts Institute of Technology and a member of New Jewish Agenda in Boston, Massachusetts.

MICHAEL T. KLARE is Director of the Five College Program in Peace and World Security Studies in Amherst, Mass. He is author of *War Without End* and *American Arms Supermarket.*

JENNIFER LEANING is the chair of the long-term planning committee of Physicians for Social Responsibility. Dr. Leaning is also a former member of the national executive committee of PSR.

NGO VINH LONG is an author and social historian specializing in China and Vietnam. He has been a political activist for Third World causes since 1964.

JACK O'DELL is a member of the Executive Committee of SANE, the International Liaison for the Rainbow Coalition, and Chairman of the Board of the Pacifica Radio Network.

CHRISTOPHER PAINE is Senior Policy Analyst for Physicians for Social Responsibility.

DAN PETEGORSKY is a staff member of the Mobilization for Survival in Boston.

CHARITO PLANAS is a Filipino leader living in exile in the United States. She speaks frequently throughout the United States about the struggle for freedom and independence in the Philippines.

TONY POLUMBA is a staff member of the Boston Mobilization for Survival and serves as New England facilitator of the National Mobilization for Survival.

STUART SCHAAR is Associate Professor of Middle East and North African History, Brooklyn College, CUNY.

BOONE SCHIRMER taught at Boston University and Goddard College. He is author of *Republic or Empire.*

PAUL F. WALKER, Ph.D. is national security analyst with Klein Walker Associated, Inc. in Cambridge, MA, former National Education Director of Physicians for Social Responsibility, Arms Control Research Director for the Union of Concerned Scientists, member of the Boston Study Group, and co-author of *The Price of Defense.*

More Resources From New Society Publishers

WATERMELONS NOT WAR! A SUPPORT BOOK FOR PARENTING IN THE NUCLEAR AGE
by Kate Cloud, Ellie Deegan, Alice Evans, Hayat Imam, and Barbara Signer; Afterword by Dr. Helen Caldicott.

Five mothers in the Boston area have been meeting regularly for four years to give each other support, to demystify nuclear technology into terms parents *and children* can understand, and to find ways of acting which will give their children a future. The result is *Watermelons not War! A Support Book for Parenting in the Nuclear Age.*

Articles describing this project appeared in *Ms. Magazine*, *Whole Life Times*, and *Sojourner*.

Large format. Beautifully illustrated. Annotated Bibliography. 160 pages. 1984.
Hardcover: $19.95
Paperback: $9.95

OUR FUTURE AT STAKE: A TEENAGERS GUIDE TO STOPPING THE NUCLEAR ARMS RACE
by Melinda Moore & Laurie Olsen, Citizens Policy Center

"The problem with getting my friends involved with the nuclear issue is that they don't know enough about it or even where to get information. I am a teacher now. I give them plenty of information whether they like it or not."
—Lena Flores, 17

Informative, beautifully illustrated and photographed resource for education and action. Includes personal statements by teenagers themselves. Handy glossary and chronology for teenagers seeking to understand the nuclear arms madness. Ideal for school, church, and community groups.

Illustrated. 68 pages. Large format. 1984.
Hardcover: $19.95
Paperback: $7.95